Coaching for Professional Development

Coaching has emerged as one of the most significant aids in developing managers and executives in the professional world. Yet there is a degree of dissatisfaction with performance coaching models and a desire to connect more with creativity and the imagination. In *Coaching for Professional Development: Using Literature to Support Success*, Christine A. Eastman suggests that literary works have a part to play in bringing about a change in coaching culture. Using a series of examples from key literary texts, she argues that literature can help coaches enhance their skills, find solutions to workplace problems, and better articulate their own ideas through innovation and imagination.

Eastman argues for literature as a coaching tool, detailing how using stories of loss, failure, alienation, and human suffering in a coaching dialogue brings positive results to organizational coaching. *Coaching for Professional Development* considers how reading fiction helps us to imagine lives outside our own and how this sensitivity of language brings out the unconscious within us and others. Eastman discusses how she guided her students to embrace literature as a positive influence on their coaching practice through literary texts. Chapter 1 begins by exploring how reading Melville's "Bartleby, the Scrivener" allowed her students to understand the importance of metaphor in their own coaching, with Chapter 2 illuminating how Cather's "Neighbor Rosicky" addresses the role of emotion. After this, Eastman considers how John Cheever's multilayered story "The Swimmer" and James Baldwin's "Notes of a Native Son" provide rich stimulus for coaching students in understanding failure, how Miller's *Death of a Salesman* shows how our family relationships are reflected in our office dynamics, and how the reactions of her students engaging with Lampedusa's *The Leopard* are more effective than the traditional coaching tool, Personalisis, in revealing their personality. She finally looks at Shakespeare's *The Tempest* for exploring themes of power and manipulation in a coaching context. By applying coaching models to fictional scenarios, Eastman demonstrates that coaches, HR professionals, and students can successfully extend the boundaries of their coaching, strengthen their interventions, and enhance their understanding of theory.

Coaching for Professional Development: Using Literature to Support Success is a unique approach to coaching with engaging case studies throughout that brings together higher education and industry. It will be key reading for coaches in practice and in training who wish to enhance creativity in their work, advisors and teachers on coaching courses, and HR and L&D professionals working in organizations seeking to implement a coaching culture.

Christine A. Eastman is Senior Lecturer in the Business School, Middlesex University, UK, and winner of the Universities Association for Lifelong Learning trophy in recognition of teaching excellence. She has worked with national and international businesses such as Halifax, Toshiba, SAP, SONY, and Nationwide (USA).

"In this book, Christine argues that to be a good coach it is not enough to follow a particular coaching model (e.g. the GROW model). The missing element is a deeper emotional awareness and that the 'process of reading is 'emotionally educational'. So, for example she suggests by analysing the complex emotions of the central character, Willy Loman in Miller's *Death of a Salesman* coaches can arrive at a deeper understanding of 'unhappiness at work'.

Having worked with Christine at The Institute for Work Based Learning, Middlesex University, I have seen first hand how introducing students to literature have benefited their practice and in this book she shares the literature introduced and how it has made a difference. I thoroughly recommend this book as a valuable addition to the coaching literature"

– **Dr Peter Critten**, formerly Project Manager Work Based Organisational Learning, The Institute for Work Based Learning, Middlesex University

"This is a timely and engaging book. I'm absolutely convinced by Christine Eastman's argument that the experience of reading and interpreting literature – which is the experience of imagining different life possibilities – brings significant benefits to clients and coaches alike. Through a series of sensitively articulated case studies, Eastman reveals the possibilities and potential of a new practice of coaching. This book will be of huge value to coaches and teachers of coaching, in both academic and business contexts, who are looking to extend and deepen their coaching practice."

– **Neill Thew**, University of Sussex / Cru Leader Development

"This book reveals valuable insights on almost every page. Christine Eastman convincingly makes the case for literary study and appreciation in professional coaching. The writer of fiction is engaged in making sense of character and human experience through sensitive and allusive language, and Eastman's argument that the coach has much to learn from these writers is abundantly supported, especially by the student case studies which form the backbone of the book. Eastman is an accomplished literary scholar, and draws on an impressive breadth of reference from criticism, biography, social and political theory, psychology and neuroscience. Her work will add a new dimension to professional coaching."

– **Professor Bill Jones**, Editor, Universities Association of Lifelong Learning, University of Leicester

Coaching for Professional Development

Using Literature to Support Success

Christine A. Eastman

Routledge
Taylor & Francis Group
LONDON AND NEW YORK

First published 2019
by Routledge
2 Park Square, Milton Park, Abingdon, Oxon OX14 4RN

and by Routledge
52 Vanderbilt Avenue, New York, NY 10017

Routledge is an imprint of the Taylor & Francis Group, an informa business

British Library Cataloguing-in-Publication Data
A catalogue record for this book is available from the British Library

Library of Congress Cataloging-in-Publication Data
A catalog record for this book has been requested

ISBN: 978-1-138-05725-8 (hbk)
ISBN: 978-1-138-05727-2 (pbk)
ISBN: 978-1-315-16494-6 (ebk)

Typeset in Times New Roman
by Apex CoVantage, LLC

To Samuel, truly *il migglior fabbro*

And to all my fantastic students in the United States, the United Kingdom, Spain, Greece, the Netherlands, United Arab Emirates, Israel, France, Singapore, Hong Kong, Canada, Germany, Austria, Poland, Russia, Slovakia, and Turkey. You have taught me to be a better coach, writer, and teacher. With heartfelt appreciation.

Contents

Acknowledgements

The extract from "The Swimmer" by John Cheever printed in Chapter 3 is from "The Swimmer" by John Cheever, published by Jonathan Cape. It has been reprinted by permission of The Random House Group Ltd. ©John Cheever 1979.

The extract from *Death of a Salesman* in Chapter 4 is from "Act One" from *Death of a Salesman* by Arthur Miller, copyright 1949, renewed @ 1977 by Arthur Miller. It has been used here by permission of Viking Books, an imprint of Penguin Publishing Group, a division of Penguin Random House LLC. All rights reserved.

The excerpts from *The Leopard* in Chapter 5 are from *The Leopard* by Giuseppe Tomasi di Lampedusa, translation copyright © 1960 by William Collins & Co. Ltd. and Penguin Random House LLC. Copyright renewed © 1988 by William Collins PLC and Penguin Random House LLC. Used by permission of Pantheon Books, an imprint of the Knopf Doubleday Publishing Group, a division of Penguin Random House LLC. All rights reserved.

I am grateful to the publishers for permission to reproduce these extracts here.

Introduction

> There are certain queer times and occasions in this strange mixed affair we call life when a man takes this whole universe for a vast practical joke, though the wit thereof he but dimly discerns, and more than suspects that the joke is at nobody's expense but his own
>
> – Herman Melville, *Moby-Dick*

Coaching for Professional Development: Using Literature to Support Success is a book about experiment or experimental chutzpah, if you will. In my quest for a bold and iconoclastic way of coaching, I decided on the experiment of using literature as a coaching tool, and I must admit that the enterprise originated to some extent in an act of self-indulgence. I love literature, have taught literature, and have an irrepressible desire to use literary works in my practice as an educator. This book explores the value that literature can bring to coaching. My background as an American literature specialist suited my purposes: I wanted to use stories of loss, of failure, of alienation, and of human suffering – stories that had long preoccupied me in my own exploration of the terrain of the American literary canon – in a coaching dialogue. In this introduction, I explain my rationale for using literary texts in a coaching dialogue, and I offer an appraisal of what these kinds of text can bring to organizational coaching. Furthermore, I discuss my choice of texts and amplify the meaning of how I use the word "canon." I also consider the role of biography in coaching and how the process of conceptualizing one's life in narrative terms intersects with and can be enhanced by literary reading.

Let me begin by relating a story that confirmed my long-standing and hitherto untested theory that literature could be used as a coaching tool. I had long encouraged students from diverse disciplines to read literary works as part of their research programs. Working at two universities, first as the director of applied professional practice and then as a senior lecturer in work-based learning, I wanted to enrich students' inquiries by harnessing the power of literature to support them in reflecting on their social values and in developing new ways of seeing the world. My work with the students profiled in this book is no different, with the exception that my focus here is on coaching. In this book, I develop a theory of coaching with literature based on exploring the analogies between coaching practice and the act of reading. The students profiled here, drawn from large multinational organizations, are sponsored by their companies to complete master's degrees in professional practice. Their master's projects invariably have a coaching focus. In the chapters that follow, I discuss how I guided diverse groups of these students to embrace literature as a positive influence on their coaching practice. The results of my work with various cohorts suggest that literary works can enhance how coaches and their coachees conceptualize workplace challenges, reflect on their personal trajectories, and devise solutions for the problems they encounter. My case for literary works as a coaching tool is based on qualitative analysis of my students' evaluation of the effectiveness of the literary strategy in their coaching practice. My method of eliciting the students' feedback through anonymous questionnaires and semistructured interviews presents a number of limitations. In particular, the methods I used to collect the data to gauge the effectiveness of my pedagogical strategy do not offer a complete picture of how literature can be used in coaching practice. Given that I rely on my students' feedback to generate a broad picture of the successes and challenges of my strategy in diverse organizational contexts, my evidence is contingent on the detail and objectivity of my students' reporting. I am their instructor, so there is always going to be a reluctance to dismiss my ideas when students think their grades lie in the balance. However, I have been able to supplement the evidence provided by my students in my interactions with professional coaches. When I was invited to give a workshop on how I use literature in coaching to a group of professional coaches from around the UK who worked in universities and in private practice, I recognized that such an occasion would be a litmus test for the validity of my literary approach to coaching. These professionals, not being students dependent on me for a grade, were free to dismiss my ideas as bunkum. I explained my technique and invited these professionals to let me know in no uncertain terms if they felt my approach to coaching was not workable in the real-world contexts they encountered in their own practice. I outlined my thoughts on John Cheever's "The Swimmer," a literary work discussed in Chapter 3 of this book. I had distributed the story among the workshop participants a week in advance because I was interested in whether they agreed that reading and discussing "The Swimmer" could facilitate a coaching conversation.

I was not surprised that the coaches found the story, in their own words, "beautiful," "haunting," "disturbing," and "intriguing" and that they appreciated its ambiguity and "layeredness" as one coach put it. We discussed critical interpretations of the story and how I used it with coaching students. We looked at how Cheever "manipulated" emotion, and I shed light on his background and turbulent life that is revealed in Blake Bailey's biography of him. I was astonished at how readily these professional people – psychologists, lecturers, experts working in the medical field, organizational development gurus – appreciated the value of adopting a literary perspective in coaching. A vital piece of feedback from my workshop with these professional coaches was that as long as an explanation of why a piece of literature was chosen and the context of this literature was provided, literary works apparently offered great potential as a tool for maximizing the impact of a coaching session. I subsequently reflected on some of my students' challenges, difficulties, and resistance to using literature in coaching and came to the conclusion that in my zeal to get them to read a story I loved, I had not always explained the rationale for doing so as adequately as I could have.

The coaches I encountered in my workshop were enthusiastic about my emphasis on metaphor. We discussed how the use of metaphor could support people to communicate seemingly incomprehensible or incoherent emotions, making feelings more concrete and less vague and impoverished. I shared one of my tentative theories that writing and coaching originated in a similar impulse: the desire to interpret, to make sense of, to analyze a situation, and to bring illumination and awareness to the fore. To my mind, writing and coaching share a drive to make the unconscious conscious through a sensitivity to language, behavior, and motivation. For these professionals not only to grasp my intention and to approve of what I was trying to achieve but to come up to me later in the day or to email me later wanting to know more about how they could use a literary approach in their coaching was both thrilling and humbling. The premise of *Coaching for Professional Development* is that reading fiction helps us to imagine lives other than our own, which is incidentally an implicit goal of coaching. My discovery of this latent nexus between coaching and reading came about through the simple desire to share my love of classic literature with students to help them grow as coaches. My aim here is to weigh up the benefits and explore the challenges I confronted in encouraging my coaching students to use this innovative coaching strategy. The book points to some of the ways my literary approach to coaching might be implemented in an array of organizational contexts and seeks to present a case for the value of integrating a process of reading and reflecting on literature into coaching practice.

The following accounts – a series of case studies exploring how literary works were used in a range of coaching contexts – are offered in the spirit of experimentation with which my idea of using literature in coaching arose. These are audacious experiments in a field of study that is, at times, contested, polarized, and even defensive. This book argues for the need to use literature as a basis for coaching and explores, at the same time, the intimate connection between the two, a connection that up to now we have unwittingly neglected.

Background to *Coaching for Professional Development*

The idea of using literature in coaching stemmed from a previous research project that explored how literary texts might be integrated into a work-based learning curriculum. For years I had worked with professionals from all walks of life and had sought to illustrate to them how they might benefit from a creative engagement with literary texts in their area of expertise or discipline. I encouraged mariners to read Richard Henry Dana's *Two Years before the Mast* or Herman Melville's *Redburn*. I directed teachers to John Edward Williams' *Stoner* or Chaim Potok's *The Chosen* and canine trainers to Fred Gipson's *Old Yeller* or Jack London's *White Fang*. I had a group of aviators who lost no time devouring Antoine de St Exupéry's *Vol de Nuit* (*Night Flight*) about the perils of early mail flights in South America. These postgraduate students were at the top of their professions – managing their own businesses, directing privately and publicly owned organizations, running retail, financial or commercial concerns – and were expected to produce research projects that examined their work critically and analytically. I was looking for a way of helping them to question assumptions, to resist simplistic answers, and to become better communicators. I persuaded them that reflecting on the lives of fictional characters was a means to achieve these goals. I was not expecting anyone to read a novel simply as a work of art or to appreciate it as a literary specialist. My belief was that an engagement with literature would help students to produce better projects and to learn more about themselves and others' worlds. The resulting improvement in the quality of their work convinced me of the value of my pedagogical approach. Their work was of a higher standard than the work of students who had preceded them and who had not worked with literature, and their formal feedback reported extremely high satisfaction on the course, a satisfaction they attributed to learning new and innovative ways of investigating their work-based problems.

When I started to work with cohorts of students from the sales industry, I was unsurprised that the majority of their project investigations gravitated toward coaching. Coaching promises great benefits to companies, and many students were enthusiastic converts to its advantages: clearer communication, improved performance, better teamwork, and a focused goal of building on strengths and minimizing weaknesses. As a concept, coaching was subject to a wide range of diverse interpretations among my students. In the introductory session to my course with coaching students, I encourage them to find common ground among their divergent interpretations of what coaching is and how it works. I ask them as a group to agree on a series of tenets that underpin their collective understanding of the nature of coaching. The following is an illustrative example of the ideas my different cohorts are able to agree on:

- Coaching provides people with a better understanding of what they are doing and how they can do something differently if things are not working well;
- Coaching encompasses improving practice through reflection and inquiry;
- Research is essential if coaching is to develop into a highly regarded profession.

My students tend to embark on the course with the belief that a coaching culture at their organizations can nurture continuing development and bring fresh perspectives to their practice. The challenge for me is to provide a means of bringing a creative perspective to their coaching practice and to help them to articulate the advantages of their practice through improved writing skills. I do not want them to confine themselves to using research approaches that are prescriptive, simplistic, neat models that offer little scope for stretching their imagination. Literature in my own work as an educator has therefore become a teaching tool that can stimulate rigorous inquiry into students' practice and that can help them to deliver and articulate the benefits of a more nuanced and sophisticated mode of coaching. Close attention to the coaching relationship means attention to people's stories, and attention to people's stories can ideally be accessed by a rich and rewarding engagement with a literary text: narrative is the liminal place within the human condition, and as coaches we would be seriously remiss to ignore the role it can and should play in our lives. *Coaching for Professional Practice* makes a case for the value that literary works can bring to coaching.

Definitions

When I help my students craft their 12,000-word coaching projects on examining ways of improving their practice and that of others in their organizations, I am adamant that they define their terms. Since most of the students are involved in some aspect of sales, terms such as KPIs (key performance indicators), Blue Ocean Strategy (capitalizing on profitable propositions), and ROI (return on investment – a resultant financial success following a specific strategy) crop up frequently. When discussing coaching in an organizational context, students deploy a range of buzzwords and concepts such as "action learning," "transformational leadership," "performance coaching," and "leadership coaching." Their written work sometimes sags under the terminological weight of unexamined concepts that generate a superficial impression of academic profundity. I encourage my students to explain the terms that undergird their discussion for the simple reason that definitions matter because clarity matters. It is in this spirit of terminological clarity that I shall define the concepts that appear in the following chapters. When I discuss my enlisting "canonical American writers" in my efforts to illustrate the diverse ways an ordinary coaching interchange can be transformed into a rich and dramatic experience, I am drawn to the editor-in-chief of the five-volume *Norton Anthology of American Literature*, Nina Baym (2007), and to her prefatory remarks on the anthology's canonical enlargement:

> Teachers and students remain committed to the idea of the literary – that writers strive to produce artefacts that are both intellectually serious and formally skillful – but believe more than ever that writers should be understood in relation to their cultural and historical situations.
>
> (xviii)

In my work with coaching students discussed in the following chapters, the authors with whom I chose to work are predominantly eminent American writers such as Herman Melville, Willa Cather, John Cheever, James Baldwin, and Arthur

Miller. But writers as diverse as Maxine Hong Kingston, Charles Simic, Lydia Maria Child, and Alberto Rios are considered members of the intellectually serious and formally weighty pantheon of American literary craftspeople that could be used by coaches interested in a literary approach. My only caveat is that the literary piece or excerpt must be complex enough to be subjected to interpretive questions. The writer must be an expert in telling a good story, what Christopher Linforth (2011, xiv) calls a "technically proficient" piece with "narrative complexity," "thematic resonance," and "strong characterization" all present.

My last chapter profiles a literary work that exhibits all of these qualities but is taken from Italian literature. My general emphasis on American literature in this book simply reflects my personal experience and expertise. I would suggest that the most effective works for enhancing a coaching dialogue are those that resonate most with the coach or coachee in question. Coaches need to be able to transmit their interest in a literary work to their coachees for the text to emerge as a valuable tool. The titles that appear in the subsequent chapters are offered, then, not in the spirit of prescription but rather of illustration. My inclusion of an Italian text is designed to capture this sense of flexibility in designing the materials for a literary approach to coaching. I was convinced that it was incumbent upon me to include Lampedusa's great novel because it constitutes an exceptionally eloquent example of how literature can anatomize even the most fleeting of human emotions. After all, although we read for comfort, for entertainment, for the sheer pleasure of experiencing beautiful language adeptly employed, reading fiction serves – I would argue – ultimately to satisfy our curiosity about how other people live. It is this conviction that underpins my epistemological concerns in this book and that guides my choice of exemplary authors. I want to make a claim for what literature can do: the fictional experiences that we read about can trigger reflection on our own stories and, especially in an educational context, can help us articulate these stories more cogently.

As regards definitions, I need to make a distinction between coaching and mentoring: I have written a coaching book. It is neither a manual nor a self-help text but a work comprising five narratives that detail what happened when I used literary texts to encourage my students to look at themselves more closely, to think more critically and reflectively, and to write better. This is not a book about literary theory but about what literature can offer us in order to address our very human need to cope with the things that happen to us. This is therefore a practical book that makes the case that life's ambiguities and the all-too-frequent gulf between our expectations and how life turns out are aspects of human experience dramatized vividly in literature. Using literature in coaching helps us to recognize the "unknowableness" of life, assisting us as we navigate complexity, ambiguity, and irrelevancies. Literature properly used, can, this book argues, make us better coaches.

One final definition is in order here. If I had to be pinned down to define coaching, I would offer the following: "the art of helping others to make sense of the ordinary and the extraordinary" – that is, those same facets of life that are illustrated imaginatively and compellingly in fiction. Hannah Arendt (1958) reminds us of a maxim of ancient Greece: we have only lived fully when we have stories about our experiences to relate. As committed coaches, we encourage our coachees to see the coaching process as meaningful, and literature becomes the ideal tool to examine actions, experiences, and emotions, rendering a meaningful link between the lived and the fictionalized life. As one of my more astute students put it, "the story in front of us is a way of talking about our own problems and blockages *without* talking about our own problems and blockages."

Biography

Coaching for Professional Development explores stories such as "Neighbor Rosicky" and plays such as *Death of a Salesman* as it investigates transformational coaching theories. The book is also drawn from a range of other sources, for example biographical. The act of "capturing" a life, especially that aspect of existence Park Honan (1979) calls the sense of "livingness," presents insurmountable challenges at times. People's lives invariably elude us:

> We have no single word for the sense of experiencing life not just today, or this hour, but on the curious moment-to-moment knife edge of time. Life seems to depart as soon as it begins so there is no stasis and every present is a present-that-was.
>
> (117)

Biography is intimately tied with fiction in this book because of the importance of biography in coaching. The perspective I bring to bear on the works by Willa Cather, John Cheever, and Arthur Miller is illuminated by the work of their biographers – James Woodress, Blake Bailey, and Christopher Bigsby – who help to elucidate these authors' motivations in constructing their fictional characters. I have drawn on biography to provide a flavor of the authors' lives with the aim of capturing how the practice of writing feeds on personal experience. Encouraging coachees to use literary texts as vectors of self-expression is a process that can be enhanced by bringing to light the relationship between written expression and life experience. As coachees are made aware of the life behind the literary work, they can begin to reflect on the processes – both metaphorical and direct – by which they might articulate their own concerns.

At the coaching workshop I have discussed earlier in this introduction, I touched upon Cheever's life, his alcoholism, his repressed homosexuality, and his literary jealousies as a means of entering the cultural and social concerns of the era and the writer's reaction to such concerns. Both in coaching and in literature, there will inevitably be problems of interpretation: fleshing out a work's creator can help students with little training in the reading of fiction to grasp the work better. In the past, I have always tried to separate artists from their art, possibly because of the concern that students might identify the attitudes and behaviors exhibited by fictional characters with those of the writers themselves. It is too easy to dismiss an ethically complex work as immoral when we assume that characters' opinions and acts are a cipher for those of the author. A student who had previously enjoyed *Lady Windermere's Fan* and *The Importance of Being Earnest* during a taster course on Victorian plays came to class to tell me that she would not be returning because she had discovered that Wilde's lifestyle and attitudes were not to her liking. A class on feminist theory saw a couple of students exit in disgust after digesting certain particularities of the crime writer Patricia Highsmith's less-than-conventional behavior. When I taught literature I was keen to emphasize how vital it was to separate creator from creation. However, a biographical perspective can be used profitably in coaching. The results of the case studies explored in the following chapters testify to the fact that the more coaching students know about the author, the richer their encounter with the work becomes. At the coaching workshop, people were eager for biographical recommendations on Cheever. His writing made them want to know more about the man. A biographical concern is central to coaching, and it constitutes, moreover, a natural point of departure for coaches keen to apply literary works in their practice.

Audience and writing

Coaching for Professional Development is aimed at academic staff in higher education, particularly those working in professional practice, work-based learning, business, and, of course, coaching. The literary model outlined in this book is designed to be adopted by professional coaches in a creative and comfortable way that suits their specific purposes and the needs of their clients. Psychotherapists and counselors developing their commercial awareness and business coaches challenging themselves to go beyond functional or technical models will find the model outlined in this book both novel and potentially transformative in their coaching practice. The literary model is not rooted in any psychotherapeutic school but instead draws on elements of existential, person-centered, cognitive-behavioral, and gestalt coaching. The book sets out a case for using literary fictional texts to enhance the coaching dialogue. I intend to demonstrate that using fictional characters in a coaching intervention can harness imagination, encourage growth, enrich a coaching curriculum, and, especially for professional practice and coaching students, close the gap between theory and practice. The fictional narrative approach has a purposeful application in advancing coaching beyond training models while at the same time offering coaches professional development. The literary model is particularly effective in facilitating a space of transit for imagining other lives. In their everyday practice, most coaches want to understand their coachees' and clients' contexts. Mapping out the threshold between the real and the imaginary – between the client's case and the fictional case – trains coaches to probe their clients' situations, to understand what they want to achieve, and enables their clients to do the same.[1]

The literary coaching model set out in the following chapters is particularly valuable because of the attention it urges we pay to language. Language plays an important role in the coaching process. An attentiveness to what clients say – how they describe their scenarios, challenges, problems – and the images and phrases they use is central to coaching. A significant component of the training I offer my student-coaches is designed to encourage this attentiveness to language. I ask my students to keep a journal (as many coaches recommend), with the subtle difference that I point my students toward Giuseppe Tomasi di Lampedusa's journal as a model to which I encourage them to aspire. Lampedusa's correspondence in *Letters from London and Europe* is penetrating, sharp, and funny. Naturally we cannot all have the talent for language that Lampedusa possessed, but we can develop an eye for detail. The detail Lampedusa brings to bear on the world around him culminated in his 1958 masterpiece *The Leopard*, a novel whose applications for coaching practice are discussed in Chapter 5. Lampedusa developed, honed, and polished this eye for detail in his *Letters*, which became his "journaling." An eye for detail, that crucial ability to peer into another's mind, is our ultimate objective in coaching. Promoting learning and behavioral change in coaching is predicated on promoting intentional change. For a coach to effect deliberate, demanding change in a client, there needs to be a focused attention on the recipient's vision and values (Howard 2015). In encouraging attention to observational detail via journaling, the coach can elicit information about a client's vision and values. A client, attentive to the working of her internal and external worlds, can develop a better understanding of these visions and values and be able to articulate them with greater precision and acuity.

Students

The data used to flesh out and corroborate the impact of the coaching model outlined in this book are drawn primarily from students' voices. I have also drawn on coaching and other pertinent literature, but the main evidence offered for the effectiveness of this literary model works is from feedback from students who have applied it in their very own practice. I have solicited this feedback via Skype interviews and the students' written testimony. The majority of the students profiled in this book were working on projects – 12,000-word inquiries into their practice that they wrote according to specifications similar to those of social science journal articles with sections on the literature review, methodology, discussion, analysis, and recommendations. These were mature students, sponsored by their companies to undertake a report or project reinforced by a wide range of academic reading and triangulated by interview and questionnaire analyses.

I integrate literature into the syllabus and required reading. Additionally, many of these students took on the literary reading discussed in these chapters as supplementary literature they wished to use to gauge whether the literary route could enhance their practice. Most of the students came from organizations that had no formal coaching program and wanted to bring about a climate that was more receptive to coaching. Many of them were qualified coaches and were convinced that organizations with a strong coaching ethos would be better places to work. One group came from a company with a well-established coaching program that relied on specific behavioral and personality analysis tools. With one or two notable exceptions, these students were the most resistant to my literary approach, possibly because they had been acculturated to dominant schools of coaching that seemed to them to admit little scope for distinct techniques. They were somewhat institutionalized in their reluctance to go beyond safe and prescriptive behavioral assessment tools that, although tried and tested, did not always tell them what they did not know and often kept them within the rigid boundaries of their coaching abilities. I wanted them to explore the terrain beyond those boundaries.

As regards the number of students who tested the literary approach, out of forty students across the various cohorts, I had twenty-four participants. I also interviewed three doctoral students, two of whom were writing up coaching doctorates. As I explain throughout the following chapters, *Coaching for Professional Development* was conceived as a response to student dissatisfaction with performance coaching models. I perceived in my students a desire to connect more empathically with their imagination and creativity, and I conceived a literary approach to coaching that would allow students to respond to the works of others as well as to draw on their own experience.

A performance coaching model has its uses and can instigate reflections on performance and behavior, but many of my students seemed to be clamoring for a way to support more complex coaching questions such as, how should I live? They were struggling with how to transform themselves in the workplace and in life. Literature offers an innovative model for professional development as it encourages us to address issues of identity, life themes, and narrative representation. Underpinning these issues is emotion. To my mind, the power of stories lies in their ability to tap into our emotions. Examining emotions in stories can in turn help to bring greater clarity to our lives. Coaching always contains the possibility of depth: the session should be about "becoming," about the possibility of transformation. The theme of transformation is evident in each of the texts I explore in the following chapters. Without an in-depth emotional explanation, without the examination of why we are feeling what we are feeling, we will never reach our full transformational potential.

Jenefer Robinson (2005) argues that there is a kind of evaluation in every emotional encounter we have. It would, therefore, be reasonable to persuade those in a coaching scenario to follow the progress of an unfolding emotional process. Robinson points out that we cannot adequately understand literature without being aware of our emotional responses. Literature, in this sense, is remarkably similar to life: we cannot understand ourselves or our clients without a close attentiveness to our emotional responses. For Robinson, the process of reading is emotionally educational: "we would do better to stay away from the generalizations of philosophers and psychologists, and turn instead to the detailed studies of emotion that we find in great literature" (99). My choice of texts was dictated by their intense emotional richness and their potential to support coaches and coachees to reflect on their emotional responses and learn from such responses.

What follows

I want to preface this section with a discussion of the more and less successful aspects of my encouraging students to use literature in coaching. One of the hurdles I encountered with my coaching students was their reticence to persevere with more linguistically complex works of prose. Herman Melville's "Bartleby, the Scrivener: A Story of Wall Street" had a few admirers, but on the whole, many students were put off by their initial impressions of Melville's writing. Melville's language, rooted in the mid-nineteenth century and crafted through his immersion in Shakespeare, the Old Testament, and a host of metaphysical and ancient Greek philosophers, is not the easiest to approach for students without a literary background. I fear that by failing to choose a more accessible text for my students to use, I undoubtedly put off many potential converts to my literary coaching method. I am not suggesting that coaches avoid using difficult texts in their practices, but tailoring the choice of text to suit the profile and needs of coachees is an important first step in overcoming initial resistance. Rather than to use the entirety of "Bartleby" in a coaching session, an alternative approach would be to choose carefully selected passages from one of Melville's works. Nathaniel Philbrick (2013), in his slim volume extolling the virtues of Melvillean philosophy and prose while making a case for reading *Moby-Dick*, sensibly makes the following suggestion:

> *Moby-Dick* is a long book, and time is short. Even a sentence, a mere phrase will do.
>
> The important thing is to spend some time with the novel, to listen as you read, to feel the prose adapt to the various voices that flowed through Melville during the book's composition like intermittent ghosts with something urgent and essential to say.
>
> (9)

Coaches who want to use literature in their practice but feel they are not yet ready to take on an entire composition could fruitfully follow Philbrick's advice on how to read Melville. Using part of a longer text – an image, a metaphor, a dialogue between two characters – can illuminate a coaching objective just as compellingly as a longer composition.

Related to the difficulties surrounding language and the length of literary works as barriers to their productive use in coaching is the idea of expectations. Many of my coaching students who were approaching literary texts as coaches expected to treat the literary characters as clients in need of coaching. Chapter 1 shows how many of my coaching students read "Bartleby, the Scrivener" in too literal a frame of mind and failed to grasp Melville's use of irony and humor. They had difficulties in engaging with the text on a metaphorical level: they read Melville's description as if it were a real-life account of a dysfunctional workplace rather than as a metaphor for Melville's thematic concerns. In a sense, they felt that they had to coach Bartleby. What I needed to have done with these students was to manage their expectations in approaching the literary work and the coaching activity. I wanted them to read the story not as coaches but simply as readers. They were not to coach Bartleby but rather use Bartleby as a springboard for coaching somebody else. One way to guard against overly literal approaches to coaching with literature is to begin with a preliminary session to gloss salient aspects of an author's biography and literary reception – nothing complicated – just a few facts that would help a student or coachee or client to enter the world of the story with greater ease. My students found that when a selected excerpt from "Bartleby" was prefaced by a brief discussion of the themes of the text, they were able to use the excerpt more effectively to elicit reactions from their coachees. The background to the story and the brevity of the excerpt enabled their coachees to respond more thoughtfully as they discussed the office tensions, imagery, and language contained in the excerpt.

I chose "Bartleby" because I thought the story of a "walled-in" employee whose apathy and disengagement create serious workplace problems would be the ideal text through which to enter a deeply dysfunctional world and learn lessons from exposure to it. My rationale was that the story had the potential to support coaching discussions on personal struggles, appropriate and inappropriate behaviors, and identity issues. "Bartleby" became a divisive read because of its textual difficulty. Written in the mid-nineteenth century, its prose presented challenges to students, with many of them irritated by having to look up archaic or uncommon words or being forced to read more than once a particularly dense, metaphysical passage. Moreover, the short story is not particularly short, so busy professionals tend to prefer not to dedicate great time and effort to deciphering an enigmatic narrative touching upon the psychological and social transformations captured in Melville's snapshot of American antebellum culture.

Students who read and engaged with the story reported that the eponymous character's issues were too "deep seated" to be treated by a coach. Many of the students took Bartleby's dysfunction literally and talked about how human resources would have to deal with him and that the threat of litigation would be imminent if "proper channels" of employment law were not followed exactly. On the other hand, there were a few students who were convinced that reading "Bartleby" could support the coaching process, particularly in the recruitment area, what one student named "the process of identifying a Bartleby before it's too late." Overall, students found it difficult to identify with the characters in the story. If it is difficult to identify with a character, there is indeed an obstacle to the kind of sympathetic identification needed for empathy that I believe is essential in coaching. As a "coaching text," "Bartleby" is not ideal. My experience in using it with my students and their experience in using the text in their organizations taught me the importance of being circumspect in choosing literary texts and in managing participants' expectations of the activity.

Willa Cather's "Neighbor Rosicky" garnered comparatively few complaints. It is immensely readable: some of the students told me they used it as bedtime reading for their children because of its "fairy-tale qualities" and the fact that it is "a straightforward, gentle story about morals, values and how to live a good life." In fact, if time is not an issue, you might want to try excerpts or even the full work of *The Professor's House*, *My Ántonia*, or *The Lost Lady* with their highly engaging mastery of style and the expansiveness of feeling captured by Cather's portraits of her characters' psychology. Cather's themes of heroic aspiration, stoicism, passion for creativity, and the challenges of being alive are molded into distinctive, lyrical prose that, from my experience, students find charming and compelling.

The experience of working with Willa Cather's short story "Neighbor Rosicky" was starkly different from that of "Bartleby, the Scrivener." My choice of this straightforward tale was motivated by the fact that this group of telecommunications salespeople mainly comprised nonnative English speakers. Cather's prose style is simple and unencumbered by metaphysical meandering. "Neighbor Rosicky," in particular, the story of a Czech immigrant living in America who looks back over his fruitful life, seemed the ideal text to use to discuss themes of low morale, poor management, and a disengaged workforce that felt shunted into the sidelines of the organization. The coaching students with whom I worked using Cather's text revealed in our face-to-face seminars and Skype sessions that they did not feel valued by the company. Cather's story explores alienation, isolation, and what it means to want to be part of something *bigger* – a family, a community, a society, a country. Many in the group bemoaned the company's recent takeover. It had been, they said, "like a family," but now the company had been subsumed within a larger "impersonal" organization; they no longer enjoyed their earlier sense of belonging.

The feedback I received from students on both reading and using the story as a coaching tool was positive. The values Cather emphasizes – those of loyalty, courage, and determination – resonated with this group. They were able to use the story as a connection between Anton Rosicky's concept of the city as impersonal, cold, and fraught with danger with the way their company felt to them then. They made an emotional leap in their own reading and in their coaching sessions with their colleagues, and they were able to use the story as a framework for articulating their hopes and plans for the company as part of a transformational coaching process in team discussions. The practice of using the story with these students confirmed my conviction that we should be unafraid to work with imagery and metaphor in coaching. The literary coaching strategy I outline in this book might seem to go against the grain of contemporary reading habits, which certainly appeared to be the case with "Bartleby." In my work with students, I have found often that there are individuals who enjoy reading for leisure and that there are others who read for knowledge. Both groups of readers nevertheless share an interest in discovering unknown writers, especially fictional writers about whom they have never heard. The literary coaching strategy is aimed to satisfy the needs of both habitual and utilitarian readers by encouraging both groups to read little-known texts in unconventional ways. The element of surprise can trigger deep personal reflection in coachees and places the literary text in the service of self-knowledge.

John Cheever's short stories are equally well suited to a literary coaching approach. Cheever's prose is clear and unencumbered, his observations astute and wise, and the ambiguity of his stories that deal with the themes of loss, failure, and alienation make them appropriate entry points for coaching discussions. "The Swimmer," the story I explore in Chapter 3, is able to accommodate both personal and universal readings. My students used it to reflect on how managers need to understand and empathize with individuals in their teams. The story is ideal for demonstrating the role literature can play in illuminating the challenges most of us are likely to encounter at work or in life generally.

Among the texts I used with my students and that form the basis of my discussion in this book, *Death of a Salesman* is unique in that it is a play and was therefore written to be watched rather than read. Schlöndorff's 1985 production is freely available online and brings Arthur Miller's play to life in a compelling dramatization. The theatrical and linguistic depth of Miller's creation is artfully rendered in Schlöndorff's production. Miller's depiction of an absurd universe in which meaning is elusive and aging and failure break the human spirit resonated with the salespeople to whom I introduced the play. In addition to using the film version with my students, I selected an excerpt of dialogue between Willy Loman and his wife, Linda, in order to illustrate how words such as "values," "morality," "distrust," and "self-awareness" become fully fleshed-out realities in the hands of a dramatist of Miller's stature.

Using John Cheever's "The Swimmer" and Arthur Miller's *Death of a Salesman* yielded equally positive results. Both texts are more contemporary examples of twentieth-century writing that is more accessible to non-literary specialists than Melville's "Bartleby." Both Cheever and Miller explore many of the themes that are particularly relevant in twenty-first-century corporate life – loneliness, self-deception, alienation, identity. In his development of the themes of competition, the cutthroat nature of sales pressure, conformity, and the balance between family and working life, Miller especially evokes the very preoccupations that dominate corporate coaching. His and Cheever's texts address work-based politics, professional tensions, and life's complexities in engaging and poignant ways that can capture the imagination of corporate coachees. Both Cheever's short story and Miller's play are multi-layered and open to a variety of interpretations. They are ideally suited to evoking readers' and spectators' personal memories and narratives and can help to bring about a bond that enables coaches and coachees to speak freely about their experiences. Both stories foreground the theme of "failure," an idea often glossed over in corporate dialogue but that bubbles beneath the surface of workplace anxiety. Commenting on the ambiguity of Cheever's protagonist Neddy Merrill and his fate depicted in "The Swimmer," one of my students noted: "we are left to choose the character's destiny." The ambiguity of Cheever's story not only accounts for its power, it also helps to explain why literary texts are particularly well suited to the role of stimulating and enhancing the quality of coaching dialogue. A story such as Cheever's allows readers imaginatively to explore the options open to a character as an analogue for the paths open to them in their own lives. A character in a predicament encourages our reflection on the decisions with which we are faced in our own lives. Works like Cheever's and Miller's with their tragic gaze on the crossroads of human action can help to break workplace taboos. Echoing the determined optimism of American cultural life, as it is parodied in these two texts, many organizations cloak themselves in self-conscious, relentless buoyancy that can become wearying to their employees. There is no place for disappointment, defeat, or bitterness, and the mere whiff of these dour states can bring calumny down on employees who bring anything other than an upbeat tenor to their working life. Works by Cheever and Miller give readers permission to discuss the disappointments of life: these works bring failure out into the open and allow coaches and coachees to inhabit a space in which it is appropriate to talk about things that are negative, sad, or even tragic.

Experience has taught me that the texts that people are most willing and able to engage with are those that have a degree of relevance for their personal and intellectual interests. For example, coaching students exploring diversity in coaching found the robust and energizing prose of the African-American essayist and novelist James Baldwin particularly appealing. A fiery political commentator, Baldwin reflects on issues of identity in his writing. His essays are stark and angry portrayals of the failure of race relations in mid-twentieth-century America, and his writing can be used to shed fresh insight on how individuals negotiate the choices they face in their life and on the perils of succumbing to destructive emotions. Baldwin's work helped students to engage in rich and moving discussions about their place and identity at work and in society. They saw no lack of relevance in essays relating events from the 1940s.

Some of my students read Lampedusa's *The Leopard* and were able to use the novel with their colleagues to try to come to terms with the complexities of experience and particularly with the difficulty of change. *The Leopard* is a writerly novel, lyrical and at times linguistically and thematically challenging. As happened when I used "Bartleby" with some of my students, there were some who found Lampedusa's work daunting. My experiments with Lampedusa confirmed my intuition that literary texts need to be paired thoughtfully and productively with their audience in a coaching discussion. There is no one-size-fits-all syllabus for coaching with literature; rather, different texts appeal to different groups and individuals, and it is helpful if there is a level of thematic coherence in the texts under discussion and the issues at play in the coaching exchange. The master's coaching students with whom I used Lampedusa were resistant on the whole. Many suggested they were unable to "enter" it. The doctoral students in general were far more enthusiastic about *The Leopard.* They admired Lampedusa's prose and believed that it could support their own writing. If addressing a practical, goal-focused aspect of behavioral change, using *The Leopard* might not be entirely appropriate. But for my doctoral students who were undertaking more research-oriented reflections on organizational change, Lampedusa emerged as a more fitting interlocutor for their work.

Each of the chapters that follow is structured around one of the literary works introduced above. Chapter 1 outlines the case for the value literary works can bring to coaching in the context of an account of what happened when I asked students to read "Bartleby, the Scrivener: A Story of Wall Street." It discusses Robert Coles's experiences at Harvard University using literature to support his students in thinking more critically and argues, furthermore, that engaging with literature can engender empathy for others. My discussions encompass my rationale for choosing "Bartleby" as a coaching text, the limitations of behavioral tools such as DISC, and feedback from students who used the story as a coaching tool in their own practice.

Chapter 2 presents my work with a student cohort employed at a large global firm in the telecommunications sector. It draws on James Woodress's biography of Willa Cather in a discussion of how Cather's work can be used in coaching. I discuss how my choice of Cather's text with these students was informed by their learning needs that emerged in my discussions with them. As I discovered the students did not feel supported at their organization, I began to reflect on how a text such as Cather's "Neighbor Rosicky" could address the role of emotions in coaching. I draw on the work of Tatiana Bachkirova and Elaine Cox to make the case that the emotional void in organizational coaching can be filled by engaging with literature such as "Neighbor Rosicky." I use Woodress's biography of Cather to explore how Cather's method of getting under the skin of her characters can help coaches who are unsure of how to work emotionally with clients. My discussion on "Neighbor Rosicky" also touches on how coaches can use myth to explore the dark side of human experience.

Chapter 3 details my work with John Cheever's "The Swimmer," a story I have used extensively with both taught-postgraduate and research students. Short, easy to read, and multilayered, Cheever's story lends itself to coaching discussions on the themes of failure, family, and management. In this chapter I explore how my students found Cheever's story a rich stimulus for reflection on difficult subjects such as melancholy, loneliness, self-deception, alienation, and the vagaries of the human condition. Cheever's profound understanding of his own and others' sense of failure can help us to explore how to live a more emotionally meaningful life. The chapter describes what happened when I gave students an excerpt to use in their coaching practice: they relate what worked, what didn't work, and the reasons why. I discuss the role of memory and touch upon Saint Augustine's *Confessions* in an analysis of the vital role played by memory in the coaching process. I draw on Blake Bailey's biography of Cheever and particularly on Bailey's insights into Cheever's self-destructive neuroses in my account of how coaches can use "The Swimmer" to support their clients to perceive their world in a more probing and thoughtful way. In this chapter, I also relate a coaching student's use of James Baldwin's "Notes of a Native Son" in his interrogation of race and diversity at his organization.

Chapter 4 explores how Willy Loman, the protagonist of *Death of a Salesman*, can spur reflection and self-interrogation in the area of sales coaching. I explore how we can use Willy Loman's family dynamics to examine the dead hand of conformity in office life, and I analyze the ways in which the roots of our early family life are inextricably entwined in office dynamics. I use Christopher Bigsby's biography of Arthur Miller in a discussion of the sociohistorical context of the play, and I illustrate how an awareness of this context can help coachees' to respond productively to Miller's work. I describe how the play's themes of success, failure, and the death of the American dream resonated deeply with a group of sales coaches. I relate students' reactions to reading and watching the play, and I analyze their emotional responses to Willy. I make a case for literary fiction as an alternative to self-help manuals, showing how such manuals offer comparatively simplistic and ultimately unsatisfactory solutions that are unable to foster the deep reflection and emotional exploration, which are central to the literary coaching model.

My final chapter posits the theory that coaching and writing are inextricably linked and argues that this connection is central to the value of literary works in coaching practice. I analyze writing blocks and illustrate their similarity to coaching blocks. I explore the nexus between writing and coaching in a discussion of *The Leopard.* I report on the strong feelings elicited by Lampedusa's text, on a spectrum ranging from numbing boredom to glowing adoration. I evaluate the coaching tool Personalisis in a comparative contrast with a literary approach to coaching, illustrating how getting coachees to engage with *The Leopard* might ultimately be far more effective in generating a fine-grained profile of an individual's personality than the comparatively generalized templates assigned by multiple choice Personalisis selections. The psychological appeal of the Personalisis tool has much in common with astrology. Individuals enjoy seeing the quirks and strengths of their personality and performance reflected back at them. But the danger of self-legitimizing coaching tools such as Personalisis is that, like horoscopes, they entail a sense of determinism. Pigeonholing idiosyncratic human beings into fixed categories may be comforting in the short term, but it can, in the long term, foster a sense of powerlessness together with the tendency to see personality traits as fixed and unchanging. Reading a text like *The Leopard* in a coaching context can encourage the deep personal reflection that is instrumental to managing change, both of the self and of the organization. *The Leopard* has been used widely in discussions of change management, and the protagonist Tancredi's dictum, "If we want things to stay as they are, things will have to change" (Lampedusa 2007, 19) has the power to capture the imagination of coachees grappling with the vicissitudes of change.

I used *The Leopard* in a series of seminars with doctoral students in the field of coaching who were struggling to articulate their ideas and to craft academic prose. I chose Lampedusa's text to illuminate the connection between writing and coaching. *The Leopard* foregrounds its author's concern with the texture of language. Reading such a text is an initiation in the aesthetic experience of conceptualizing writing as a means of self-discovery. Writing and coaching can both be characterized as vehicles of discovery. My doctoral students were receptive to the lessons evoked by Lampedusa's prose and began to see the possibilities of developing metaphor and other figures of speech in their own writing. The students were able, furthermore, to replicate the heuristic benefits of the text in their own coaching practice. A head teacher told me that she had set chapters of *The Leopard* as required reading for staff who were, in her words, "resisting change." Like "Bartleby," *The Leopard* has its disadvantages as a coaching tool. It is a complex work of literature that presents challenges for nonspecialist readers. However, when pitched to doctoral-level students, particularly those interested in ameliorating their writing, it was unparalleled.

In the final section of the book, I look ahead to using Shakespearean sonnets, dialogues, and soliloquies from the plays as vectors for exploring the themes of power and manipulation in the context of coaching. Shakespeare is a fitting continuation of the coaching experiments in which I have used writers like Melville, Cheever, Baldwin, Cather, Miller, and Lampedusa. Many of the writers I profile in this book are influenced consciously or unconsciously by the language, voice, and theatricality of the great playwright. Shakespeare's sophisticated and knowing attention to his characters' psychological, spiritual, and moral life is never far from these writers' creative minds. Melville was an omnivorous reader of Shakespeare (Philbrick 2013). Cather studied Shakespeare intensively at university and, as an undergraduate, published an essay on the equating of art and religion in his work (Woodress 1987). One of Cheever's earliest stories is entitled "Homage to Shakespeare" and discusses Cheever's degenerate grandfather. Cheever remarked that Shakespeare's plays "seemed to light and distinguish [his grandfather's] character and his past. What might have been defined as failure and profligacy towered like something kingly and tragic" (Bailey 2009, 10). Baldwin's first theater experience was a 1936 Orson Welles production of *Macbeth* with an all-black cast. He wrote forty years later as he reflected on his career that theater, and in particular the black actors' portrayal of Shakespearean characters in *Macbeth*, drove him to the pulpit and energized his writing career (Baldwin 2000). Miller performed in Shakespearian historical dramas in college productions and remarked on the perfection of *King Lear* in its demonstration of how pain can be reshaped into meaning (Bigsby 2008, 670). Lampedusa was an avid anglophile, well versed in Shakespearian drama, fond of quoting from Shakespearian sonnets in his correspondence (Lampedusa 2010). Just as one would be hard pressed to find a writer not influenced by Shakespeare's art, it would be difficult to find anyone in organizational coaching who had not been exposed to Shakespeare at school: his work is universal, and his themes of class, hypocrisy, ridicule, identity, and disguise are ideally suited to fomenting workplace discussion.

In the final section, I discuss some of the ways *The Tempest* might be used in a coaching setting. One of the last plays Shakespeare wrote, *The Tempest* revisits a familiar plot structure – a ruler cast from power, a shipwreck, and eventual triumph – and invests the story with a striking intensity and vivid dream-like quality. The unforeseen catastrophe of shipwreck – loss, disaster, and terror after happy progress and smooth sailing – is a powerful metaphor for thinking about careers and the perils and fears that plague so many of them. Most professionals can identify with the feeling of having pitched up on an unknown shore with few allies, little support, and diminished status. This play, like many others by Shakespeare, is a powerful dramatization of the sensation of having been stripped of one's identity while stumbling in unfamiliar territory. With a valedictory poignancy, *The Tempest* is one of richest and strongest embodiments of Shakespeare's poetic imagination.

The Tempest, we will see, is another tool in the arsenal of interventions for organizational coaching. The interventions described in the course of this book are, at their core, linguistic interventions, both made up of words and predicated on the conviction that words matter. In this spirit, I will use the words of one of my students to bring this introduction to its close. This passage is taken from an evaluation of my coaching program and novel approach to using literature as a coaching tool:

> In our organization, and I suspect in many others, managers over-schedule their coaching rotations and don't have time to coach properly. This increases the likelihood that a directive, prescriptive, and even mechanistic conversation will happen. A lack of preparation adds to this problem as coaches rarely review their last coaching session. Sharing a piece of literature can focus you – both coach and coachee – on the task and it allows for a period of reflective analysis that is crucial to the coaching process. If everyone had the opportunity to discuss just a few themes from a story as interesting as "The Swimmer," we could be able to engender the kind of coaching culture we aspire to.

Coaching for Professional Development suggests that literary works have a part to play in bringing about a change in coaching culture. In the chapters that follow, I privilege my students' voices as a window into the paradigm shifts in coaching practice currently underway in many of their organizations, and I trust that their example may serve as a blueprint for other coaches willing to make tentative steps in a literary direction. Our minds and bodies are taxed by an avalanche of adverse factors every day at work – simplistic solutions, fierce competition, organizational restructuring – and coaching offers workable and positive enabling tools to address such challenges. Treat this book as a tribute to the power of literature. It is designed to help coaches to see how they can use literature in coaching and to leave them emboldened to start a literary conversation.

Note

1 I use "coachee" and "client" interchangeably throughout the book. My students had the former, but many readers may have the latter.

References

Arendt, Hannah. 1958. *The Human Condition*. Chicago: University of Chicago Press.

Bailey, Blake. 2009. *Cheever: A Life*. New York: Picador.

Baldwin, James. 2000. *The Devil Finds Work*. London: Vintage.

Baym, Nina, ed. 2007. *The Norton Anthology of American Literature*. New York: W. W. Norton.

Bigsby, Christopher. 2008. *Arthur Miller: 1915–1962*. London: Weidenfeld and Nicolson.

Honan, Park. 1979. "The Theory of Biography." *Novel: A Forum on Fiction* 13 (1): 109–20.

Howard, Anita. 2015. "Coaching to Vision Versus Coaching to Improvement Needs: A Preliminary Investigation on the Differential Impacts of Fostering Positive and Negative Emotion During Real Time Executive Coaching Sessions." *Frontiers in Psychology* 6 (article no. 455): 1–15. https://doi.org/10.3389/fpsyg.2015.00455

Lampedusa, Giuseppe Tomasi di. 2007. *The Leopard*. Translated by Archibald Colquhoun. London: Vintage.

Lampedusa, Giuseppe Tomasi di. 2010. *Letters From London and Europe (1925–30)*. Translated by J.G. Nichols and foreword by Francesco da Mosto. London: Alma Books.

Linforth, Christopher, ed. 2011. *The Anthem Guide to Short Fiction*. London: Anthem Press.

Philbrick, Nathaniel. 2013. *Why Read Moby-Dick*? New York: Penguin.

Robinson, Jenefer. 2005. *Deeper than Reason: Emotion and Its Role in Literature, Music, and Art*. Oxford: Oxford University Press.

Woodress, James. 1987. *Willa Cather: A Literary Life*. Lincoln: University of Nebraska Press.

Chapter 1

Leadership and its absence

Herman Melville's "Bartleby, the Scrivener: A Story of Wall Street"

In the Introduction, I gave an outline of the conceptual axes that underlie the case this book makes for the value that literary works can bring to coaching. In this chapter, I intend to flesh out the premises on which this case for literature rests. The first premise is that reading literature brings cognitive benefits: we can learn from literature and be improved by it (Lamarque 2008). The second is that reading literature has emotional benefits and plays an important role in helping us to understand ourselves, our relationships, and our responses to the world around us (Robinson 2005). These cognitive and emotional benefits correlate with the principal tenet of coaching, that is, the notion that coaching is instrumental in the realization of human development. An emotional process I deem highly desirable in coaching is that of empathy, which is the basis of intersubjective experience and a mode by which we can access other individuals' mental states. Without empathy, the process of knowing oneself and facilitating self-knowledge in others would be considerably impaired. It is difficult to see how, without empathy, people could ever truly know themselves, own themselves, be themselves, and help others do the same. These four steps of knowing, owning, being oneself, and helping others in this pursuit of self-knowledge and self-possession are, according to Stokes and Jolly (2014), the four essential components of leadership coaching. I shall argue here that these four steps are instrumental not only in leadership coaching but in all coaching and that these four steps are, furthermore, central to reading literature and to discussing it. Knowing and defining the self and activating these processes in those with whom we interact: such are the basic commonalities shared by reading and coaching that explain the myriad ways literature can enhance the coaching process.

This chapter enlists the character Bartleby, one of the most enigmatic and tragic characters in American literature, to illustrate how using literature in coaching will help us to empathize – to give us the possibility of understanding another "from the inside" (Smith 2011, 111) – so that we can become better coaches: more sensitive, imaginative, responsive, at ease with unease, in short, so that we might embody the true meaning of a transformational coach. The coaching students with whom I used Herman Melville's short story and whose reactions are charted in this chapter adhere to no particular coaching model but rather capitalize on aspects of a range of varied approaches to coaching – psychodynamic, solution-focused, person-centered, narrative, developmental, leadership. My aim with these students was to investigate how empathy could be engendered by engaging with literature in pursuit ultimately of a more effective and challenging coaching experience. There are two coaching processes at play here: I was coaching these students to overcome work-related and academic challenges; these students were, at the same time, coaching colleagues in their organizations and were applying the literature-based coaching methods I had been using with them. In this chapter and throughout the book, although we will come across a wide range of approaches to coaching, it is worth noting that I am not advocating for the advantages of any one strategy over another. I will, however, address the prevalence of personality tools such as DISC as part of an overall coaching strategy in organizational life. Just as coaching has been seen as a valuable tactic as part of an overarching scheme for developing people in organizations, personality assessments are in widespread use in organizations with claims of direct benefits to individuals, including improved performance by nurturing maturity and productivity and by developing strengths and working on limitations. DISC supporters claim that the tool helps employees to be better attuned to each other's emotions and therefore enables them to be more effective conflict managers and communicators (Sugerman 2009). Its stated aim of focusing on patterns of external, observable behavior is, to my mind, a serious limitation, and it is certainly not a universal panacea for any organization's learning needs.

This chapter will discuss how students from a Fortune 100 company that relies heavily on this assessment tool as part of its coaching program read Herman Melville's "Bartleby, the Scrivener, A Story of Wall Street" as a means of complementing and enhancing their coaching conversations. I will cover why I chose this particular text and how the students reacted to reading it. My discussions here are informed by Robert Coles's experiences of using literature at Harvard University in courses that were not thought of as natural sites for literary exploration, as well as by a range of philosophical and neuroscientific insights into empathy and the emotions. I will then draw out the connections between empathy and coaching by bringing in voices from the fields of philosophy, literature, and psychology. Finally, I aim to demonstrate how engaging with "Bartleby" will help students express themselves with more clarity, going beyond the mechanical, lifeless prose they are too often accustomed to reading.

My objective in this chapter is to make a persuasive case for reading and engaging with the characters from a mid-nineteenth-century, not-particularly-accessible story, to enrich the coaching experience in organizational life. The difficulty of the literary text is significant. All too often, organizations look for schematic, quick fixes to problems. Certain aspects of coaching are not immune to prescriptive, unimaginative, mechanized approaches, but I think that we should encourage people to engage with more complex art. Human beings and their motivations can be extremely complicated, and we need to support coaches to think beyond stereotypes. Bartleby himself is a multifaceted character who elicits a range of feelings in readers, such as frustration, rage, and even self-identification. When we explore the creation of a complex character who has been molded by a writer with a great intellect and capacity for understanding human motivation, we too can train ourselves to understand others better and to be more empathic. Understanding others and being more cognizant emotionally is not an obstacle to rationality but is indeed a central part of what it means to act rationally. As social animals, human beings are inescapably bound up with interpersonal, cooperative structures. Part of what it means to be human is to interact with other people in order to achieve one's goals. Sensitivity to other individuals' emotions and empathic modeling of other individuals' minds are not superfluous, then, as is commonly assumed in the organizational context; becoming more attuned to others enables us to make better decisions, and developing techniques for other-oriented thinking constitutes a significant enhancement of learning and an important goal of coaching. Melville's nuanced, ambiguous text encapsulates the "unimaginably many details in any person's situation" that we too often are unable to grasp fully (Morton 2011, 324). "Bartleby" captures the mystery of the human self, and any endeavor that deals with human emotions must recognize that we are first and foremost mysteries, ever resistant to tidy psychological and behavioral boxes.

The great novelist and short story writer Eudora Welty once remarked, when asked about her purpose in writing: "The goal of fiction is not to point the finger in judgment, but to part a curtain, that invisible shadow that falls between people, the veil of indifference to each other's presence, each other's plight" (Yardley 1996, 13). My intention here should not be interpreted as a criticism of anyone's particular coaching practice: we are all striving for better self-awareness and the fostering of self-determination and personal development. My work should be read instead in the spirit of adding another dimension to the coaching experience. This chapter is based on the contention that understanding our emotions lies at the core of the coaching intervention. Reading and engaging deeply with literature helps us to understand our emotions better as well as to engender empathy for others. Therefore, using literature in coaching has self-evident benefits. In addition to these more self-evident aspects of discussing literature in coaching is the fictional characters' distance from the "real" discussion. It feels less frightening and dangerous to discuss a character's lack of motivation or disengagement or relationship problems than to discuss one's own. Noël Carroll muses, "Perhaps one reason we are so free with our sympathies toward fictional characters is that, since we need not act on their behalf, their needs never threaten to fall foul of our interests" (Carroll 2011, 173). The potential distancing mechanism offered by a literary-based coaching dialogue has its obvious uses in the hierarchical, competitive, excessively corporatized world of modern business. First, though, I will turn to the story of "Bartleby," its history, and its enduring significance over 150 years since it was published.

"Bartleby, the Scrivener: A Story of Wall Street"

In order to help situate Herman Melville and his short story "Bartleby" in their historical and literary contexts, a potted history of Melville's literary career is in order. The significance of Melville and his literary work can be illuminated, furthermore, through a survey of the critical reception of "Bartleby" from both contemporary reviewers and those penned over the last eighty years by writers working in the fields of folklore, biography, American literature studies, psychology, and psychiatry. "Bartleby" has fascinated, frustrated, mystified, and delighted reviewers, critics, and general readers since its inception. Over a number of generations, the critical foci of interest have shifted: at first, the meaning and purpose of the story were mined in order to shed light on the mores, motivations, and nature of the American "character"; subsequently, critics have used "Bartleby" to reflect on the relationship between work and psychological health. It seems that every generation, field, and discipline has found something relevant in the story of a lowly scrivener and his potentially tragic abhorrence for the workplace.

By the time Herman Melville turned to writing short stories for publication in the American periodicals of the time, he was already, in his eyes, a "failed" writer. After the initial success of his first novel, *Typee*, a substantially fictionalized account of his life with the natives of the Marquesan Islands, he failed to find a reading public. His subsequent books, including his masterpiece *Moby-Dick*, generated little interest with reviewers and readers and even less financial revenue for his publishers. He was therefore forced by straitened pecuniary circumstances to try his hand at short fiction. His first attempt at a short story, "Bartleby" was published in *Putnam's Monthly*. The story provoked much favorable discussion. In 1856, the New York *News* called it a "gem" and "beautifully written" (quoted in Higgins and Parker 1995, 471). Elsewhere, it was proclaimed "capital," "quaint," "readable," "equal to anything from the pen of Dickens" and possessing "unquestionable merit" (quoted in Higgins and Parker 1995, 473–80). Melville's intention in all of his works was to find a way of exploring the contradictory and unsettling elements in American culture in a subversive way. He needed to express what on the surface could be read simply as a story; but if the careful reader looked beneath, a deeper meaning could be discerned, a bit like the objectives of good coaching.

Most critics now take for granted Melville's multi-layered meanings and technique of expressing unpopular views in deeply embedded symbols (Fisher 1977). Writers on Melville from every decade since its publication have an opinion on the "enigma" of "Bartleby," and just as many others are attuned to his dark humor. In her seminal study of American humor, Constance Rourke (1959, 203) counts Melville as a "legend maker," a writer who uses humor sardonically to convey the terror of "impending death," a technique that had been a staple of the comic legends of the country. "Bartleby" exemplifies the "strange or rebellious" types in the mid-nineteenth-century popular comedy. Rourke was writing in the 1930s, during the American Depression, and was offering her readers a "usable past," an interpretation of American literature as one rooted in American myth. Rourke was connecting with folklore to uncover a national, cultural tradition. In place of a genteel literature of polite manners and conventional morality, the literature that Rourke and many of her fellow 1930s writers studied was literature as an expression of life lived in America by common men and women (Murphy 1988). No critics of "Bartleby" contemporaneous with the period during which the piece was written touched upon the fertile symbolism – psychological, social, economic, and metaphysical – to which modern critics and commentators tend to be particularly attuned.

When "Bartleby" was published, although it earned the epithets "vital," "imaginative," and "splendid," there was little analysis of the story's real purpose. However, many of the reviewers were not completely blind to Melville's intentions. In fact, charitable interventions by well-to-do lawyers in the affairs of struggling young people were a common mid-nineteenth-century literary trope. Moreover, the depiction of paralysis after a crisis was the standard device in popular novels of the period – *Uncle Tom's Cabin* being an obvious example. The story can be summarized succinctly. An unnamed lawyer narrates the story of his last hiring to his firm on Wall Street. The two scriveners and a lackey already there are described in humorous (but rather pompous) detail, and the reader is cognizant that the lawyer deems his office flunkeys a collection of misfits. His new scrivener, Bartleby, seems at first to be hardworking and promising but, with no apparent trigger, reacts with the refrain "I would prefer not to" to any request to do a task. Bartleby's use of the refrain soon spirals out of control. Soon he would "prefer not to" go home, vacate the office, even eat, until he is carted off to the Tombs (New York's asylum) and dies presumably of starvation. The story narrates the lawyer's repeated efforts to address the deteriorating situation and to try to understand why Bartleby would "prefer not to." As I noted, contemporary reviewers focused on the language and the style of the story rather than paying any attention to what might be termed the coded messages of Melville's creation.

Subsequent biographers and critics were keen to unearth the deeper meanings of the story, especially in the 1940s and 1950s at the height of psychoanalytical criticism in the United States. For Newton Arvin, "Bartleby" dramatizes not the "pathos of dementia praecox" but "the bitter metaphysical pathos of the human condition itself" (Arvin 1950, 243). Richard Chase (1949, 183) sees that as an American man, Bartleby is alone in the wilderness. He has no place to go, no fulfillment in life, as he "stubbornly asserts the negative aspects of his 'freedom of will' and decides to withdraw from life itself." The psychoanalytical tradition consecrated by Freud furnished attractive material for critics commenting on "Bartleby" from the beginning of the twentieth century. H. Bruce Franklin (1963, 243) argues that we can never know who or what Bartleby is: he could be anything from "a mere bit of human flotsam" to a "conscious and forceful rejecter of the world" to the "incarnation of God." Because of Melville's well-documented disappointment particularly after the failure of *Moby-Dick*, Newton Arvin (1950, 234) is able to connect Bartleby's disintegration to that of his creator. H. Bruce Franklin (1963, 246) can liken Bartleby to a crucified Melville. Richard Chase (1949, 148) is able to draw parallels between Melville's fractured relationship with his disgraced bankrupt of a father and the lawyer's and Bartleby's strained father–son relationship. Leo Marx (1953) sees Bartleby's colorless, blank wall as highly symbolic of man's limited vision, a vision that reflects Melville's despairing state of mind. Marx (1953, 620) is convinced that Bartleby parallels Melville's fate as a writer "who forsakes conventional modes because of an irresistible preoccupation with the most baffling philosophical authors."

More recently, writers have contextualized Melville's story for a modern readership. Sheila Post-Lauria (1993) is concerned with the story's socioliterary value. "Bartleby" is stylistically challenging. It is multitextured and ambiguous so that Melville can examine work hierarchies, class divisions, and the nature of acquiescence and submission in the workplace without being overtly critical of prevailing societal practices. I will return to the ambiguous nature of the story when I discuss students' reaction to it and their thoughts on how it could be used in coaching discussions. Corey Evan Thompson (2015) is also interested in the story's social context. He reports that by the 1830s, the average American was drinking more than four gallons of pure alcohol a year and that there was rampant alcohol abuse at the time Melville was writing "Bartleby." The story can be read – rather literally, I think – as a warning against using alcohol as an escape. Such alcohol abuse is exemplified by the lawyer's scrivener Turkey, who drinks to escape his mind-numbing, alienating work. He ekes out a depressing, soul-destroying existence, and alcohol is his coping mechanism. Thompson makes an important point that "Bartleby" is not focused so much on any character but on the nature of work.

Rosemary Garland-Thomson (2004) is convinced the story is about self-determination. Bartleby faces a world with a limited range of options and decides to make a free choice to die: "his options and the consequences of his choices are severely circumscribed and over-determined by the ideologies that declare him both unfit for the social world and suffering hopelessly as a result" (Garland-Thomson 2004, 783). Wai Chee Dimock (1997) posits that the reader never finds out what ails Bartleby because we need to focus on the narrator's response to Bartleby's disruptive refusals. Bartleby is deliberately a cipher because he represents a threat to the ordered world of a productive, rational, and impersonal workplace. The narrator "parades" his empathy, makes a "sentimental effort at empathy," but demonstrates throughout "a lack of imagination inflected by stereotypes and bias" (Dimock 1997, 792–3).

Robert Schultz (2011, 586) emphasizes Bartleby's lack of control in his work and life as he draws parallels between Bartleby's lack of agency and the "dehumanizing" nature of the market economy. Gertrud Mander (2005) sees Bartleby's resistance as a survival strategy. Mander (2005, 218) is a psychotherapist who is fascinated by Melville's tale because of "the tragic fate of its strange and haunting hero who reminded [her] of some of [her] most difficult and perverse patients." I will be exploring these and other critical discussions of the story to the extent that they can illuminate my arguments concerning the ways in which reading "Bartleby" can provide lessons for richer and more meaningful coaching conversations. In the sections that follow, I will expand and draw on some of the critical reactions to the short story outlined here in order to amplify discussions on empathy, the emotions, the coaching relationship, and strategies for improving writing skills through engagement with literary works.

A literary route to coaching and some remarks on empathy and neuroscience

Robert Coles (1989), the eminent psychiatrist and educator, who taught courses at Harvard law, medicine, and business schools, realized that literature was a fruitful way of seeing the world and probing the moral and social dimensions inherent in these disciplines. He found that the conceptual materials provided by studies in psychiatry, psychoanalysis, and the social sciences were woefully inadequate in capturing the complexity and ambiguity of life: they were unable to provide a sensitive enough lens through which to view the world. Early on in his career when he was a resident on the psychiatric ward of Massachusetts General Hospital, he was attempting to treat patients with phobias. Most of the time, senior psychiatrists talked about "formulating" a case, "conceptualizing" the problem, and exploring "the psychodynamics at work" (Coles 1989, 5–6). In contrast, one of his supervisors valued the stories of the patients and urged Coles to listen to these stories: "The people who come to see us bring us their stories. They hope they tell them well enough so that we understand the truth of their lives. They hope we know how to interpret their stories correctly. We have to remember that what we hear is *their story*" (Coles 1989, 7; original italics).

One of his patients who had been diagnosed as having a rigid personality and a serious character disorder paced the ward all day. Instead of relying on the conventional or prevailing practice of categorizing a patient's ailments and "treating them," Coles decided to ask her to tell him a few stories about her life – as he put it, "moments in it you remember as important, as happy or sad" (Coles 1989, 11). Prompted by his supervisor, Coles recognized the crucial role narrative plays in people's lives. He remarked on the noticeable difference in her: he had paid sustained attention to her life, and she had responded by telling him her story, pouring forth both pleasant and unpleasant details, becoming a person with a story to tell rather than a patient with a "presenting history" (Coles 1989, 14). He learned that all too often, patients come with "preconceived notions of what matters, what doesn't matter, what should be stressed, what should be overlooked, just as [psychiatrists] come with [their] own lens of inquiry" (Coles 1989, 14). The treatment encouraged abstract, concise histories with a diffuse attempt to probe core issues. It appeared to Coles far better for the psychiatrist to delay his interpretations, to attend to how a patient organized her story, to give the patient the time and space to be truly heard as a person.

Years later at Harvard Business School, dismayed by the restrictive syllabus, Coles introduced novel reading as a strategy to address the confusion and lack of direction exhibited by many of the young people in his classes. He explains his rationale: "We all remember in our own lives times when a book has become for us a signpost, a continuing presence in our lives. Novels lend themselves to such purposes; their plots offer a psychological or moral journey with impasses and breakthroughs, with decisions made and destinations achieved" (Coles 1989, 68). One of the books Coles had his students read was F. Scott Fitzgerald's *The Great Gatsby*. The themes of shallowness, hypocrisy, polished emptiness, scrabbling up the ladder while leaving others to pick up the consequences of their poor decisions afterward were themes students could use to look inwards and take stock of their lives. He introduced the reading of novels in his courses because he saw the potential that literature had for guiding, warning, and offering us wise perspectives. The lessons he had learned on the psychiatric ward, lessons about attending to a person's story, were transferred to his university students. Imaginary characters could serve as spiritual counselors for readers: "Every medical student, law student, or business student, every man or woman studying at a graduate school of education or learning to be an architect, will all too quickly be beyond schooling, will be out there making a living and too, just plain living – that is, trying to find and offer to others the affection and love that give purpose to our lives spent here" (Coles 1989, 160).

Leaving aside the very obvious links between the goals of coaching and what Coles values from engaging with literary works, there is a particular benefit in reading literary texts not as a critical exercise but in reading them to regard the characters as voices that accompany our lives, voices that may help us to untangle the moral contradictions and murky ambiguities at work or at home. Coles relates the story of an English literature student disillusioned with the insistent textual analysis required in his other classes. The student found many of the literary discussions pretentious, abstract, and overly analytical. He preferred to use his own instincts to enter a literary work. For example, he said that when he had moral issues to address, he would imagine what characters from *Anna Karenina* or *Middlemarch* would do in his situation. They were "people" for him, and they were able to guide him to make choices (Coles 1989, 203).

Equally, exploring characters from "Bartleby" does not necessitate the usual critical apparatus from a module in English or American literature. Like Coles, I am interested in a story's immediacy and how it connects with the human experience. I see "Bartleby" as a learning tool for coaching, a means for people to confront issues and challenge themselves, as well as a tool to examine barriers to success and objectives to improved performance. We learn from a variety of ways – from observing others, from our own experience, from feedback. Literature is a useful way to review our own experience and our own stories. Psychology in the psychoanalytical tradition has long exploited a treasure trove of insights from literature as it has mined the intricacies, idiosyncrasies, and so-called neuroses of the literary talent behind the work.

Coles (1980, 207) reminds us of Freud's obsession with creative writers. Freud had considered Dostoevsky's talent "exhausting" (Coles 1980, 207). His daughter Anna Freud claimed that most psychoanalysts were envious of literary creativity. It is important to bear in mind, as Coles does, the dangers inherent in psychoanalytical literary criticism, particularly in its reductionism or oversimplification of "exceedingly complex issues" (Coles 1980, 208). He reminds us of Flannery O'Connor's dictum, "It is the business of fiction to embody mystery through manners" (Coles 1980, 208), as she admonishes us that the modern obsession with neat analysis and clean resolution will invariably be resisted by the mysteries of fiction. Coles does not accuse just psychoanalysts of reducing literary accomplishment to a mechanical technique, he sees linguists such as Noam Chomsky as equally at fault. Coles (1980, 211) argues that we attend to the cognitive and linguistic skills of writers because of *how* they write: "some of us have God-given visual or linguistic capabilities – brains a touch more able to use words, or visualize and reproduce externally what is visualized."

Coles's plea not to reduce literature and its creators to the products of abnormalities and attendant victimized, wounded, or otherwise disturbed individuals has a great deal of resonance for the coaching relationship. As coaches, we are not looking to heal anyone else. We are not looking at each other as human receptacles containing identifying traits of strengths and weaknesses that need to be weighed and found admirable or wanting. Coaching, in any of its practices, is concerned with human beings with all of their foibles, narcissisms, pretentions, biases, and mysteries. We are not tasked nor should be tasked with reducing human beings to discernible parts but rather with attempting instead to empathize with them, because it is only through empathy that we can understand one another. Before I move on to the experiences my coaching students had with "Bartleby" and how they reconciled its use with their present personality assessment tools, I first want to look at the neuroscience implicated in my use of literature as a coaching tool.

Dick Swaab is a renowned neuroscience researcher who has been widely acclaimed for his work on sex differences in the brain, depression, and Alzheimer's disease. Swaab (2014) reminds readers that Darwin discovered that our moral awareness is nurtured by social instincts that underpin group survival. The capacity to "recognize and share the feelings of others" is the basis for all moral behavior (Swaab 2014, 250–1). Swaab points out that we have moral networks in our brains: neurons such as mirror neurons (which provide the basis for empathy) reside in the prefrontal cortex and in other regions of the cerebral cortex (Swaab 2014, 250–1). The prefrontal cortex is where our emotions are linked to moral concepts so that any damage it sustains can unleash antisocial behavior of varying degrees. Abnormalities in the prefrontal cortex are found in the brains of psychopaths, a phenomenon that explains a psychopath's utter indifference in the face of his victim's fear, pain, or pleading for mercy. Our moral networks residing there encompass the notion of empathy (as well as emotions such as guilt, pity, pride, envy, disgust, and so on, depending on the interaction between brain regions). Empathy in its most general sense means having the ability to relate to the feelings of others. In the case of moral judgments, one's emotions have a decided impact: "An area in the brain's frontal lobe, the ventromedial prefrontal cortex, is crucial to solving moral dilemmas [. . .] individuals with damaged prefrontal cortex weigh [emotional decisions] in a clinical, highly detached way. They don't experience emotions like empathy or sympathy" (Swaab 2014, 330).

Cognitive neuroscientist Alvin Goldman (2011) provides further insight into the concept of empathy. He reminds us that writers and researchers exhibit a range of approaches to empathy, some of which will be more germane to my study than others. Empathy has a considerable history in philosophy and psychology. Some see it as restricted to affective or emotional states. Cognitive scientists break it down into different shades of empathy – an empathy for touch, or an empathy for pain, for example. Others define it as the basis of altruistic behavior. Those studying Asperger's view the condition as an empathy deficit. Goldman's concern is in discovering if there is one route to empathy or more than one. If a person watches another person being touched, in the person watching, the "same brain areas are activated [as] in the person being touched" (Goldman 2011, 36). Goldman discusses how this finding is implicated in the discovery of a variety of systems in the brain that have "mirror properties" (Goldman 2011, 36). One distinctive route to empathy is, therefore, the mirroring route. The other route, the reconstructive route, is far more complex and involves a lot more effort: "When empathizing with another, you often reflect on that person's situation, construct in imagination how things are (were, or will be) playing out for him, and imagine how you would feel if you were in his shoes" (Goldman 2011, 36). It is the important role played by empathy in our experience of art, in this process of imagining other people's experiences, that invests artistic objects with potential value as a coaching strategy.

Why "Bartleby"?

The potential uses of "Bartleby" in organizational coaching derive from the story's poignant portrayal of the plight of the employees in this Wall Street office. The depiction of the hardship entailed by working in the office – what Post-Lauria (1993, 200) describes as "the survival of the individual caught within the rigidly structured financial world" – is plain for sensitive readers. Such readers are able to discern the distance of authority, the suppression of individuality, the walled-in and "stuck-ness" of being in an office, which resonate just as much now as they did more than 150 years ago. Bartleby creates chaos because he has little control over his life (Schultz 2011). The lawyer-manager demonstrates "his superior abilities" in surviving the Wall Street dog-eat-dog world by "wielding authority over others" (Post-Lauria 1993, 200). One of the scriveners, Turkey, uses alcohol as a means to numb himself from the alienating and repetitive work (Thompson 2013). The lawyer-narrator views Bartleby, indeed all of his employees, as acquisitions who are machine-line entities lacking independent thought and whose actions are "completely prescribed" by the parameters of the closed-in, walled-off office (Schultz 2011, 592).

Gertrud Mander (2005, 221) finds she is able to use the story of Bartleby since the protagonist of Melville's story is, like many of her patients, "in therapeutic terms, a victim of an environment in which the vulnerable individual is reduced to narcissistic withdrawal and an unremitting repetition compulsion." Mander

(2005) deals with cases like Bartleby in her psychiatric practice and is able to diagnose a "defiant resistance as a protective shield in the service of a fragile self" (226), an individual "crying out to be diagnosed and treated" (218), someone who has regressed to his "psychic core" when confronted by "nameless dread" (225). I am certainly not suggesting that organizational life is populated by Bartlebys in need of intensive and prolonged therapy, but I do believe that Bartleby's condition – albeit in an exaggerated form – exemplifies the struggle many of us have with office dynamics. Melville's depiction of the lawyer's bafflement in the face of Bartleby's intransigence also exemplifies the attempt to understand another who resists comprehension. How prevalent is the situation in which one employee finds another inscrutably enigmatic? Bartleby may resist our understanding, but using fictional characters can be, as Mander points out in the context of her psychiatric work, the link between theory and practice. In a very practical way, Mander uses fictional characters in her discussion of a range of case studies examining the complexity of individual psychopathologies. She thereby circumvents the need to write about her real patients, which is complicated by issues of confidentiality. The term "depression" appears these days to cover any manner of feeling down; it is used often very broadly and with little accuracy. There is a large body of evidence to suggest that neurobiological factors can increase a person's disposition to suicide: depression is a complex disorder that has many gradations (Sequeia et al. 2007). Indeed, there could be unmotivated individuals in the office, individuals like Bartleby, who "prefer not to" act as part of a team or to take on responsibilities or to help out in some way who can call themselves "depressed."

Smith (2011, 106) observes that a given author's "precise delineation of a character's state of mind" frees us from clichéd diagnoses and stereotypical ideas: "Our experience of engaging with characters in fictions and other narratives cannot be understood on the basis of empathy alone. But every type of response [to fiction] – purely cognitive understanding, 'acentral' sympathetic responses, contagion mimicry, 'in his shoes' imagining, and, yes, empathy – plays a role in the account of the psychology of fictional response as a whole." Empathy can be "refined" through an engagement with literature (Smith 2011, 111). It can also help us to empathize with fellow beings who are "radically" different from us (Smith 2011, 111). To know what it is like to be another human being is of course valuable in itself: to explore an extremely dysfunctional character like Bartleby is an undeniably difficult coaching workout. Even if we accept the argument that understanding real people and understanding literary characters are very different processes, it has been demonstrated that "empathy has intrinsic value in general in our experience of narrative," and the "episodes of empathy" could strengthen a person's capacity for empathetic response (Smith 2011, 113). Bearing in mind the relationship between the cultivation of empathy and the reading of literature, we are now well placed to turn to a discussion of how this kind of literary reading might be used in empathy training in the coaching context. My students' reaction to Bartleby – this walled-up creature, this victim of office hierarchy, this inadequate everyman trapped in the human condition – bears out the intuition that coaching Bartleby turns out to be an enriching exercise, but my experiment with "Bartleby" also generated some unexpected results.

Preparing for "Bartleby" and DISC

The coaching students on my course are tasked with completing a 6,000-word project proposal in their first term and then a 12,000-word project in the second term. It is an MA course in coaching, so although the students work primarily in the sales division of a financial services conglomerate, their project themes lend themselves to an exploration of topics in the humanities. Investigations in areas such as gratefulness, appreciation, courage, and mindfulness demand a wide range of reading in disciplines other than in psychology and business studies. Students are permitted by their organization some latitude in their choice of inquiry: their objective is to make a case for a more productive and efficient team, unit, or workforce by putting forward their investigation as a means of illuminating the path to achieve this goal. Therefore, a student promoting the efficacy of mindfulness to help employees to be happier and more productive in the workplace will read widely around the topic of mindfulness, gather data from her colleagues through interviews, questionnaires, or surveys on what her colleagues think about the topic, analyze the data, and then put forward recommendations based on her research on how mindfulness training, for example, as strongly endorsed by her data findings, should be implemented perhaps as a pilot program in her company or in a department of her company.

The irony has always struck me that however much latitude in inquiry choice is offered to the students, their first-draft proposals discussing their literature reviews invariably cling to rigidly codified best-selling "business guru" or "self-help" books. They are not initially comfortable with my suggestions to explore more challenging academic work from journal articles or literary reading, particularly reading that doesn't immediately strike them as relevant. I circulated a chapter of Alexis de Tocqueville's *Democracy in America* for them to read and discuss before one of our online seminars. I thought it would be fruitful to identify the parallels between large organizations and democracies. In chapter 7 of volume two, de Tocqueville (2010, 418) states,

> Chains and executioners, those are the crude instruments formerly used by tyranny; but today civilization has perfected even despotism itself, which seemed however to have nothing more to learn. [. . .] Under the absolute government of one man, despotism, to reach the soul, crudely struck the body; and the soul, escaping from these blows, rose gloriously above it; but in democratic republics, tyranny does not proceed in this way; it leaves the body alone and goes right to the soul.

Freedom of thought can be compromised in democratic societies because going against the majority opinion is sometimes very difficult for people to do. Likewise "groupthink" is prevalent in organizational life: people may be willing to abandon independent thought to ensure a more orderly and productive organization with the attendant advantages of material prosperity.

At the time, our discussion seemed one sided with me doing a lot of the expounding and questioning and then filling in answers after long, uncomfortable gaps. Yet on separate follow-up small-group Skype sessions, I discovered that students had read more de Tocqueville and were keen to discuss the implications of his ideas on the "tyranny of the majority" in their work. Some even wrote about their own observations on prejudices and bias. I subsequently went on to introduce students to a range of reading from Orwell, Machiavelli, Spengler, Solzhenitsyn, and other philosophical and political writers who I thought would challenge their thinking. Nevertheless, I was cautious about introducing fiction, thinking it perhaps would be perceived as a step too far. My mind was changed by my growing confidence that using fictional characters in a coaching intervention could be a viable organizational strategy. Other coaching students I was teaching from other organizations were reporting increasing success with my strategy, a story I will relate in subsequent chapters. I was also minded to take the plunge by the frequency of times the students referred to "leadership issues" in their organization. My determination was fortified by the growing impression that the psychometric personality and behavioral assessments that appeared to be the cornerstone of their coaching practice were self-limiting and unimaginative. It also struck me that the organizations from which my students hailed made grandiose claims about the efficacy of personality and behavioral assessments such as DISC and Personalisis. DISC, in particular, widely used at this specific organization, struck me as having self-fulfilling elements that appealed to people's vanity. I found its similarity to horoscope predictions both inescapable and uncomfortable.

DISC is an evaluation of behavioral and motivational styles that breaks people's personality down into four quadrants. Broadly, Dominant means you tend to be direct and guarded. Other characteristics include making quick decisions, being results oriented, blunt, restless, and impatient. Influencer means you tend to be direct and open. You are also outgoing and persuasive – not task oriented but someone who tends to procrastinate. Steady people tend to be indirect and open. You are known as dependable and technically competent, but you are a poor delegator who prefers routine over change. Conscientious people lean to being indirect and guarded. You are a thorough, attentive perfectionist who prefers little to no people contact. Additionally, you are rigid and overly detailed and want to define the limits of authority yourself. Although I didn't specifically ask for a DISC assessment on Bartleby, I was pretty confident that students would peg him as a C. These are the four basic personality types, but there are additional "personality blends": D/I – creative and logical (the former being more dominant than the latter); D/S – driven and flexible; I/C – having good will and being poised; S/C – self-confident and successful; S/D – patient but reacting negatively to change; S/C – persistent and setting your own pace; C/I – a perfectionist with decisions based on precedent; and C/S – a sensitive person looking for hidden meanings (Slowikowski 2005, 835–43).

The idea is that after the assessment is completed, employees will know their basic personality type and their possible personality blend so that they can focus on maximizing their predominant behavioral tendency or modifying their style weaknesses to adapt to particular situations. Knowledge of these basic personality types and blends theoretically enable teams to "create a mission that accounts for and makes use of the different personality types" (Slowikowski 2005, 842). The premise of this instrument is to enable better communication because conflict resolution will be enhanced by the formation of more compatible teams. Knowing a team's personality type and blend will help leaders to recognize "the keys for inspiring and influencing team members and will support individual team members to find out what makes people tick and then to use their strengths to enhance the team" (Slowikowski 2005, 835). Jeffrey Sugerman (2009, 152) provides a case study of an organization that needed to "streamline its processes," effect "lean thinking," and "engender a cohesive, successful work environment" by focusing on its people. The company found that the DISC model was useful in allowing "nonjudgmental communication" and helping the company to understand "the priorities and motivations" of all colleagues so that managers could effectively mitigate conflict and colleagues could better communicate with each other and deal with change more productively (Sugerman 2009, 152). Sugerman is clear, though, that companies should be careful not to put too great an emphasis on the results of psychometric assessments.

The multitude of psychometric instruments claiming to harness the power of psychology so that people can understand each other and communicate better – DISC (Thomas Personal Profiling System), TAT (Thematic Apperception Tests), FIRO-B, Picture Frustration Test, Gordon's Personal Profile Inventory, and more – has grown into a multimillion-pound industry predicated on the value of these tools as accurate predictors of individual behavior. Sreenidhi and Fernandes (2014) point out that many organizations make great claims for the objectivity and validity of these assessments, their value in determining a person's aptitude for a job, and their accuracy in taking out the guesswork in predicting an efficient, well-matched team. Sreenidhi and Fernandes (2014, n.p.) advocate a more holistic approach in the use of these assessments: some of these assessments classify people into rigid categories, pigeonholes that people tend subsequently to fall back on as a source of excuses for poor performance; the assessments can even "cramp the complexities of human personality into an artificial and limiting classification scheme."

It is Sreenidhi and Fernandes's final objection that I would like to focus on mainly. With few exceptions, my coaching students appeared in favor of DISC as an effective model to work with in coaching. Their responses when I asked them if they found DISC effective in team building ranged from unqualified enthusiasm to pragmatic acceptance: "It helps us to communicate more effectively"; "It measures both our natural and adaptive states"; "In a heavily regulated industry that is beholden to strict legal standards it has its uses"; "It is an easily usable toolset";

"Because it breaks personality down into quadrants, we are able to understand each other's strengths and weaknesses"; "It is very helpful for our sales professionals to establish trust and build rapport." It was only when I challenged them by suggesting that DISC focused on patterns of external, observable behaviors, and that this type of behavioral manifestation was probably not the best way of accessing the motivations of other people, that they acknowledged its limitations. I accept that companies need to make the necessary investments to produce desired outcomes, that they constantly need to explore ways to improve performance, and that they need to understand what motivates people, but I remain unconvinced of the unqualified efficacy of these personality assessment tools. The complexities of the human personality cannot be divided or blended into quadrants, nor are they always external and observable. More often than not, our presenting behavior is either consciously or unconsciously removed from tangled, conflicting, and intricate patterns beneath the surface, invisible not only to our colleagues and to the organization but even to ourselves. A text like "Bartleby" used to support coaching conversations opens the possibility of discussing his behavior and that of his employer in a more fine-grained analysis. Literary texts enable exploration of the irrationalities and confusions that simply cannot be captured by broad category-based assessment tools. It is through a coaching relationship that acknowledges and honors these irrationalities, confusions, and paradoxes inherent in our humanity that we can come close to understanding each other. Using a text about the workplace and the misunderstandings that arise in the workplace will have a far more powerful impact than simply skimming the surface with these generalized psychometric assessments of each other.

In asking how coaches can make a positive contribution to an organization, Barbara Kaufman (2006, 291) found that coaching needs to be "grounded in the interdependent nature of others." She also discovered that executives, when asked what they really could have benefited from when they started their current positions, stated that the most value would have been gleaned "from the guidance of a 'truth-teller,' someone willing to alert them to cultural landmines and unwritten norms, and candidly to point out role expectations and performance areas in need of course correction" (Kaufman 2006, 287). In terms of critical scrutiny, the DISC or TAT or Myers-Briggs model is no substitute for the kind of "truth-telling" coaching that many executives and others are crying out for in the workplace. To my mind, "Bartleby" goes right to the heart of the "leadership issues" to which my coaching students allude. The multilayered weaving of social and literary themes interrogates "leadership issues" throughout the story: the reader sees Bartleby as challenging the authority of his employer, and the reader begins to question the authority of the narrator and lawyer. The lawyer's "leadership skills," or rather lack of them, can serve as an opening to a "truth-telling" conversation about an organization's style or identity. "Bartleby" contains the material for so many potentially powerful discussions in the workplace on leadership, responsibility avoidance, colleague envy, management and interpersonal skills, learning from failure, trust, and ethics. Mordecai Marcus (1962, 366) touches upon an odd but nevertheless plausible facet of leadership – that the lawyer's sporadic "vindictive" responses to Bartleby's passivity suggest "an anger against a force which has invaded himself." A truthful coaching conversation could analyze this story to reveal not only the subtexts and significance in the relationship between "leader" and "followers" in "Bartleby" but also in one's existing workplace.

I asked a half dozen (out of twenty-six) students to read the story and to attempt to use it in a coaching session with one of their colleagues in the workplace. I suggested an excerpt they might get their coachee to read at the beginning of the session, and I set a series of sample questions they might use to initiate discussions. I wanted these students to focus on the story's potential to support a coaching dialogue about leadership as well as personal struggles, morality, appropriate behavior, and core identity among other themes. I wanted the students to use "Bartleby" as a case study on dysfunctional behaviors. I asked only those students who I thought would be able to grapple with the mid-nineteenth-century language and who I suspected would be able to organize their time to read a long, complex story, as well as have the confidence to use the text in their coaching sessions and the conscientiousness to respond thoughtfully to a questionnaire I devised in order to gauge their perceptions of how effective "Bartleby" had been in their experimental coaching sessions. Because of their already demonstrable academic skills, particularly in critical reflection, I did not think this exercise would be too much of a burden on top of their work and the MA course, both on a full-time basis. My questionnaire was structured around a single premise: In what ways have you found "Bartleby" to be effective in a coaching conversation? One of these students, Lucy, exhibited a reaction to "Bartleby" that is illustrative of the responses of the majority of the other students. Lucy told me a story that was depressingly similar to all of the other student responses to the story. Of course, this striking similarity has its own story to tell, and I will attend to its implications as well.

In my training sessions prior to encouraging the students to use "Bartleby" in their own coaching practices, I explained that my central research question was whether reading literature, particularly this story, created a more fertile ground for a coaching exchange. I reported the evidence that reading literature generated productive emotions in readers, and I discussed how coaching might be conceptualized as a means of creating the type of emotions that help people to understand each other better. My contention, I explained, was that reading literature would enable the coach and coachee to see more clearly what their emotions were telling them. Because our emotions guide our responses, literature could serve as a simulative bridge between our emotional life (confusion, anger, frustration, joy – the whole range of emotions) and the workplace: How do I get on better with my colleagues? How do I generate a more motivated team? How do I deal with the peaks and troughs of the job? In my own coaching discussions with these students, I demonstrated how reading "Bartleby" could be an enlightening exercise in getting people to open up about blockages, lack of communication, ennui, and power dynamics. In my own sessions with the master's students, I used "Bartleby" to address competencies such as thinking imaginatively about contemporary business issues. The students, including Lucy, were receptive in our individual discussions on "Bartleby." I referred to certain aspects of the text and persuaded them to make connections with their own workplace experience. But when the students attempted to replicate in their own coaching dialogues the literary-based discussions in which we had successfully engaged on our own, they encountered a problem. During our discussions, they had seemed able to engage with the text in an abstract way, but in their written responses following the practical application of the reading activity with their own coaches, they displayed a certain inflexibility of thought and a tendency to see the reading activity in terms that were overly literal. Lucy's response to my questions, "Do you or your coachees have personal struggles similar to Bartleby's?" and "Are there specific strategies you could use in building confidence in a coachee such as Bartleby?" is illustrative:

> As coaches I know we have all encountered a client who has challenged our coaching capabilities. Turkey epitomizes the more mature worker in today's workforce who has been set in his ways is unlikely to change without there being repercussions associated with his actions. His quality of work seemed to diminish after returning from with what we refer to as lunch; in 19th century times this was dinner. And descriptors of his face made me wonder whether a little bit of imbibing of some alcohol may have been part of the daily routine that impacted his quality of work as well in the afternoon – ink spots. His quality of work seemed otherwise acceptable in the morning. I don't believe building confidence in Bartleby is possible by a coach until his deep seated issues are addressed and definitely not by a coach.[1]

It seemed that while my students had been receptive to discussing their workplace when I had drawn comparisons with "Bartleby" in our initial sessions before using the questionnaire, they were unable to replicate the depth of reflection they had attained, perhaps unconsciously, in their own practices as coaches and their subsequent reflection on this practice. There was an evident gulf between what the students were capable of under adequate guidance and their subsequent perception of the utility of the activity they had, unwittingly perhaps to them but very obviously to me, successfully undertaken in our earlier exchanges. All of the responses mentioned the obvious manifestations of the character-employees' dissatisfaction in work. The students focused on the characters' temperament, their emotional tone, and their inability to adapt to their environment. In the special case of Bartleby, the general consensus was that his issues were too entrenched, or, as Lucy put it, "deep seated" to be treated by a coach. In my questionnaire I also asked if they had been able to use Bartleby's struggle as a way of entering questions of personal morality and of interrogating "appropriate behavior." Lucy's response to this question was the most detailed and touched on similar themes that emerged in the responses of my other students:

> This question poses for me a dilemma in that more than one issue seems to be involved. Morality from my perspective takes into consideration one person's

beliefs when placed upon another as a form of judgment. Judgment is an area coaches are trained to avoid, with intention accepting the person as whole and assumes the client is capable of finding the solution from within him or herself with the help of coaching where appropriate. However, in the workplace, using more my Human Resources background vs. coaching, when a work performance issue is identified then addressing this is not a moral issue and must be dealt with if performance improvement is to be achieved. Insubordination and drinking during work hours are areas that must be addressed but coaches at [our company] would not be involved with this type of process as you'll read next. Insubordination – Bartleby's rigid use of "I would prefer not" – would not be a coach matter but would be expected that a manager would address this with the area [a specific department that deals with serious employee matters].

Although initially, I could see a manager working with an internal coach to help formulate the conversation that might ensue to address the insubordination. If no progress resulted with the associate (i.e., Bartleby), then [this department] would be consulted for next steps; verbal followed by written warning and finally to employment dismissal. Living in his employer's rented space is almost inconceivable in today's environment though I suppose a person could decide to live there hiding away in a restroom or some space where one might sleep and bathe in a sink in a lavatory area.

At our company security guards stroll the premises all night long so I'm not sure how long one such as Bartleby could go undetected. There are very distinct lines in today's workplace where managers, as well as coaches, are not authorized to go and matters are elevated to the Human Resources function for collaboration with the manager to resolve. Drinking, by the way, could fall under the ADA (Americans with Disabilities Act) and would be handled with the greatest of finesse to avoid litigation through improper handling of the matter. In this particular case the behaviors described are of such an odd nature that one would consider mental health issues may be involved and neither managers nor coaches are qualified to address this type of scenario. Never mind the legal ramifications of attempting to do so and causing harm to the associate or others in the workplace. I recently dealt with a manager who was confronted with an associate with anger management issues and made statements that implied he could cause harm to himself or others. She was attempting to address this and my coaching to her was that she was in over her head and that she needed to get HR involved. This manager ignored my strong suggestion and a couple of weeks later another incident such as the first erupted at which point she did involve HR. The associate was "encouraged" to contact EAP (Employee Assistance Providers) for assistance. He has done so and is making tremendous progress in dealing with this situation. He feels better about himself and is not at risk of losing his job. He thanked her for doing what no other employer has ever offered to do for him and that was to seek the appropriate help that was needed. The proper coaching in this instance was to recognize when you are not the qualified resource to facilitate the necessary change.

Lucy's thorough and considered response highlights the issues of judgment and the distinction between coaching and morality, or more precisely work performance and morality. As Lucy explains, in a large organization with stratified departments and teams dealing with a codified set of responsibilities, the outward manifestations of Bartleby's dysfunction would fall under the aegis of human resources. As this is an American company, there is the potential involvement of the EAP (employee assistance providers) and the threat of litigation if proper channels are not followed. All of the students who responded to my questionnaire mentioned the EAP, the legal ramifications of the scenario, and the likelihood of HR involvement. Only Lucy addressed morality, albeit briefly, while the other respondents focused on "appropriate behavior." I wondered whether the lack of attention given to the concept of morality was the fault of my question, which, in hindsight, I realized conflated morality and behavior, or if that lack of attention signified something more important. But there is a larger question dominating this discussion: Why did Lucy and her colleagues take the story so literally? There was no attempt to engage with the story on an allegorical level even though my own discussions about the story always made it clear that Melville wanted to highlight the plight of workers at the time and was restricted by the literary conventions of his period so had to resort to metaphor and other figures of speech to mask his points about the powerlessness of the working class in contemporary society. The students seemed institutionalized in their literal reactions to what should have been an attempt to empathize with Bartleby's situation (and that of his colleagues). The Bartleby exercise, despite the promising work in class in advance of the students' application of the literary texts to their own coaching sessions, did not work as I had intended. Students used it as a coaching case study rather than an opportunity for a more philosophical reflection on what makes other people tick. My questions addressing empathy and morality led to literal rather than more thoughtful interpretations.

Noël Carroll (2011) makes points about empathy that are relevant to the question of morality. His premise is that there are limits to empathy. He reminds us of Stephen Pinker's uncontestable observation: "The body is the ultimate barrier to empathy. Your toothache simply does not hurt me the way it hurts you" (Pinker 1997). Naturally, another person's world will never be fully accessible to our minds. Moreover, it is going to be even more difficult to enter a fictional character's world that resists access: we may have scant affinity for a character like Bartleby because we have no handle on him. To Carroll, empathy is relational. When we discuss empathy, we draw on the similarities between our world and that of a character.

Literary discussions on empathy liberally highlight the attractive (and unattractive) qualities of many nineteenth-century characters. The difficulty here appears to lie in the characterizations of Bartleby and the lawyer: they are simply unsympathetic (as distinct from merely unattractive) characters: the lawyer is supercilious, impersonal, and self-absorbed; Bartleby is frustrating and cipher-like. Carroll argues that we must find a character "worthy of our emotions," or, in another sense, he must be morally worth our attentions: "Morality, especially of a fairly widely shared and nearly universal variety, gives the popular fictioneer the interest, or project, or loyalty, or touchstone of allegiance upon which audiences from similar cultures, or even sometimes dissimilar ones, converge" (Carroll 2011, 174). The characters in Melville's text are perhaps not deserving of our benevolence, and therefore we are not bound to them emotively. They seemingly resist our examination from a moral perspective.

Lucy points out that from her perspective, morality "takes into consideration one person's beliefs when placed upon another as a form of judgment." Of course, the aim of coaching is not to judge, but our judgment is always with us. Lucy could not engage with the story on an emotional level because she did not find any of the characters "worthy" of her emotions. As this was the case with all of the other students, I am left with no other conclusion than that a subtle, complex, nineteenth-century tale is probably a step too far in corporate coaching. Because Melville is not clear to the reader about his characters' beliefs or ideas about morality, the average twenty-first-century non–literary-trained reader is hardly going to identify with these cipher-like characters. And because they cannot identify with them, there will be serious limitations in using the story to deepen empathy in coaching. Without empathy, not only will there be a lack of coaching expectation or achievable results, but the coaching relationships will remain unexplored and even avoided.

Another of my questions elicited examples of specific questions my student-coaches could ask to promote beneficial change in Bartleby's worldview. Lucy, again the most detailed of respondents, gave the following response:

> These are questions that I might begin discussions with the lawyer and I am making the assumption that the lawyer has already shared with me what he's tried with Bartleby that has not worked. Bartleby, if you were in my shoes and confronted with behavior such as your own, what would you do? Bartleby, how do you think I should handle the situation that will provide a successful outcome for both of us since this is a business I am attempting to manage here? What recourse are you leaving me other than to have you forcefully removed from these premises? I am not a trained therapist so I would be speculating on all sorts of matters to confer on what problems Bartleby might be facing. This could all stem from matters in his personal life that have contributed to his extreme avoidance of wanting to interact with other human beings.
>
> There are too numerous of examples that fall in the "could be" of what problems Bartleby has. And, without knowing how to explore his past through trained therapeutic questioning, more harm than has already been heaped upon him that has resulted in his current state, I would not venture to

address this. I'm sure in the mid-19th century employers would not have had employee assistance providers ("EAPs") that an individual such as this would be strongly encouraged to reach out to vs. mandating one to do so. In today's environment, this would be encouraged initially and then mandated only in the face of the insubordination as the employer is being left with no alternative. As I have already stated I would not attempt to coach Bartleby directly. However, I will attempt to consider an answer to your question. Bartleby, I am perplexed as to what may have happened in your past (this is where coaching should not go – the past because that is the work of a psychologist/therapist trained to explore such situations) that has brought you to this current state. In light of your employer's angst over your work performance not being entirely satisfactory, in that you pick and choose what you will and will not do, exploration of alternatives has been proposed. Your employer has engaged me to work with you in this regard. (This again violates my own code of ethics with regard to coaching. A coaching engagement is one that should be entered into willingly and unless Bartleby is willing to work with me and this is mandated by the employer the matter of trust exists and is unlikely to develop when forced upon someone.) On a scale of 1–10 how willing are you to explore options that may be better suited to your liking? (Given the rigidity of "I would prefer not to" throughout – I think we know the answer and why I feel this is not the realistic approach to have a coach vs. psychologist/therapist intervene.) However, in the absence of understanding or exploring your past, perhaps you would be open to talking with me about what alternative avocation you may want to consider. (Some questions in coaching are stated as a sentence with a pause and allow the individual to consider what has been said and respond. Silence can be a very effective coaching tool. Doubtful it would have any impact on Bartleby!) If anything the Bartleby story may be used to help manager/coaches understand when an issue is one that is not conducive to coaching and requires a referral to EAP. Unfortunately, I am at a complete loss for reflecting on the deep seated issues Bartleby is facing because I think this one does require a therapist and not a coach. Perhaps: Bartleby, your employer very much wants to help you and unless we find a way together to help you get past the obstacles (preferred not when asked to proof the copies along with the other workers in the law office) that are preventing you from working with others, I'm afraid the outcome is not one that is going to be conducive to your remaining employed here. Why don't you take some time over night to think about what might be getting in the way of your interacting with others. I'll come back tomorrow and we'll begin our discussion of what you believe these obstacles to be. How does this sound to you? (In coaching it is critical that buy-in is achieved. In fact, if it were not for the dysfunctional personality of Bartleby, questions would be asked to get Bartleby to come up with his own solution but since he is so limited with the words he uses, I would offer suggestions to see if I could open the door for change.)

Lucy wrote more extensively than others, but everyone touched upon the themes described above. They all recognized the importance of the need to negotiate with each other in an attempt to comprehend others' actions while coaching. Lucy's response encapsulates the problem that Morton (2011) identifies in grasping the motives of those we perceive as dissimilar to us. There are deep obstacles "to the kind of sympathetic identification required for empathy" (Morton 2011, 321) when we encounter barriers of unfamiliarity. We can empathize with unpleasant characters if we are able to grasp how they decide what they do (even if it is an ugly deed). Morton cites the example of Macbeth. Perhaps in the case of Bartleby, the inscrutability of his actions eludes our attempts to make an emotional connection: we just cannot get past his barriers, although Lucy makes a valiant attempt to do so.

My final question concerned the concept of change and how it was addressed in the story. Again, all the responses were similar, and here, everyone noted the issue of "avoidance." The following is Lucy's response:

> I think this is one of the most interesting questions you pose. I believe the concept of change was addressed but it was not change that occurred where one would have desired to see change. Bartleby is who the reader wants to see change. Instead we see the lawyer acquiesce and come to accept that he was willing to tolerate the eccentricities of Bartleby for the fine work that he is able to produce and let the "prefer not to" wait until another time (i.e. indefinitely). The lawyer actually feels pity for Bartleby in that he does not go out at all, not even to eat, and that he works day and night and seems to have no other life than being a scrivener. It is not until the lawyer discovers the abnormal situation of Bartleby actually living in the law office that he is confronted with the severity of the problem and having to address the situation that can no longer be tolerated. He has an office to run and other lawyers and clients may come to the office so this could not continue.
>
> This raises another topic in Melville's story that could be a coaching topic and that is avoidance. Coaches can play a role in helping someone to overcome this type of obstacle. In the story the lawyer could not find a way to enforce Bartleby to leave the premises. He even commanded that he do so and when this did not work the lawyer left instead. He did not have the heart to throw Bartleby out on the street or have him arrested so he chose to leave. We don't know what type of mental health options were available in the 19th century but in today's environment the lawyer might be coached to explore how he could help Bartleby by connecting him with the right resources. In the end, the next tenant lawyer had him arrested and he went to an asylum. The reader gets the sense this was something the lawyer had a hard time dealing with and thus paid to have someone try to care for him with meals every day. A very tragic ending for both of them.

Lucy is alert to the fact that the lawyer acted toward Bartleby with a lack of alacrity that might have exacerbated the situation. Although none of the students responded explicitly to the barriers that frustrated entering the mindset of a character like Bartleby, we can see encapsulated in Lucy's narrative how barriers and procrastination are linked. The lawyer is reluctant to overcome his barrier to empathizing with Bartleby; therefore, he avoids the situation until it becomes too disruptive to avoid. Reading "Bartleby" produces startling responses to questions relating to morality, judgment, leadership, and change. The fact that the students found it nearly impossible to identify and empathize with the characters, as they testified in their subsequent reflective responses to my questionnaire, reveals a great deal about the obstacles to the kind of sympathetic identification required for empathy and, by extension, coaching. It seemed that the students in our own one-to-one coaching sessions, when I initially introduced the text, had been happy to use "Bartleby" as a spur for reflecting on their own workplace problems. In those earlier exchanges, their gaze had been firmly fixed on their own emotional state and personal development. However, when I encouraged the students to direct their gaze toward the protagonist of Melville's story in their own coaching practice and their subsequent reflections guided by my questionnaire, the students manifested a certain unwillingness or inability to sympathize with the character. By referring to the institutional structures in place to deal with potential Bartlebys in her workplace, Lucy was merely avoiding getting involved too personally. Bartleby was too much of a challenge, both for her and for her coachees. He was too radically different, alien, so that my students were unable to shift their perspective to his, to see the world through Bartleby's eyes, as a first step toward "coaching" him. It was not simply Melville's prose that was inaccessible but the character himself.

But although Bartleby remained resistant to coaching, there were other aspects to my students' engagement with Melville's text that yielded greater benefits. Reading "Bartleby" did have some tangible impact on the students' writing skills. Exposure to the style of a literary craftsman like Melville aided the students in reflecting on their own writing and put them on the path to expressing themselves with greater clarity and vigor.

The writing case for reading "Bartleby"

I do not intend to make any exaggerated claims for the students' writing skills being vastly improved by reading "Bartleby." My claims will be modest but noteworthy. I first want to explain my strategy in the context of the students' project work. Many academics have bemoaned what they perceive as a diminution of the crucial role good writing plays in academic work and the increase of poorly expressed student output. We in higher education are familiar with the proliferation of academic writing units and of their necessity. Mature, working students who are in elevated positions in their company are able to communicate reasonably well. They do have difficulties, however, in recognizing that the aim of academic writing is to produce prose characterized foremost by clarity and simplicity. They are bombarded by journal articles, particularly in the business realm, replete with awkward sentence constructions, incomprehensible jargon, and contorted, overcomplicated phrasing. With few exceptions, students new to academia believe that density and obscurity are the hallmarks of scholarship.

Literature is a natural handmaiden to teaching writing skills when the works demonstrate a cohesive style and high level of critical analysis. Literary writers tend to be experts in telling a good story and are technically proficient. Not only is there a closer connection between well-versed readers and skilled writers, those who read become more attuned to the subtleties of language, narrative complexity, thematic resonance, and characterization – all qualities present in fiction and all foremost considerations for producing a coaching project. I encourage students in the skill of close reading, which I define as paying attention to what is written on the page. It means not only reading and comprehending the meaning of each printed word but being sensitive to the connotations and nuances of the language employed by skilled writers. There are four levels of attention that I encourage: linguistic attention (noting vocabulary and figures of speech); semantic attention (looking deeply at word connotations); structural attention (thinking about the relationship between words in the text); and cultural attention (reflecting on how the text relates to the conditions in which it was written). It requires practice for students to become aware of their own composing processes through attending to the stylistic features of fictional writers. It is, as McCord (1985, 748) notes, through the process of reading that students can become better writers: "unless students learn a way of reading that enables them to discover signs of the composing process they are not only discouraged by what seems an impossibly high standard of writing but left in ignorance of how to go about the process of producing such an essay."

I asked the "Bartleby" readers among my cohort of coaching students to examine the following excerpt, which we discussed subsequently in Skype session follow-ups:

> "Bartleby! quick, I am waiting."
>
> I heard a slow scrape of his chair legs on the uncarpeted floor, and soon he appeared standing at the entrance of his hermitage.
>
> "What is wanted?" said he mildly.
>
> "The copies, the copies," said I hurriedly. "We are going to examine them. There" – and I held towards him the fourth quadruplicate.
>
> "I would prefer not to," he said, and gently disappeared behind the screen.
>
> For a few moments I was turned into a pillar of salt, standing at the head of my seated column of clerks. Recovering myself, I advanced towards the screen, and demanded the reason for such extraordinary conduct.
>
> "Why do you refuse?"
>
> "I would prefer not to."
>
> With any other man I should have flown outright into a dreadful passion, scorned all further words, and thrust him ignominiously from my presence. But there was something about Bartleby that not only strangely disarmed me,

but in a wonderful manner touched and disconcerted me. I began to reason with him.

"These are your own copies we are about to examine. It is labor saving to you, because one examination will answer for your four papers. It is common usage. Every copyist is bound to help examine his copy. Is it not so? Will you not speak? Answer!"

"I prefer not to," he replied in a flute-like tone.

It seemed to me that while I had been addressing him, he carefully revolved every statement that I made; fully comprehended the meaning; could not gainsay the irresistible conclusions; but, at the same time, some paramount consideration prevailed with him to reply as he did.

"You are decided, then, not to comply with my request – a request made according to common usage and common sense?"

He briefly gave me to understand that on that point my judgment was sound. Yes: his decision was irreversible.

It is not seldom the case that when a man is browbeaten in some unprecedented and violently unreasonable way, he begins to stagger in his own plainest faith. He begins, as it were, vaguely to surmise that, wonderful as it may be, all the justice and all the reason is on the other side. Accordingly, if any disinterested persons are present, he turns to them for some reinforcement for his own faltering mind.

"Turkey," said I, "what do you think of this? Am I not right?"

"With submission, sir," said Turkey, with his blandest tone, "I think that you are."

"Nippers," said I, "what do you think of it?"

"I think I should kick him out of the office."

(Melville 1969, 48–9)

This is an ideal passage to scrutinize for a range of reasons: it has the advantage of being brief; it encapsulates the office dynamics between the lawyer and his staff; and it provides a flavor of the style – sentence structure, word choice, content – of Melville's writing. In this excerpt, we discern that Bartleby has become an employee that "prefers not to" do anything. There are obvious office tensions now between Bartleby and the other copyists. I asked students to focus on any imagery they found striking or remarkable. They pointed out the lawyer becoming "a pillar of salt." Students recognized its biblical significance and wondered if such imagery had its place in academic writing, and in particular, in writing on coaching. They asked if they had "permission" to use imaginative description. They decided that it was preferable to use a brief, striking image that captured someone's feelings precisely than to regurgitate the usual clichés for the lawyer's emotional response to Bartleby's refusal: "confused," "dumbstruck," "frozen."

The biblical image not only contextualized the writing as being from a time when readers would immediately recognize such allusions, it also provided an exactitude to the lawyer's feelings. "There is no waffle," as one student put it.

With further probing, I was interested to hear the students emphasize how relevant the setting was to them. It was agreed that Melville had captured the kind of office politics that would be unavoidable in a frank coaching conversation. The frustration and barely suppressed rage on behalf of the lawyer who is meant to exhibit the characteristics of a leader is eloquently expressed: he speaks "hurriedly"; he demands "the reason for such extraordinary conduct"; he turns to any "disinterested persons" and asks them for "some reinforcement for his own faltering mind." My students acknowledged the importance of word choice in capturing the tenor of a coaching dialogue. Most of us instinctively know a good writing style when we see it: it is immensely valuable to reacquaint oneself with good style by the exercise of close reading. Furthermore, there are distinct lessons on leadership we can take from this brief excerpt. The language the lawyer uses can be analyzed and discussed as part of a larger discussion on leadership issues and the danger and abusive possibilities inherent in a so-called leader's language.

As the students pointed out, the lawyer "demands," "advances," could "thrust" someone "ignominiously" from his presence: there is material in "Bartleby" to explore themes of power misuse, authority abuse, and equality and neutrality in coaching. Coaching can make employees feel more valued and connected with their organization, but it is unable to help people to understand and improve their working relationships without a concerted focus on clarity. A close reading from "Bartleby" enables students to concentrate on language. It also helps us to see that words can mask or reveal what is going on in the thoughts of another person. I have found that there needs to be more than a slavish adherence to a prescriptive model of personality assessments or of behavioral prediction tools. No training kit will capture the rich and meaningful emotions literature reveals through an author's treatment of his fictional characters or produce the more sophisticated interpretations and considered judgments that coaching deserves.

I have expressed doubt whether narrow and prescriptive models, such as many personality assessments, are able to foster meaningful coaching conversations. Literature, in contrast, encourages us to have empathetic responses to its fictional characters, and, in the hands of a highly skilled writer, we are powerless to resist its onslaught of emotions. Empathy is an important aspect of coaching: if we want to understand our fellow colleagues' behavior and motivations and help them to be productive and happy in the job, empathy can be a route to such means. We may not be able to empathize with Bartleby or his frustrated and mystified boss, but there is cognitive value in a story that enables readers to feel what it is like to be in the closed-in Wall Street offices of these nineteenth-century scriveners. Moreover, there is value in being able to attend to the language, imagination, and themes of the story. Coaching is, as my observations from working with a wide range of organizations have demonstrated, perfectly feasible to do without any literary input. But my question is this: is it desirable to do without the "truth-telling" value of literature, of beautifully crafted, wise stories? The call of stories and their usefulness and moral support seem perfectly matched to the aims of coaching. Perhaps a story like "Bartleby," from an alien time and populated by alien beings, is simply a step too far from many coaches and coachees' comfort zones. However, there are, as we will see in the next chapters, literary works that can foster the kind of empathetic perspective shifting that makes for successful coaching dialogue. Stories may sometimes be difficult and may often produce unexpected results; but it is through the unexpected that an imaginative flash can suddenly appear, a moment of clarity and self-vision earned through arduous empathic processes. Stories like "Bartleby" certainly do not offer a one-size-fits-all, practical solution to coaching challenges, but we would be remiss to neglect the coaching potential of a good story.

Note

1 The student responses collated here are drawn from recorded follow-up interviews in addition to the written responses they submitted to my questionnaire. Permission has been granted by the students to use their responses here in an anonymized form.

References

Arvin, Newton. 1950. *Herman Melville*. London: Methuen.

Carroll, Noël. 2011. "On Some Affective Relations Between Audiences and the Characters in Popular Fictions." In *Empathy: Philosophical and Psychological Perspectives*, edited by Amy Coplan and Peter Goldie, 162–85. Oxford: Oxford University Press.

Chase, Richard. 1949. *Herman Melville: A Critical Study*. New York: Palgrave Macmillan.

Coles, Robert. 1980. "Psychology and Literature." *New Literary History* 12 (1): 207–11.

Coles, Robert. 1989. *The Call of Stories: Teaching and the Moral Imagination*. Boston: Houghton Mifflin.

Dimock, Wai Chee. 1997. "A Theory of Resonance." *PLMA* 112 (5): 1060–71.

Fisher, Marvin. 1977. *Going Under: Melville's Short Fiction and the American* 1850s. Baton Rouge: Louisiana State University Press.

Franklin, H. Bruce. 1963. *The Work of the Gods: Melville's Mythology*. Stanford: Stanford University Press.

Garland-Thomson, Rosmarie. 2004. "The Cultural Logic of Euthanasia: 'Sad Fancyings' in Herman Melville's 'Bartleby'." *American Literature* 76 (4): 777–806.

Goldman, Alvin. 2011. "Two Routes to Empathy: Insights From Cognitive Neuroscience." In *Empathy: Philosophical and Psychological Perspectives*, edited by Amy Coplan and Peter Goldie, 31–44. Oxford: Oxford University Press.

Higgins, Brian, and Hershel Parker, eds. 1995. *Herman Melville: The Contemporary Reviews*. Cambridge: Cambridge University Press.

Kaufman, Barbara. 2006. "The Role of Executive Coaching in Performance Management." *Handbook of Business Strategy* 7: 287–91.

Lamarque, Peter. 2008. *The Philosophy of Literature*. Malden: Wiley-Blackwell.

Mander, Gertrud. 2005. "Defiant Resistance in the Service of the Impoverished Self: Herman Melville's 'Bartleby': An Illustration of Clinical Casework." *British Journal of Psychotherapy* 22 (2): 217–26.

Marcus, Mordecai. 1962. "Melville's Bartleby as a Psychological Double." *College English* 23 (5): 365–8.

Marx, Leo. 1953. "Melville's Parable of the Walls." *Sewanee Review* 61 (4): 602–27.

McCord, Phyllis. 1985. "Reading Non-Fiction in Composition Courses: From Theory to Practice." *College English* 47 (7): 744–62.

Melville, Herman. 1969. *Great Short Works of Herman Melville*. Edited by Warner Berthoff. New York: Perennial Classics.

Morton, Adam. 2011. "Empathy for the Devil." In *Empathy: Philosophical and Psychological Perspectives*, edited by Amy Coplan and Peter Goldie, 318–30. Oxford: Oxford University Press.

Murphy, Geraldine. 1988. "Romancing the Center: Cold War Politics and Classic American Literature." *Poetics Today* 9 (4): 737–47.

Pinker, Steven. 1997. *How the Mind Works*. New York: W. W. Norton.

Post-Lauria, Sheila. 1993. "Canonical Text and Context: The Example of Herman Melville's 'Bartleby the Scrivener: A Story of Wall Street'." *College Literature* 20 (2): 196–206.

Robinson, Jenefer. 2005. *Deeper than Reason: Emotion and Its Role in Literature, Music, and Art*. Oxford: Oxford University Press.

Rourke, Constance. 1959. *American Humor: A Study of the National Character*. Tallahassee: University of Florida Press. First published 1931 by Harcourt, Brace and Co.

Schultz, Robert. 2011. "White Guys Who Prefer Not To: From Passive Resistance ('Bartleby') to Terrorist Acts (*Fight Club*)." *The Journal of Popular Culture* 44 (3): 583–605.

Sequeia, Adolfo et al. 2007. "Patterns of Gene Expression in the Limbic System of Suicides With and Without Major Depression." *Molecular Psychiatry* 12 (7): 640–55.

Slowikowski, Mary Kay. 2005. "Using the DISC Behavioral Instrument to Guide Leadership and Communication." *AORN Journal* 82 (5): 835–43.

Smith, Murray. 2011. "Empathy, Expansionism, and the Extended Mind." In *Empathy: Philosophical and Psychological Perspectives*, edited by Amy Coplan and Peter Goldie, 99–117. Oxford: Oxford University Press.

Sreenidhi, Sam Kris, and Owen Fernandes. 2014. "The Benefits of Using a Holistic Approach in Behavioral Assessment Interpretation." *International Education, Training and Consulting. IBSM International Conference of Business, Management and Accounting*, 91–100.

Stokes, Jon, and Richard Jolly. 2014. "Executive Leadership and Coaching." In *The Complete Handbook of Coaching*, edited by Elaine Cox, Tatiana Bachkirova, and David Ashley Clutterbuck, 244–55. 2nd edn. London: Sage.

Sugerman, Jeffrey. 2009. "Using the DISC Model to Improve Communication Effectiveness." *Industrial and Commercial Training* 41 (3): 151–4.

Swaab, Dick. 2014. *We Are Our Brains: From the Womb to Alzheimer's*. London: Penguin.

Thompson, Corey Evan. 2013. "The Prodromal Phase of Alcoholism in Herman Melville's Bartleby the Scrivener and Cock-a-doodle-do." *The Explicator* 71 (4): 275–80.

Thompson, Corey Evan. 2015. *Alcohol in the Writings of Herman Melville "The Ever-Devilish God of Grog"*. Jefferson (NC): McFarland and Co.

Tocqueville, Alexis de. 2010. *Democracy in America*. Indianapolis: Liberty Fund.

Yardley, Jonathan. 1996. "A Quiet Lady in the Limelight." In *More Conversations With Eudora Welty*, edited by Peggy Whitman Prenshaw, 3–13. Jackson: University Press of Mississippi.

Chapter 2

The space to tell one's story

Willa Cather's "Neighbor Rosicky"

In the previous chapter I gave an account of some of the challenges that arise when using literary works in coaching. Herman Melville's "Bartleby" did not stimulate the level of personal reflection and abstraction that I had intended. The story provoked predominantly literal responses among my postgraduate coaching students, who tried in essence to coach Melville's dysfunctional protagonist rather than take a metaphorical leap and perceive aspects of Bartleby in themselves and encourage their coachees to do the same. This chapter narrates a comparatively effective endeavor to introduce coaching students to a work of literature that was able to trigger the reflective processes that seemed elusive with the "Bartleby" cohort. Here I contemplate the power of stories to get people to tell their own story, and I explore the reasons why a short story like Willa Cather's "Neighbor Rosicky" might succeed in setting that narrative impulse in motion, whereas Melville's "Bartleby" might sometimes fail to do so. The chapter presents a chronicle of the work I did with a cohort of students working for a large global firm in the telecommunications sector. This was a small group of nine males and one female engaged in inquiries about how coaching could improve aspects of their business. All but two of the students were nonnative English speakers, so I decided to introduce a piece of literature that I thought undemanding and accessible. Students worked in Columbia, Germany, Spain, Portugal, Russia, and the UK, and all were concerned about employee morale, which had plummeted after the company had changed from Swedish to Japanese ownership. This is not the place to detail the reasons the students believed the company had altered for the worse under its new ownership: my concern is instead how the literature with which they engaged was able to illuminate their coaching reflections and interventions. All of the students were investigating a range of coaching strategies: one student responsible for operations over a large area in South America was exploring the potential of coaching remotely; another student, exasperated by his direct management, whom he deemed "distant and unconcerned," was interested in the role of emotional intelligence in coaching. We worked together for a year, meeting four times face to face in the organization's London headquarters and the rest of the time in virtual small-group sessions or on one-to-one calls. The responses to my own literary intervention were gathered by questionnaire or by informal interviews on Skype. All of the students participated in the exercise, believing it would add value to their coaching practice.

"Value," or more accurately "values," is an important word in the following narrative I will relate. When I was first introduced to this group of master's-level students, the word and its cognates surfaced again and again in our discussions. Students did not feel "valued" by management. Their "values" were not properly addressed. "Valuing" each other as colleagues appeared to be diminishing. The "value" of direct and simple communication had been lost in a tsunami of administrative tasks and bureaucratic directives. While supporting them as they embarked on their projects that would survey the academic literature in their field, describe their methodology and data collection, analyze their data (from questionnaires, surveys, interviews, and observations), and finally make practical and feasible recommendations for change to their organization, I decided that reading Willa Cather's "Neighbor Rosicky" would enlarge their understanding of their enquiries and help them to improve their practice by asking questions of the text that could be applied to their own practice. Their understandable preoccupation with values is perfectly addressed by Cather's story of a farmer who reflects on values just before he dies: his own values, those of his neighbors, and the conflict of values between rural and urban life. Cather was adamant in her belief that "economics and art [were] strangers" (Woodress 1987, 189), a belief that reflected my students' workplace concerns. Absent from their inquiries was any reference to increased productivity or falling share prices or more streamlined ways of handling business. Their concern was for the art of being in the workplace – how to create solid and satisfying teamwork, how to communicate with greater clarity, how to demonstrate to colleagues that they valued each other's hard work, patience, and good-humored support.

"Neighbor Rosicky" seemed to me the ideal text to introduce a fictional approach to a coaching scenario. The students were seeking, above all, a sacred space, and this story – born out of deep and abiding love of the "promised land" of nineteenth-century America, infused with societal and cultural values of the American dream of natural harmony and human potential, and created from a romantic vision of manifest destiny – seemed to me an unparalleled match for people who had been demoralized and dispirited by corporate exigencies. The students expressed alienation and isolation, an identity crisis for which "Neighbor Rosicky," with its reverence for the values inherent in the pastoral ideal, seemed an antidote.

I will discuss values, the divided life, and the parallels between Willa Cather's philosophy and writing techniques and coaching. I will explore how "Neighbor Rosicky" can provide richness to coaching by stimulating more satisfying conversations on values, myth, and spiritual well-being. I will address the role of emotions in coaching and the role of literature in evidence-based coaching. I will describe the crucial role values play in Cather's fiction as well as the role of myth and the unconscious both in Cather's fiction and in coaching in general. I will turn to questions of Cather's early career as a journalist and ask if we can learn anything about writing from her experience. I address how her writing can help students write and coach better. Throughout this chapter I will draw on James Woodress's biography of Willa Cather, *Willa Cather, a Literary Life* (1987), which not only painstakingly details her letters, speeches, reminiscences, interviews, and critical reception but also provides a scholarly investigation into the parallels between her life and fiction. Finally, I will let the students' voices speak for themselves. My primary concern is that the emotional context of coaching in some organizations is woefully insufficient. Here, then, is the story of how I used a simple folk tale in a targeted way to fill the gap a group of coaching students was looking to fill in an emotional sense. This is the story of how to embrace the sacred without fear.

Values, the divided life, and parallels with coaching

Cather's most persistent preoccupation in her writing is values. From the outset of her career, it is an overarching theme that runs through her work to her mature fiction: her main concern is the inevitable conflict between materialism and spirituality. When she was briefly a schoolteacher in Pittsburgh, she described the appalling conditions in Potterville, the stockade where the immigrant laborers lived. Toiling at the Carnegie steel plant, they lived seventy to a timber-framed shanty. Cather recalled that the splendid Carnegie library was used only by management: the constantly employed mill hands had no leisure to enjoy this benevolent gesture bestowed by the steel magnate. She was fascinated by division, the two halves, those who lived divided lives (Woodress 1987).

Her first novel, *Alexander's Bridge* (1912), tells the story of a man torn between his wife and his mistress. We learn that there is a fissure in his moral nature as Cather incisively examines what he values, deciding that he is unable to "harmonize desire with possibility" (Woodress 1987, 219). In his restless dissatisfaction with life, the protagonist exhibits a divided nature: he yearns for and seeks something that he can never find. Cather's interest lies in what she perceives as the moral division in man's nature, an inability to reconcile contradictions in his character. The rather unappealing protagonist with his flimsy morals was defended by Cather: she insisted that writers needed to see into a character deeply and that they must not be circumscribed by what they admire: there needs to be an attempt to comprehend fully motivation, values, and conflicted desires.

A précis of *Alexander's Bridge* should help to elucidate and set my further points in context. Alexander Bartley has become a world-famous engineer. He has built a bridge across the St. Lawrence River and is exceedingly good looking, and seemingly happily married. On a business trip to London he meets again an actress with whom he had been in love and takes up the affair again. Cather illustrates his year of living a double life, a divided existence that mirrors the crack that emerges in the bridge he built. He has been warned the bridge is weak and, upon inspecting it, is plunged into oblivion as the bridge finally collapses. In an interview with the *New York Sun*, Cather explained her objective in writing the story as illustrating a connection between the metaphor of the bridge and the vocation of its builder:

> This is not the story of a bridge and how it was built but of a man who built bridges. The bridge builder with whom this story is concerned began life a pagan, a crude force, with little respect for anything but youth and work and power. He married a woman of much more discriminating taste and much more clearly defined standards. He admires and believes in the social order of which she is really a part, though he has been only a participant. Just so long as his ever kindling energy exhibits itself only in his work everything goes well, but he runs the risk of encountering new emotional as well as new intellectual stimuli.
>
> (Woodress 1987, 218)

The bridge is a symbol for the tangible accomplishments of Cather's protagonist. It stands for his hard work, a victory over nature by human ingenuity, just as the protagonist's wife tames her husband's rusticity through her refinement. But the crack suggests the precariousness of the triumph. Emerging concomitantly with the failing bridge, the divide between the protagonist's former self and his current nature will resurface in Cather's story. It is these tensions in human personality that Cather captures in her story, the gulf between real and assumed selves. And it is these same tensions that coaching dialogues in the workplace must navigate.

The testimony of a student from another organization given during a Skype conversation sheds light on the role of literary works in helping to bring to the surface the conflicted personalities often suppressed in the workplace. The coaching student had read James Baldwin's essay "Notes of a Native Son" on my suggestion because he was investigating culture and race at his organization and how his company addressed diversity in the workplace. Baldwin's voice had been a revelation to him. The honesty, power, and controlled anger of his prose made my student realize that Baldwin's work was pivotal in his inquiry. He had asked a member of his team to read the essay as a basis for an upcoming coaching session. His colleague expressed relief that someone – even sixty years ago – understood what it was like to be "Janus-faced." The colleague felt "splintered" by having to present to others at work the persona of someone he was not because he thought that his "real self" was unable to convey the correct amount of distance and stature for him to be thought of as a leader by his team. I will relate my student's use of Baldwin's writing in my next chapter: Baldwin's eloquent howl of rage at civilization feels like a companion piece to John Cheever's barely suppressed disgust at society. What Baldwin and Cheever share with Cather is their attuned sensitivity to the inner conflicts that simmer below the surface of our public personalities. It is this aspect of these authors' characterization to which my coaching students are invariably attracted, and it is this aspect of their work that makes their texts particularly appropriate vehicles for coaching dialogue and for reflecting on workplace behavior.

As Cather became a more experienced writer, she was convinced that "the material [must] dictate the organization and structure of her novels" (Woodress 1987, 232). Form must follow function: the essential matter of the story comes first. The parallels with coaching may not seem obvious at first, but the principles are the same. The story must take precedence over the mechanical details and presentation. It was unimportant if her presentation was episodic, a loose series of telling incidents that became a narrative. She was never averse to making digressions either. For example, it was not extraordinary for her to skip ten years before resuming the thread of the central narrative. I maintain that coaching too must be respectful of people's organic whole, their essences, and their stories, no matter how digressive or fragmented. There are similarities between creating a meaningful novel and getting the most out of the coaching experience. Cather had followed the precept that whatever had been teasing the mind for years needed to be worked up into a story. She believed that the "shapes and scenes" that had been in her mind would create something far more "vivid and vigorous" than the mere transference of an immediate impression (Woodress 1987, 241). In the coaching sphere, there have been critical tensions between rationality and emotion in the workplace, tensions that have origins in Western philosophical thought, in which rationality trumps emotion (Bachkirova and Cox 2007). Organizations, for the most part, present themselves as rational, reasonable entities. However, there is no denying human beings are emotional creatures and that our emotions, in particular, support our decision making. Cather's fiction is acutely sensitive to her characters' emotions: there is much we can learn from how she handles emotion in her characters and how she manipulates emotion in her readers.

Bachkirova and Cox (2007) make a compelling argument concerning the emotional context of coaching in organizations. People at the top of the company hierarchy are expected to be leaders, to be able to act rationally, and to evaluate others and events dispassionately. Yet they are also expected to respond with a high degree of emotional intelligence. Coaching of course is not psychotherapy or counseling, but it is undeniably an emotional process, even in an organizational context. Bachkirova and Cox (2007, 609) found that the views coaches had on emotion reflected "a multiplicity of attitudes to emotion in personal and organizational context." They concluded that it was valuable in a coaching strategy or intervention to be able to reflect on one's attitude to emotion. There were undeniably ambiguous attitudes to emotion in organizations, and those attitudes created fluctuating postures with regard to emotion among the coaches questioned. Bachkirova and Cox's (2007, 610) respondents recognized the crucial role played by coaches' "personal history and the dynamics of individual development" on their theory of emotion: people's backgrounds and experiences provide a unique voice in organizational life.

Coaching with emotion in organizations could be captured by exploring the contested role of emotions in the workplace *at a distance*. If we allow literature and its attendant discussions of how different characters react to each other and events, we can mitigate the discomfort some coaches experience in addressing potential raw, negative, and even ugly emotions (such as envy, rage, and hatred). By using the distance of literature, coaches can encourage their coachees to get under the skin of another while avoiding addressing the problems of the coachee head-on. For example, coaches might guide their coachees to explore their envy of a colleague by reading *Alexander's Bridge* and discussing the issue of envy illustrated in the story rather than by tackling the workplace problem directly and trying to contain it. Such a method for approaching the workplace problem might seem like a recipe for avoidance, a vehicle enabling problems to be circumvented rather than addressed. However, the discussion of a problem through the literary work can be more productive than a direct confrontation for a number of reasons. First, uncomfortable, personal, and emotional issues are often best approached with tact by eliciting the coachee's narrative rather than by demanding it through interrogation. Literature can be a productive means of eliciting narratives. In their reading of a literary work, coachees can be encouraged to make links with their workplace experiences in a more abstract setting that can seem less hostile than a dialogue immediately focalized on personal problems. The second reason why literature can be a more beneficial way of approaching coaching dialogue is that its effect can endure long after the coaching session. Literary works have a tendency to lodge themselves in the mind, in a way. They can encourage prolonged reflection long after the initial reading or coaching dialogue has taken place. Literature is, then, a way of coaching beyond the parameters of a coaching session. It has the potential to make coaching, and the insights obtained from it, an integral part of our reflective lives, as we interrogate our own behavior and attitudes under the stimulus of a literary work and the guidance of a coach who urges us to make links between the work and our own lives. Literature can become, in this way, a space for moral reflection, which can enhance the richness and pervasiveness of coaching dialogue.

Cather was frank in her anatomizing, stating that "getting inside a new skin was the finest sport she knew" (Woodress 1987, 255). A writer like Cather provides valuable instruction for how coaches can address the problematic nature of less pleasant emotions surfacing in coaching. To draw an analogy between, on one hand, Cather's techniques of eschewing "immediate impressions" for what is "vivid and vigorous" from her memory and history and, on the other hand, working with emotions in coaching, I would suggest that Cather's method of "getting inside a new skin" can help coaches who want to distance themselves from any notion of therapy as well as those coaches who are comfortable yet unsure about how to work emotionally with coachees. Whether conscious or not, voiced or not, coaching is the art of getting inside a new skin. Coaches may or may not have a clearly articulated strategy of working with emotions, but their endgame is invariably to get to know what motivates their coachees. They need to be able to explore another person's heart, mind, and soul as much as the other person will consciously or unconsciously allow. The value of using literature in coaching is that an expert artist, a diviner of souls, an explorer of hearts, an anatomizer of minds has already done the hard graft. The characters created by Cather, for example, become the buffer, the safe space between coach and client: no one needs to reveal, become exposed, present vulnerabilities. Cather's characters are those that are revealed, exposed, made vulnerable: they become examples of emotional excess or impasses on which a coaching dialogue can center without directly involving the current participants. Another clear advantage of using Cather's literature is that she did not write intellectual novels – there are no obscure references or deliberately difficult passages. Her writing is straightforward and uncomplicated. She privileged storytelling over any experimental plot devices: her work is emotional and nurturing, drawing on the stories of her youth and impregnated with the deep and wide classical reading she loved, especially Homer and mythology. Above all, her abiding interest is in how human beings communicate with each other. She explores how we misunderstand each other in every aspect of life, especially in the working environment. This desire to avoid misunderstanding seems to my mind to be systematically expressed also in literature on coaching.

Literature and coaching

Cather's expertise at evoking emotions is an aspect of her craft that has been noted admiringly by many critics (Woodress 1987). Moreover, if one is to judge by the reviews on Goodreads, she is received extremely favorably by the general public. I recently conducted a survey of her novels on Goodreads and was impressed by an overwhelming percentage of five-star reviews, with many readers praising her mature understanding of human psychology, her ability to craft cautionary tales of what can happen when people live lives without reflection, and her adroit characterization of the realities of life and their emotional pools of light and darkness. If coaching is expected to respond to the demand of emotionally astute ways of enhancing performance and helping clients to negotiate change skillfully, coaches need a way of supporting their clients to make sense of the world and of their position in it.

Shipton and Sillince (2012) point out the peripheral role emotions have played in organizational-learning literature as they detail the results of a five-year study to ascertain the emotions people experience during organizational learning. In the one organization they followed, they concluded that researchers needed to adopt "a more emotionally centric perspective" to highlight where and how organizational learning occurs: emotions should be seen as "integral to, rather than separate from, the cognitive dynamics that underlie learning and change in organizations" (Shipton and Sillince 2012, 507). Organizational learning occurs when people's emotions – frustration, anxiety, excitement, pride, and the complexity of these emotions – are validated by the organization. The focus needs to be on "the sharing of success stories, role modeling, coaching focused on surviving failure, communicating and sharing exciting big picture perspectives. Acknowledging that emotions exist is a necessary first step" (Shipton and Sillince 2012, 506).

It is this crucial first step in acknowledging the existence of emotions in which a literary work such as Cather's can be instrumental in organizational learning and in the coaching dialogues that drive it. Cather's plots are secondary to her interest in character. In her ability to get the reader to feel, she evokes with consummate skill how her characters see their world, how they feel, for example, frustration, anxiety, excitement, pride. Her characters are not heroic figures but seemingly ordinary people who, more often than not, like the people coaches work with in organizations, have to learn to live with change, to learn how to adapt to novel conditions, and to learn how to accept the inevitable. Her stories work out personal problems, especially how to live in a world in flux. She may have the lightest of touches, but as one critic perceived, she leaves behind "deep conjecture and pictures which are realer than your own life" (Woodress 1987, 388). My students' reactions testified to the role Cather's art plays in people's emotions. Students reported physiological changes, for example, feeling calmer and at peace when reading the story of Anton Rosicky. Sometimes it is simply good enough to offer a halt, a pause, a slowing down in busy executives' lives, giving them time to reflect on their own emotions while appraising another's trials and tribulations. Even though Rosicky is a figment of Cather's imagination, and my students knew that, they were able to reflect on his fate and be affected by the narrative.

"Neighbor Rosicky" and evidence-based coaching

Anthony Grant (2016, 77) argues that "evidence-based coaching" has become a phrase incorporated into the terms of reference for many coaching practitioners, in much the same way as a phrase like "return on investment": evidence-based practice promises data that can be statistically analyzed and quantifiable. Evidence in coaching originates from places that may well be extraneous to the empirical research of science-based disciplines: "all kinds of information can count as evidence, just as long as it is valid, reliable and relevant" (Grant 2016, 77). Evidence becomes information. Grant puts forward a nuanced view of evidence-based coaching practice, arguing that a broader, less reductionist view of evidence-based practice is best. After all, coaching is not medicine: "Indeed, given that much coaching does not follow prescribed or manualised treatment regimes, the medical model may be a somewhat inappropriate framework from which to develop an evidence-based approach to coaching" (Grant 2016, 77). If, as Grant (2016, 82) reminds us, the main goal of coaching is in illuminating "observable behavioural change," Willa Cather's work seems ideal to use in a coaching scenario. We have seen how Cather's *Alexander's Bridge* might be used as a distancing mechanism in coaching dialogue. In the subsequent sections, I am going to explore how "Neighbor Rosicky" might be used as a tool to observe behavioral change. I will relate how my students' responses to this narrative characterized by emotion, feeling, and the subtle use of myth and symbol enabled them to discuss change and work out personal issues at work. My contention is that a story such as "Neighbor Rosicky" can effect a more powerful coaching dialogue by appealing to emotions that guide us to perceive our world in a more probing and thoughtful manner.

Written in 1928 and collected in the volume *Obscure Destinies* (1932), Willa Cather's "Neighbor Rosicky" is the story of an ordinary man who, facing death, reflects on the meaning and value of his life. An émigré who has escaped from the slums of the Old Country to settle in America's Midwest, Anton Rosicky is horrified by city life. He has come to value the tough but rewarding life as a Nebraskan farmer and considers his life with his large family idyllic. Before he dies, he wants to make sure that his son's domestic life is put right. The son's wife is disgruntled and frustrated by farm life, and Rosicky takes pains to nurture his relationship with his daughter-in-law so that she can begin to recognize the richness and beauty of their rural existence: he wants her to perceive the value of what he values. Their growing relationship is movingly detailed as Rosicky listens to his daughter-in-law Polly's dissatisfactions and strives to make her more of an integral part of his happy family. Polly reflects on Rosicky's actions at the end of the story: "Nobody in the world, not her mother, not Rudolph [her husband], or anyone really loved her as much as Rosicky did. It perplexed her. She sat frowning and trying to puzzle it out. It was as if Rosicky had a special gift for loving people, something that was like an ear for music or an eye for colour. It was quiet, unobtrusive; it was merely there, you saw it in his eyes" (Cather 1992, 615–16).

The story explores themes such as honesty, integrity, hard work, honor, spiritual wealth, and emotional depth – all themes that coaches can invite coachees to reflect on in order to facilitate awareness of any underlying emotional barriers facing either of them. The story can be used to contemplate how to live a more meaningful life, for what happens in "Neighbor Rosicky" is, quite simply, a coaching dialogue. Rosicky coaches his daughter-in-law in the ways of his world and encourages her to become a beneficial member of her household and community. The story, outwardly at least, has little a twenty-first-century white-collar employee can relate to. It is set in a faraway land at a faraway time. Superficially, much has changed from the world Cather depicts to the urban centers people inhabit today. But Cather touches on themes that are imbued with a universality that can continue to speak in powerful ways. Indeed, it is precisely because Rosicky's world seems so distant that we are able to appreciate it all the more. Like Polly, we may think this world has nothing to tell us. But Cather guides us, just as Rosicky guides Polly, in making the connections between our own lives and those depicted. The gulf between the world of the story and our own encourages a reflection that is all the more powerful on our own situation and predicaments. Blanche Knopf, the wife of Cather's publisher, commented on Cather's ability to depict atmosphere and people "in such a way that they became a good deal more real than the landscape outside the window or the person sitting across the table" (Woodress 1987, 441). It is this ability to slow life down and to approach life with magnifying lens that gives readers the reflective space to think about Cather's characters and to ponder those who surround them.

Reissner and DuToit (2011, 251) maintain that storytelling can be shaped to reinforce what they see as the "serious and challenging considerations" of use and abuse of power in the workplace. They are convinced that storytelling in organizational coaching involves a degree of "story selling," which means that the storyteller has an agenda that can be "inextricably linked to power" (Reissner and DuToit 2011, 251). The coach (the writers refer only to external coaches, but their work could also be applicable to internal coaches) engages in a complex process that aims to exert power over a coachee. Similarly, an organization may seek to exert power over a coach. Either "may manipulate the situation by exercising their power of manipulation and the telling of a compelling story" (Reissner and DuToit 2011, 251) so that, in the organization's case, it absolves itself of responsibility for an employee with performance problems or, in the coach's case, to exert power over the employee by exaggerating past successes. Both coaches and coachees reveal the stories of their experiences, and storytelling appears integral to sense making in coaching.

Storytelling that is used to make meaning of personal experience is part of a transformational learning process and can support both personal and professional growth for coachees, which ultimately benefits the organization. But storytelling can also be used to manipulate a coach or coachee. Reissner and DuToit offer the example of a coach using the coaching experience to try to ensure that the organization's coaching contract can be met. In a disputatious scenario with an organization, coachees can try to get the coach to be more sympathetic to their side of the story. Reissner and DuToit (2011, 256–7) argue for better-quality stories in a coaching engagement:

> All parties involved in storytelling need to be mindful of the dynamics of power play that is inherent [in any coaching stage]. Awareness of these dynamics allows coach, organisation and coachee to navigate through these stages for the purpose of achieving the benefits of coaching for all stakeholders.

What Reissner and DuToit warn against is the potential for manipulation by those involved in a coaching contract. They advise us to address this potential abuse by recognizing and analyzing the complex nature of power dynamics, or "story selling" in the coaching process.

Reissner and DuToit raise important issues in the power relations in coaching that could be resolved without any need to examine people's "sides." Using fiction can obviate the need for any coach going down the route of "story selling." Using a fictional text can address the problems inherent in manipulating either party involved in a coaching scenario in that the use of a narrative in coaching dialogue is a way of redirecting the manipulative tendencies in storytelling. The coach's story becomes secondary to the literary story, so that a master manipulator, in the best sense of the word, is able to strengthen the coaching experience in an ethical manner. There is no need to delve into one's personal experience – the fictional text can serve as a touchstone for discussion instead.

Cather's writing and her values

Through the process of close reading, students can appreciate an author's technique. They can learn how an author manipulates a reader's emotions, and they can ask questions of the text that can be applied to their own practices. There are elements in Cather's writing that are arguably manipulative: in detecting them, we can embrace the benefits of storytelling and eschew the abuses of story selling. Narrative thinking and narrative identity are contributory concepts to coaching practice. Narrative psychology – a clinical practice that privileges a client's story – can help people to gain insights into their motivations. Narrative psychology "offers a frame for understanding the schematics behind [our] cognitive processes as well as the socio-political processes that shape our own unique distortions" (Drake 2007, 284). If we are alert to the pitfalls of story selling, we can use stories to navigate relationships, give meaning to our critical choices, and better understand our own stories. The stories we construct can help us to understand our own experiences, however distorted: "We use [our stories] cognitively, discursively, and socially to remember and organize our past, communicate about and negotiate our present, and envision and act into our future" (Drake 2007, 285). David Drake argues that it is the conversational space that is often overlooked in successful coaching work: he urges "story listening" (Drake 2007, 288) as a mode of occupying that conservational space. Literature has a part to play as a guide in opening up both coaches and clients to new possibilities. A coach's and a client's unfolding narrative can be prompted, supported, and channeled through a story such as "Neighbor Rosicky," particularly in relation to a discussion on values.

Alongside William Faulkner's Oxford, Mississippi, and Mark Twain's Hannibal, Missouri, Willa Cather's Red Cloud, Nebraska, is one of the most famous towns in America in the world of fictionalized places to which readers can make pilgrimages (Woodress 1987, 44). This town of homestead farms named after Chief Red Cloud of the Oglala tribe was where Cather grew up and where her imaginative world was formed. Her fictional world of vast, endless prairies, closely knit immigrant families, and the strong values of the worth and mystery of human experience, the importance of the countryside, and loyalty to one's hearth, was created through myth, symbolism, and her ability, as we have seen, to get under the skin of her characters. The conflict in values captured by Cather is inevitably between materialism and spirituality, especially in "Neighbor Rosicky." The story turns to Cather's memories of Nebraska in the late nineteenth century and her feelings about her beloved late father, the strong men and women who faced adversity on their unyielding land, and the people who had a deep and abiding love for this place.

My students read the story and made initial comments based on my overarching question: How can you use "Neighbor Rosicky" to discuss values in a team-building/coaching scenario? Their initial responses were emotional ones: "the story touched me"; "it triggered reflections regarding my own life which is what a good story should do"; "the reader is invited to address fundamental questions about the meaning of life and value of happiness when living in a modern, free-market economy"; "the story addresses the timeless conflict between duty and desire: we would all love to live in the countryside doing our own gardening but some of us have to work in a highly developed sequential information and service industry"; "it's interesting that the well-educated doctor who tells the story and observes the family envies Rosicky for his life and family." One student "liked" the story but argued that Rosicky was "hardly a role model for employees working for a multi-national company in the 21st century. He is almost a Disneyesque figure that we can look on wistfully and dream with for a while. Then we leave the cinema." I suspected that the gap between a twenty-first-century life as an IT professional and an immigrant farmer in the late-nineteenth-century American prairie might create this consternation: "can one afford Rosicky's principles?" the same student asked. This student makes an especially valid point: there is an acute contrast between their own highly specialized, hierarchical, and "sequential" lives in the IT service industry and the pastoral arcadia that Cather embraces. But it is perhaps because the world Cather depicts is seemingly so alien to our own lives that reading and reflecting on "Neighbor Rosicky" can support the coaching process in our twenty-first-century accelerated existence. Cather's world, because it is so alien, provides us with the opportunity to reflect on long-buried emotions of more innocent and simple times. Recognizing the distance that separates Cather's world from ours opens a reflective space for meditating on precisely what is missing from our own existence. It is through distance that the absence becomes palpable; the values that are missing or unspoken in our own lives become painfully present.

Although Carolyn Hunt (2016) is addressing the discipline of teaching when she points out that teaching is perceived as a rational activity, I believe we can draw parallels between the pedagogical demands on teaching and the demands on coaching. She suggests that coaches in the teaching profession are severely restricted by mandates of "reform and accountability" (Hunt 2016, 332). Coaching in a corporate structure is equally subjected to a discourse of power and positioning, and using emotions in coaching is still a contested area. Hunt's (2016 331) point about literacy coaches experiencing "conditions of vulnerability, which encouraged feelings of shame, guilt and fear" parallel my experiences working with coaching students in the corporate world, which is fraught with tensions that discourage any references to emotions.

One student told me that reading "Rosicky" made him think about "the barrenness of collecting new things." These are professionals who work extremely hard, traveling extensively over the globe, and, as I explained earlier, are deeply concerned about their company's revenue fall, general employee disengagement, and falling morale. As one student memorably put it, "we are in a pitfall situation where we remain puzzled and running around in insane business circles." They are well compensated, financially comfortable people who believe passionately that the company needs to connect with its employees' values for it not only to flourish but to survive. One student expanded thoughtfully on the importance of recognizing each other's value being the cornerstone of coaching conversations at his work:

> Rosicky is a hard-working farmer but he is not looking to maximise his wealth and income as the sole purpose of his life. Instead he cares for his

> family and friends and is generous even when money is tight. When he does good, he feels comfortable. We all live in a global economy driven by factors such as free markets and the necessity for growth at all costs. The reflection on Rosicky's busy neighbours tells me that there is a risk that such busyness impacts our behaviour and blurs our values. There are lessons here on defining our individual values, prioritising them and applying them to the decision we face in work and in life.

The students' emotional responses to the story – especially the response that Rosicky's life was a kind of cartoon fantasy – bring to mind the competing power structures and expectations that influence coaching work. Emotions seem to be hived off as separate from the intellectual conversations about improving practice.

Cather's criticism of the unthinking materialism that marked the 1920s resonated deeply with the coaching students' concerns about how to live meaningful lives, particularly within the strictures of bureaucratic and, at times, soul-destroying objectives and targets. As my Disney comparing student sadly asked, "Spiritual wellbeing in the 21st century workplace is an ideal, isn't it?" There is a meticulous consideration of the conflict of values in Cather's fiction. There are "good" people who value family, love, nature, and self-sufficiency pitted against shyster lawyers, ruthless ravagers of land, and unprincipled manipulators of others. Of course, good writers are able to manipulate readers' emotions, and it could be argued that their primary objective is to employ such techniques in characterization, plot, and dialogue to move their readers emotionally, to disturb their readers' equilibrium. Susan Feagin (2010) suggests that an author does not solely control the imagination of a reader. Instead, he or she manipulates a reader's emotions by mastery over structure and style. My students reported being moved by "Neighbor Rosicky." Just as in coaching, which uses "structured, focused interaction to promote desirable and sustainable change [in people]" (Cox, Bachkirova, and Clutterbuck 2010, 1), skilled novelists aim to structure their work in such a way that their focus will effect an emotional reaction in their readers.

When my students state that the character of Rosicky "touched" them, they have experienced an emotional process stimulated by Cather's artistry. Such a cause and effect claim that the arts cultivate emotional sensibilities is reinforced by David Keplinger (2016, 187–8): "The artist's role is to create a conversation between her own perception and the readers', and for a brief moment to make them one." One technique that Cather employs is her use of myth. Although castigated in her time for "supine romanticism" by the formidable early-twentieth-century English critic Granville Hicks (Woodress 1987, 469), it is Cather's thorough engagement with her classical roots through myth that my students (and generations of readers) have found particularly effective. Susan Feagin (2010) argues that the emotions play a significant role in literary appreciation, and, although I am not especially concerned with fostering a capacity for literary appreciation in my coaching students, Feagin's supposition that readers' emotions are controlled by an experienced and perceptive writer is directly relevant to my own argument that coaching expertly and engaging with literature draw on the same skills and abilities.

Myth and the unconscious

Graham Lee's (2014) point that the goal of coaching is to make the unconscious conscious provides a theoretical basis for the notion that literature has an important part to play in coaching. Drawing on the theories of Freud and Jung in particular, Lee demonstrates that psychodynamic coaching examines our unconscious strategies for building up our self-identity (which Freud calls the "dynamic unconscious"). We have built up defenses unconsciously since childhood, and the sensitive coach therefore needs to build trust and rapport with coachees, who, more often than not, are controlling their emotions in case they are not perceived as socially acceptable. The problem is intensified in organizations when coaches use "intellectualization as a way of dealing with upsetting personnel issues, projection as a way of blaming other departments for organizational failings and displacement as a way of keeping busy with unimportant details rather than tackling more important but anxiety provoking issues" (Lee 2014, 23). The job of the coach is to create a space to look at the coachee's emotions and how these emotions are labeled in language so that carefully guarded emotional distress becomes transmuted into an experience of which the coachee is aware and able then to articulate and ultimately to try to address.

One of my students, David, commented on the ability of "Neighbor Rosicky"' to connect with life lessons "that we are not always conscious of." Graham Lee's model of psychodynamic coaching provides a parallel to my coaching students' awareness of how the unconscious affects our emotions and our drives. In a pattern of thought related to Lee's psychodynamic model, David was able to link his resistance to a new company directive (that he disagreed with) to Rosicky's lack of awareness when it came to his son Rudolph:

> It is better to let your children explore life by themselves and also to become more independent. Rosicky wants Rudolph to stay working on his farm and avoid city life and working in industry. He should allow Rudolph to trust his own instincts and try out industry. He may regret it and return to the farm. It is better not enforce your own experiences on others. Let them find their own way. The problem here is that our judgment is not valued. We are told what to do rather than being allowed to rely on our own experiences.

Another student, Julian, echoed these thoughts:

> The key area here – irrespective of whether it is 19th century American farmland or 21st century Western technologically run business – is that if one has a modicum of one's sense of self, then we can't help but be reflective as we get older. I don't think Rosicky is concerned at all with the meaning of life.

> He's quite 'existential' if I can call it that. He wants everything to be beautiful and honorable and living off the land is the only way he can achieve this. His romantic perceptions and limited ambitions have possibly done his children no favors in the long run. I see someone slyly trying to impose his will as many corporations not so slyly persist on doing to their long term detriment.

Students at this company are resisting autocratic diktats or the dead hand of authority and are able to mine the story for material that consciously or unconsciously reflects their working challenges. Cather may have intended to create a sympathetic character in Rosicky, but Julian has perceived him rather differently. It is important to note that there can be a range of responses to the same text: we all respond in an individual way to a text (Robinson 2005). When I read the story, I automatically assumed Rosicky was right to urge his son to stay in farming – no matter how tough – rather than return to a faceless, industrial position in the city. The way my reading diverges from Julian's is a reflection of our individual wants and desires: our interpretations are the sum of our emotional responses to situations, into which the myths we build up around ourselves feed. No student commented explicitly on the story's mythic features: they appeared to prefer to engage exclusively with how the characters in the story demonstrated their morals and values. The story captured their imagination through its interrogation of values. I would speculate that this was the case because they are not encouraged to discuss their values at work. Coaching, as far as it is constructed at this company, is concerned with facilitating goals, building internal resources, developing solutions, and effecting change – all admirable concerns but ones that fail to go deep enough to connect emotionally with the students.

My students did not respond to the story's mythic qualities until I asked them to use a specific excerpt with their coachees, an excerpt to which I will turn shortly. Cather used myth extensively in her fiction and was fond of drawing on widely different mythological sources from Roman writers such as Ovid and Virgil to Greek myths. "Neighbor Rosicky," as most of Cather's fiction, draws on Cather's love of classical mythology. The personification of the land – wild, savage, and suffused with meaning – has its roots in mythology. Evelyn Hinz (1972, 51) detects biblical imagery in the story: Rosicky lives in close communion with nature, and the farmer is "*part* of the natural scene, that is in vegetative terms." There is a symbolic cord between Rosicky and his land, a relationship I would argue is the essence of American myth. I selected an excerpt of the text that embodied the role of myth in the novel for my students to share with their own coachees:

> The winter turned out badly for farmers. It was bitterly cold, and after the first light snows before Christmas there was no snow at all, and no rain. March was as bitter as February. On those days when the wind fairly punished the country, Rosicky sat by his window. In the fall he and the boys had put in a big wheat planting, and now the seed had frozen in the ground. All that land would have to be ploughed up and planted over again, planted in corn. It had

happened before, but he was younger then, and he never worried about what had to be. He was sure of himself and of Mary; he knew they could bear what they had to bear, that they would always pull through somehow. But he was not so sure about the young ones, and he felt troubled because Rudolph and Polly were having such a hard start.

Sitting beside his flowering window while the panes rattled and the wind blew in under the door, Rosicky gave himself to reflection as he had not done since those Sundays in the loft of the furniture-factory in New York, long ago. Then he was trying to find what he wanted in life for himself; now he was trying to find what he wanted for his boys, and why it was he so hungered to feel sure they would be here, working this very land, after he was gone.

They would have to work hard on the farm, and probably they would never do much more than make a living. But if he could think of them as staying here on the land, he wouldn't have to fear any great unkindness for them. Hardships, certainly; it was a hardship to have the wheat freeze in the ground when seed was so high; and to have to sell your stock because you had no feed. But there would be other years when everything came along right, and you caught up. And what you had was your own. You didn't have to choose between bosses and strikers, and go wrong either way. You didn't have to do with dishonest and cruel people. They were the only things in his experience he had found terrifying and horrible; the look in the eyes of a dishonest and crafty man, of a scheming and rapacious woman.

In the country, if you had a mean neighbour, you could keep off his land and make him keep off yours. But in the city, all the foulness and misery and brutality of your neighbours was part of your life. The worst things he had come upon in his journey through the world were human, depraved and poisonous specimens of man. To this day he could recall certain terrible faces in the London streets. There were mean people everywhere, to be sure, even in their own country town here. But they weren't tempered, hardened, sharpened, like the treacherous people in cities who live by grinding or cheating or poisoning their fellow-men. He had helped to bury two of his fellow-workmen in the tailoring trade, and he was distrustful of the organized industries that see one out of the world in big cities. Here, if you were sick, you had Doctor Ed to look after you; and if you died, fat Mr. Haycock, the kindest man in the world, buried you.

(Cather 1992, 611–13)

I asked the students to use the excerpt with their team members to reflect on meaning in life and on how one might lead a more meaningful life. Was there such a thing as a "meaningful life," as described by the text, or was Cather's idea merely a myth? Could the excerpt be used to trigger deeper coaching conversations in the workplace? The students latched onto the question of myth. Julian wrote the following astute observation:

> Rosicky lives the American dream, the myth that anyone can find success in this country. The irony is that he rejects all forms of materialism to instead embody Cather's myth of living off the land and finding the quest for his identity in the power and beauty of his work, farming. His will is infused with the will of nature. There may be an unnatural separation between the city and the country or the myth of the city and the myth of the country, but there are truths that we spoke about. One thing that both my coachees and I found useful in our discussions on this passage is breaking down the myths of our organisation and focusing on what is useable and helpful in our work together.

David reported back that this team responded to "Cather's universal themes of honesty, integrity, hard work, and emotional depth." He said that his coachees picked up on the imagery: "panes rattling," "bitterly cold," "dishonest and crafty" men, and "scheming and rapacious" women in the city, the juxtaposition of the harsh, unforgiving prairie winters with the ephemeral, shallow life in the city with its schemers and cheaters. For David and his team, the issues offered a way of entering a conversation about his company and his team's values: "We were unanimous in seeing that no matter how tough the atmosphere was, only by good team work and honesty could we keep out the 'bitterly cold' wind of constant change, chaotic management directives and treadmill travel. These conversations were a way of bonding us."

Dark mysteries in the human experience

When I met the students they all professed an admiration for the GROW strategy (Whitmore 1992). I was familiar with the strategy and was frankly less than impressed by its claims. When I started working with the students, I asked them if GROW (goal, reality, options, wrapping up) had been outgrown. Aimee's response was broadly representative of the group's:

> During the coaching cycle, I became aware of the limitations of the GROW model. It is somewhat simplistic because a key consideration is risk in our industry. The OSCAR model (Gilbert and Whittleworth 2009) had become more appropriate to follow because the "C" represents consequences. Now we use a combination of the models to create GRORW – growth, reality, options, risks, way forward. This model is far more explicit than GROW and OSCAR and as it is crucial to remember – a goal needs to be driven by a stated need in the first place.

Developed in the 1980s by Graham Alexander (2010) through his work with coaches in human resources and senior executives, GROW has become somewhat an industry standard. As Alexander (2010, 83) puts it, his challenge was to capture what he was doing successfully with his clients, so he developed a simple model that could be applied to all coaching:

> Within this framework the coaching is fluid, natural and artistic. The coachee is not subjected to a mechanistic linear approach. While our language requires us to describe the GROW model as linear, in fact most coaching sessions are cyclical in nature. A coach recaps earlier phases of the GROW model throughout a coaching intervention, helping the coachee to see clearly and move forward.

The challenge for me is the model's action steps. Here, as in similar models, the focus is on topics distilled into "bite-size chunk[s]" so that the "coachee can walk away with a result" and conversations don't become "frustrating, purposeless and sometimes meandering" (Alexander 2010, 84). I would counter that we gain many of our most startling insights from those very conversations, however frustrating, purposeless, and meandering. Our emotions may seem formless and difficult, but their very formlessness and difficulty give them their significance.

Returning to the responses from reading "Neighbor Rosicky," I would reiterate that students connected emotionally with Rosicky's concerns for his son and daughter-in-law, who were tempted to leave the land and go to find work in the city. Students had visceral reactions to what they perceived as his interference and the imposition of his will, although they admired and understood his reasons. Noël Carroll (2011, 169) describes how good writers can create an identification between their characters and the reader in their fiction that "organizes or filters the situations and events it presents in such a way that the features the creators select for emphasis are those that are criterially apposite to the emotional states intended to be excited by the work." Carroll elucidates the process by which the literary vignette – the sequence of settings, events, and the characters that populate the fiction – can be skillfully manipulated to activate a reader's emotions. The notion of identifying with a character emotionally, of engendering empathy for that character in a coaching conversation can have extremely powerful implications and lasting effects. Aimee told me that for her and her team, literary coaching had enriched her practice:

> Yes, I still agree that a goal needs to be driven by a stated need in the first place but sometimes we are so overworked, we are unclear about our needs. Anton Rosicky's reflections helped me and my coachees to reflect on what was happening at work. We started to talk to each other for the first time sometimes about things we wouldn't have dreamed of talking about. More than anything, we have been challenged to look at our coaching practice more imaginatively. GROW and similar models will still have a place as short, introductory coaching interventions, but if we want to dig deeper and develop stronger bonds between us, we need to connect more emotionally through this literary approach.

The problem lies in the fact that many managers and coaches may think that they are far more emotionally intelligent than they are in reality. Literary works can help to ameliorate a situation in which one flawed human being coaches another by displaying a range of complex emotional states that can help both coach and coachee identify the nature of their feelings. In the workplace, emotions tend to be suppressed, but a literary work can help to coax them to the surface. By allowing a skilled adjudicator of human emotions – a literary creator – to take a scalpel to a fictional relationship and reveal it to us in all its glorious complexity, the emotions can become a productive part of a coaching dialogue rather than a latent subtext that quivers beneath a set of frosty and formal interactions. Literary works have the potential to humanize coaching dialogue by releasing participants from the straitjacket of formal workplace appearances. The International Coach Federation's website (n.d.) states that coaching "assumes the presence of emotional reactions to life events and that clients are capable of expressing and handling their emotions." I remain unconvinced that most of us are capable of managing our emotions, which naturally can be frustrating, purposeless, meandering, and at times incomprehensible. Literary works can become a key part of a coaching toolkit enabling the expression and handling of emotions. Pedagogical exercises such as asking a coachee to describe the emotions experienced by a character in a literary work and questioning the extent to which the coachee is able to understand those emotions can set coachees on the path of deeper self-knowledge.

Students can examine the different aspects of the GROW or GRORW model – growth, risk, reality, options, and consequences – through a straightforward and transparent fictional narrative that operates satisfyingly on many levels. The themes to which coaching students are accustomed are there, but there is also resonance, complexity, characterization, and language to consider. Like any coaching model, we can subject a story to interpretive questions. What has always been important to me is to eschew simplistic, prescriptive strategies – models and acronyms – that reduce the mysteries of human nature to comprehensible and bite-size nuggets of usefulness. However, I recognize the limitations of rolling out a literary coaching program for a large multinational organization, and we touched upon the limitations and challenges faced by the literary method in Chapter 1.

A student from another organization (one that focused on DISC and other personality assessment tools) observed that a coaching program should be organized around a series of assessments: large organizations and the people in large organizations crave structure. That may be so, I answered, but is there not room for a more reflective approach other than the usual barrage of assessments? "Absolutely," she responded, but "the organization needs to find a way of 'packaging' a literary approach."

Thoughts on packaging a literary approach: is it difficult to integrate literature into coaching?

Faced with the question of how difficult it is to integrate literature into coaching, one might counter that the difficulties will depend on the nature and structure of the organization. I realized rather quickly, from my experiments with "Bartleby," for example, that getting students to read entire novels, plays, and long, difficult short stories was counterproductive in this time-poor environment. I decided to hone the material or, in pedagogical terms, create a scaffolding opportunity. I would select an excerpt from a novel, play, or short story, particularly one that encapsulated the qualities of the story that could then get the intrigued student to go on to read the whole text. After my experience sharing with students the long and difficult 1855 story by Herman Melville, I recognized that I would have to develop my learning resource thinking better. I would need to ask one or two targeted questions rather than a large number of them, and these questions would focus on the excerpt. The excerpt would contain the distinct qualities in miniature that the whole text possessed – a particular voice, for example.

If we take the excerpt from "Neighbor Rosicky" that encapsulates Cather's voice, we can then focus on Cather's language. When Cather was an undergraduate at the University of Nebraska in the 1890s, she was already sparring with her pedantic and overly analytical (as she saw them) English professors. Her passion for words and character deemed literary analysis feeble and worthless: "They [literary analysts] never feel the hot blood riot in the pulses, nor hear the great heartbeat. That is the one great job which belongs exclusively to those of us who are unlearned, unlettered" (Woodress 1987, 81). It is for the amateur reader that she crafts her deceptively simple language, a technique that we can adopt in our coaching conversations. Looking back at the excerpt I provided the students, we can see that in a mere 500 words, we are able to enter the late-nineteenth-century world of a farmer reflecting on his life. We know that he is connected to the land which is now cold, unyielding, and unforgiving, but its hardships, no matter how severe, are balm when compared to the poisonous, callous, treacherous existence in the city. From birth to death, the land becomes personified – a living entity, a knowing god, who, although harsh like the land of the Old Testament, is the security and goodness to which this farmer cleaves and desires his family to embrace. Here is a man sure of his values, undimmed by his growing frailty in his love for what and whom he considers sacred.

Cather connects the reader to emotions such as empathy, anxiety, and loyalty, just a few of the emotions the students determined would be fruitful to probe further in a coaching conversation. For example, Carlos, the student who likened Anton Rosicky to a "Disneyesque figure" admitted that Rosicky consistently demonstrates that his emotions are underpinned by his values and principles: "The reader is always aware of this character who is conscious of doing the right thing. From the point of view of a coaching dialogue, discussing this character can lead us to a discussion on our own values of course." Carlos further pointed out that Rosicky's emotions are universal and therefore relevant: "We at [our organization] can all relate to Rosicky's conflicting feelings between love of his family and the need to make money. We are loyal to our company but this doesn't feel reciprocated. At the very least the story can open up an important dialogue we all need to be having here."

There is little doubt in my mind that Ashforth and Humphrey's (1997, 98) observation that "the experience of work is saturated with emotion" is true for every organization. Taking this particular group of students, I was especially astounded by their loyalty to their organization and attendant sadness and bewilderment that it was experiencing free fall in profits and productivity. They desperately wanted their once successful organization to prosper again, yet were unconvinced that its leadership had the vision to alter the seemingly unstoppable descent.

Discussing the impact of reading "Neighbor Rosicky" during small Skype group conversations, the students agreed that because their organization appeared to behave as though emotions had no place at work and that only rationality was privileged and prized, their voices remained unheard. I would categorically maintain that coaching is not psychotherapy, and its objective is not emotional healing; however, the emotions that Cather reveals to us in limpid prose depict the universality of human emotion and provide a natural and unthreatening access to a deep engagement with our values and the beliefs we hold in relation to coaching, emotions, and true selves.

When students used the excerpt as a starting point to discuss their coachees' experiences in the company, a few commented that their coachees tried to draw a link between the city as presented in Cather's novel and their own organization as it presently was. Their metaphorical way of thinking about the novel as in some way connected with their own experience expanded to view the land Rosicky values so highly as a symbol for what their company had been and could be. The link they made was an emotional one: Rosicky values the land in the same way as they valued their company. The shared emotion of loyalty was one they were able to identify in the text, and they were thus able to be more eloquent about their own hopes and fears for the company. Cather's work is replete with the imagery, myth, and symbolism that can be effectively harnessed in coaching language: key emotions such as fear and uncertainty can be explored far more effectively using Cather's characters than using a technique that reduces the rich complexity and slippery ambiguity of human feeling to a rigid and oversimplified model. Coaching may not be about treating psychological problems, but engaging with a writer who is able to peel away the protective layers of carapace to reveal a character's true feelings can and should be an integral part of a transformational coaching process.

For the purposes of coaching, Ashforth and Humphrey (1997) define emotions as a "subjective feeling state." I am taking this definition to include emotions, feelings, and moods. I would go further and maintain that, if emotions are part of the coaching process (and there is no negating their role), coaches need to be comfortable around emotions and their purposes. There are competing theories of emotion as well. Jenefer Robinson (2005) distinguishes between judgment theorists who believe that there is some kind of evaluation present in every emotion we experience and theorists who believe that there needs to be some kind of physiological response in emotion. She concludes that emotions are processes: we never are fully in control of our emotions and can influence them "only indirectly through subsequent cognitive monitoring" (Robinson 2005, 97). Her work has important ramifications in coaching. If we think we can label and then handle our emotions, then we are evidently unaware of their complexity and their way of acting on us and influencing our behavior even when we are not entirely conscious of their impact. We are not always able to identify how an emotional process unfolds, and there appears to be a tendency to make generalizations about emotions. Robinson believes that the answer to getting a better idea of what are emotions are and how they function lies in the exploration of literature:

> If we really want to understand emotions in all their uniqueness and individuality, if we want to follow the progress of an emotion as if unfolds, if we want to understand how the different elements of the process feed into one another and interact, and how the streams of emotional life blend and flow into one another, then we would do better to stay away from the generalizations of philosophers and psychologists, and turn instead to the detailed studies of emotion we find in great literature.
>
> (Robinson 2005, 99)

If we want to get the best out of our clients, we need to understand how they emotionally connect to the workplace. Literature offers us that key.

What Willa Cather's journalism can teach coaching students about writing

In both writing and speaking, Cather's fiction provides lessons on developing a voice. Jane Danielewicz (2008, 424) makes the point that the power of a text is wholly dependent on a writer's voice or what she calls a "persona" which becomes the essence of conveying (or not) authority. If voice is "the quality of text that lends it social power" (Danielewicz 2008, 424), then we can learn much about writing from Cather's early journalism career. Under the tutelage of Samuel McClure, Cather joined such luminaries as Arthur Conan Doyle, Mark Twain, Rudyard Kipling, and Robert Lewis Stevenson as a contributor to McClure's journal, which produced fiction, memoir, and investigative pieces in the first few decades of the 1900s. Cather contributed short fiction but was also employed full time as a journalist. *McClure's Magazine* was a "supernova in the journalistic firmament" (Woodress 1987, 185) and provided a solid foundation for Cather's growing skills as a fiction editor. Although she never wanted to write articles on popular science or celebrities or have the dubious honor of shifting through interminable slush piles, looking at others' work, these tasks helped her to hone her craft and to develop her distinctive voice. She recognized that the material must always dictate the organization and the structure of a work – the shape must design itself or "form must follow function" (Woodress 1987, 232). This principle has parallels in coaching in that a coach must work with the "material" in front of her: the organization, the person, and the relationship between the two. Too often, organizations ignore their employees' intuition. Students at this particular organization wanted the leadership to acknowledge their value, their voice, their dissatisfaction with the current scenario, and their lack of autonomy. Certainly if emotional intelligence can be linked to job satisfaction and effectiveness under stress and is considered the sine qua non of effective leadership (Angelidis and Ibrahim 2011), managers that do not relate to their people, that do not listen to their voices, are not the curators of the principles that valuable employees hold dear: recognizing, understanding, and evaluating others' feelings to guide action that will navigate more smoothly through the stormy seas of organizational pressures and uncertainties.

How can coaching develop distinctive voices that can articulate the values of an organization that management seems intent on ignoring? How can voice ensure people a place of participation? Cather's long apprenticeship as a journalist provides lessons in enhancing our narrative authority. She was always impressed by her boss Samuel McClure's leadership: he believed in allowing his editors and writers autonomy. Although Cather wanted above all to be a novelist and stayed with *McClure's* for financial reasons at the beginning of her career, she appreciated McClure's management style. On a scouting trip in London for new contributory talent, she went to see Synge's play *The Rising of the Moon*. A drama critic companion asked her what she thought of the play, and she responded that she did not think it very "dramatic." He offered that "anything interesting in theatre belongs there and is dramatic" (Woodress 1987, 203). She was apparently impressed by this principle, which she used to guide her work henceforth. Applying such a principle to coaching may at first sight seem perverse and irrelevant, but with deeper reflection and consideration, the coaching dialogue contains much that is dramatic. A coach's voice must be persuasive and animated. It should enliven the discourse within any organization. Bachkirova and Cox (2007) remind us that many organizations are comfortable promoting the idea of emotional intelligence because it has been packaged as "scientifically sound," therefore a positive draw for these organizations wanting to work with emotions in the workplace. However, emotional intelligence does not generally embrace the gamut of human emotions: the more negative ones such as envy and fear (by my reckoning, highly prevalent in the workplace) do not fit into a positive leadership discourse. Bachkirova and Cox (2007, 602–3) make an astute point that emotions, being associated with "soft skills," are treated with an attitude of wariness: emotions tend to be associated with counseling and therapy, activities from which coaching in the business world is at pains to distance itself.

Bachkirova and Cox's (2007, 610) data, elicited from the personal experiences of coaches addressing emotional issues (or not) with their clients, revealed that coaches "hold a multiplicity of attitudes to emotion in the perusal and organisational context," which the authors believe reflected the complex nature emotion plays in our lives. They decide that it is difficult to recommend a specific strategy in dealing with emotions in the workplace, although they do advocate that coaches "consider their personal stance towards emotion and to examine their strategies of dealing with emotion in the coaching process" (Bachkirova and Cox 2007,

610). I would suggest that all coaches, particularly those identified by Bachkirova and Cox as coaches "who see work as a place where emotionality should be suppressed" and those who perceive emotions as "[d]angerous to play with" could benefit from the technique of using a text that can draw out emotional responses that could be then used as a buffer between coach and client. Bachkirova and Cox's respondents, who were clearly uncomfortable with the notion of working with emotions (some responded that they would be "shocked" when presented with a strong emotion [2007, 606]), could use a text as the basis for a discussion on emotions rather than feeling as though they have to address a problem directly with a client.

Returning to the excerpt from "Neighbor Rosicky," there is intense drama inherent in a character's preparation for death. Here the third-person narrative slips into Rosicky's consciousness but never loses its dramatic authority, its weightiness of belief, its perceptiveness about how others feel. We are persuaded by the strength of Rosicky's values. As Danielewicz (2008, 425) reminds us, when we write in our own voice, we are able to express our own "cultural identity through idiom and style." Cather's voice through Rosicky is ever present. She possesses her material by infusing her own values and principles into it. As coaches, we must never shy away from investing our own story in a coaching dialogue. We should not be afraid to work with imagery and metaphor and drama. Whether we are working with clients, writing about our own experiences, or addressing organizational challenges, we must strive to make others see and feel our world.

In discussing the values of a fictional character, we do not stray into vulnerable areas more suited to exploration by a trained psychiatrist. The coaching conversation can delve into emotions without the danger of either the client or the coach being too direct: the fictional piece (or nonfictional work, as we will see) acts as a transmitter that channels both positive and negative emotions between coach and coachee and is a useful technique in group coaching. Emotions, of course, are neither good or bad in themselves, but for coaches wary of entering into problematic or inappropriate terrain, a text serves as the object of any emotion in question, providing a distance, a screen, or a buffer, and mitigating any sense of excessive self-indulgence for those especially sensitive to any accusations of treating coaching as therapy.

As in great works of art, great coaching must be guided by a spiritual sense of life. "Neighbor Rosicky" is not an intellectual story, which is a strength allowing it to be used with readers who have not had the benefit of a humanities education, who do not read or feel that reading is not for them. It is a story of emotion and feeling, which, in helping us to grasp the inner life of a memorable character, also helps us to see how we can create a memorable narrative with simplicity, imagery, and economy, making all else subordinate to the person in front of us. Great coaching resists anything formulaic, anything prescriptive, anything unimaginative. Cather always thought that literature needed to break out of its mold – American writers needed to stop grinding out the same old straitjacket themes such as love and success. In a 1933 NBC radio speech, Cather opined:

> We have begun to look about us, but we have a long way to go. We cling to our old formulae; for the moment we stress the bad-girl instead of the good, the rowdy who is kicked out of his great corporation instead of the smoothly polished young man who becomes its president. We won't face the fact that it is the formula itself which is pernicious, the frame-up. When we learn to give our purpose the form for every story instead of trying to crowd it into one of the stock moulds on the shelf, then we shall be on the right road, at last.
>
> (Woodress 1987, 451)

Coaching too must go beyond the stock molds – it must look beyond the usual, the tried, and the tested. Coaching students and coaches can use "Neighbor Rosicky" as a starting point for a conversation about values: reading the story helped my students reflect more deeply on their practice and understand the role emotions have in coaching. The story can be targeted in such a way to fill an emotional gap in an organization that has a considerable number of employees that are unhappy and unmotivated, employees who are looking for a novel coaching technique that speaks to their values and allows them to explore richer, more meaningful coaching conversations.

References

Alexander, Graham. 2010. "Behavioural Coaching: The GROW Model." In *Excellence in Coaching: The Industry Guide*, edited by Jonathan Passmore. 2nd edn. London: Kogan Page.

Angelidis, John, and Nabil Ibrahim. 2011. "The Impact of Emotional Intelligence on the Ethical Judgment of Managers." *Journal of Business Ethics* 99 (S1): 111–19.

Ashforth, Blake, and Ronald Humphrey. 1997. "Emotion in the Workplace: A Reappraisal." *Human Relations* 48 (2): 97–125.

Bachkirova, Tatiana, and Elaine Cox. 2007. "Coaching With Emotion in Organisations: Investigation of Personal Theories." *Leadership and Organization Development Journal* 28 (7): 600–12.

Carroll, Noël. 2011. "On Some Affective Relations Between Audiences and the Characters in Popular Fictions." In *Empathy: Philosophical and Psychological Perspectives*, edited by Amy Coplan and Peter Goldie, 162–85. Oxford: Oxford University Press.

Cather, Willa. 1992. *Stories, Poems, and Other Writings*, edited by Sharon O'Brien. New York: The Library of America.

Cox, Elaine, Tatiana Bachkirova, and David Clutterbuck, eds. 2010. *The Complete Handbook of Coaching*. London: Sage.

Danielewicz, Jane. 2008. "Personal Genres, Public Voices." *College Composition and Communication* 59 (3): 420–50.

Drake, David. 2007. "The Art of Thinking Narratively: Implications for Coaching Psychology and Practice." *Australian Psychologist* 42 (4): 283–94.

Feagin, Susan. 2010. "Giving Emotions Their Due." *British Journal of Aesthetics* 50 (1): 89–92.

Gilbert, Andrew, and Karen Whittleworth. 2009. *The OSCAR Coaching Model: Simplifying Workplace Coaching*. Monmouth: Worth Consulting.

Grant, Anthony. 2016. "What Constitutes Evidence-Based Coaching? A Two-By-Two Framework for Distinguishing Strong From Weak Evidence for Coaching." *International Journal of Evidence Based Coaching and Mentoring* 14 (1): 74–82.

Hinz, Evelyn. 1972. "Willa Cather's Technique and the Ideology of Populism." *Western American Literature* 7 (1): 47–61.

Hunt, Carolyn. 2016. "Getting to the Heart of the Matter: Discursive Negotiations of Emotions Within Literacy Coaching Interactions." *Teaching and Teacher Education* 60: 331–43.

International Coach Federation. n.d. "The Nature and Scope of Coaching." Accessed May 8, 2016. www.coachfederation.org

Keplinger, David. 2016. "For Love of Humanities and Arts." In *How Higher Education Feels: Commentaries on Poems that Illuminate Emotions in Learning and Teaching*, edited by Kathleen Quinlan, 155–89. Rotterdam: Sense.

Lee, Graham. 2014. "The Psychodynamic Approach to Coaching." In *The Complete Handbook of Coaching*, edited by Elaine Cox, Tatiana Bachkirova, and David Ashley Clutterbuck, 21–33. 2nd edn. London: Sage.

Reissner, Stefanie, and Angélique DuToit. 2011. "Power and the Tale: Coaching as Storyselling." *Journal of Management Development* 30 (3): 247–59.

Robinson, Jenefer. 2005. *Deeper than Reason: Emotion and Its Role in Literature, Music, and Art*. Oxford: Oxford University Press.

Shipton, Helen, and John Sillince. 2012. "Organizational Learning and Emotion: Constructing Collective Meaning in Support of Strategic Themes." *Management Learning* 44 (5): 493–510.

Whitmore, John. 1992. *Coaching for Performance: Growing People, Performance and Purpose*. London: Nicholas Brearly.

Woodress, James. 1987. *Willa Cather: A Literary Life*. Lincoln: University of Nebraska Press.

Chapter 3

Coaching, memory, and emotion

John Cheever's "The Swimmer" and James Baldwin's "Notes of a Native Son"

This chapter investigates the parallels between literature and coaching and what coaching can learn from literature, in this instance from the fiction of John Cheever and from the writing of James Baldwin. I will document what happened when I shared one of Cheever's most famous stories, "The Swimmer," with students drawn from disparate groups – coaching students from a large financial services firm, students investigating coaching solutions from a telecommunications company, and individual doctoral students from a seminar I ran on effective academic writing. I will continue with my theme of how writers manipulate readers' emotions and will reflect on the lessons we can learn from their techniques that we can then apply to coaching and to our own writing. I intend to return to the long-standing dichotomy between rationality and emotions, sketching the history of rationality and bringing in the argument for the role of emotions in coaching. I will also highlight the role of memory and the narrative imperative in coaching, drawing on Saint Augustine's *Confessions* and providing the reader with some background to John Cheever's life and work. Cheever's life and work, I will show, can illuminate Augustine's lessons on using experience as a path to enlightenment and even wisdom, which is surely the ultimate aim of coaching. There are uncanny parallels between the life of this third-century saint, who writes, "I was led astray myself and led others astray in my turn" (St Augustine 1961, 71), and the alcoholic, repressed homosexual, foremost chronicler of post–World War II America. I will look at the major themes in Cheever's fiction particularly encapsulated in "The Swimmer" – melancholy, loneliness, self-deception, alienation, the vagaries of the human condition – and demonstrate how coaches can work meaningfully with these themes in their practices. I will bring in my own observations about the similarities between coaching and writing, drawing on Cheever's perspicacity, his moral conviction, and his deep understanding of his own and others' sense of failure. I hope to make sense of his alcoholic pessimism and unflagging desire for respect, being acknowledged and being loved. Underlying the discussion in this chapter is the conviction that reading helps us to learn about others, together with the belief that fiction is our most intimate means of communicating.

A good coach can learn much from Cheever's (and many other writers') habit of keeping a journal. Cheever was adamant that no impression should go to waste and that writing can keep us from despair. Cheever's intuition of the value of writing amid the desperate moments in his own life is borne out by research in the field of psychology, particularly that of James Pennebaker, who found compelling evidence that writing about traumatic experiences brings both physical and emotional benefits. Ultimately Cheever's life was a struggle – against blurred individuality, against his homosexuality, against his ravaging alcoholism. Cheever's personal demons and the ways he found of sublimating their pernicious effects through his writing offer an illuminating perspective on the practice of coaching. Cheever's struggle with life waged in a literary medium can be used to map the various ways in which coaches can help others with their struggles. Such a writer's cogent articulation of the universal contradictions of our souls can provide light where there is darkness in human relations.

This chapter will explore in detail another significant way in which reading literary works can enhance the practice of coaching. Literary works can be used in a coaching dialogue to stimulate reflection in coaches, as we have seen in Chapters 1 and 2. But the emotional and cognitive gains yielded by the process of reflection can achieve a more lasting and significant impact through the process of writing. Writing is intimately linked with successful coaching, as I intend to show in this and subsequent chapters. It is the prolonged reflection through writing after the initial coaching dialogue that can turn a eureka moment into enduring personal transformation. We can learn much about our own writing and its role in our trajectory as coaches and coachees from a close reading of a work like "The Swimmer." Cheever's clarity of detail and the techniques he used to craft his prose to suit the market provide an insight into how we can improve our own styles. Finally, I will discuss the work of a coaching student who engaged with James Baldwin's powerful rhetoric in the essay "Notes of a Native Son." Baldwin and Cheever were contemporaries, and their background and relationship, albeit not intimate, reveals much about the socioliterary world of postwar America, a period that students interested in coaching to diversity may find illuminating. Throughout this chapter, I hope to demonstrate how both fiction and non-fiction can support us to understand, empathize, and coach people better. "The Swimmer" and "Notes of a Native Son" can play crucial roles in addressing the challenges most of us are likely to encounter at work and in life generally.

Manipulating emotions

When we work with people, we are working with complexity. Part of this complexity arises from the emotions at play in human encounters. Coaching can be an emotionally charged activity. And even in the workplace situations that encourage the suppression of outward emotional responses, emotions are there, whether we like it or not, simmering beneath the surface. A philosophical perspective on emotions can help to clarify exactly what they are and why they are, or should be, central to the coaching encounter.

Peter Goldie (2000) traces writing about emotions back to Book II of Aristotle's *Rhetoric*, in which the ancient philosopher warns readers that an appeal to the emotions is sought to sway people's minds. Goldie (2000, 28) points out that once our emotional responses are engaged, "further thoughts, feelings, judgments, and actions will be influenced by [our] emotions." An emotion is an enduring complex state. It can come and go, wax and wane. It involves bodily changes, thoughts, and feelings and constitutes part of a narrative, *our* narrative. The idea of narrative is important because we need to understand the emotional components in order to make sense of our lives. Emotions, no matter how difficult or powerful, cannot be understood by detaching them from the narrative in which they are "embedded" (Goldie 2000, 16). Therefore, we can't understand our own narratives without coming to grips with our emotions.

Aristotle's (1991) misgivings about emotions are justified: these complex, dynamic, evolving states are deeply bound up in the beliefs we hold when we experience an emotion. Emotions cannot therefore be analyzed or understood in simple terms. They can be analyzed only by subtly identifying the thoughts involved in the process of experiencing emotions. Many good writers can tell an engrossing story, but some of the most captivating narratives and, from a coaching perspective, the most useful, are those narratives that analyze these complex, dynamic, and evolving states and help us to grasp perceptions that we may not have even acknowledged. Some narratives have the capacity to support us in recognizing and empathizing with their characters and their characters' emotions. Interpreting and understanding motivation, character, and points of view are predicated on our emotional responses to texts. Jenefer Robinson (2005, 107; emphasis in original) makes it clear that emotions are paramount in understanding a novel: "Without appropriate emotional responses, some novels simply *cannot* be adequately understood." Although most of the focus of this book is on short stories, her point remains. Before Aristotle, Plato had already made a clear distinction between reason and emotion in the *Republic*, complaining that poetry had a nefarious moral influence on people because it appealed to their emotions not their reason. And reason, according to Plato, was the most elevated part of the soul. Plato's celebrated relegation of poetry to the bottom of the hierarchy of human activity was predicated on the link he perceived between art and emotion. Robinson (2005, 1) observes that "there has been a widespread conviction among Western thinkers that there is some special relationship between the arts and emotions." And while poets may be ostracized from Plato's Republic, we would do well to cultivate the implicit connection between the literary arts emotion that has been intuited since Plato's time. In fact, based on the centrality of emotion in the arts, for which Robinson argues compellingly, we can actually make a strong claim for the significance of art in helping us to understand the people around us. We can extend this special relationship between art and emotion to understanding people because the process of reading is emotionally educational: "we can have our emotions aroused as we read so that we too, like the characters, are made to focus attention on certain situations and see them in a certain way. We too are influenced in how we respond by our desires, interests, and values, and we too may have our attention fixed by physiological means" (Robinson 2005, 158).

Robinson's study has serious implications in coaching people – if novels, short stories, poetry, and other texts introduce readers to emotional states that focus their attentions, desires, and interests, then their perceptions and thoughts about people may change. Robinson (2005, 159) is adamant that by observing well-crafted characters, readers "expand their emotional horizons and learn about the possibility of new emotional states."

Larry Siedentop (2014) traces the history of reason, stating that it held unassailable hierarchical assumptions in the ancient Greek and Roman worlds. Social subordinates – women and slaves, for example – were not deemed to be rational. Solely members of the citizen class – magistrates, priests, warriors – were judged to possess reason or *logos* – the power of words. Reason, so identified in the public sphere with a class that commanded and spoke persuasively, became the entity that governed over all faculties: it was for centuries interlinked with social superiority. By the twelfth century, the role of reason was assailed by more theological considerations. The task of reason became one necessary to explore faith: "Thinkers became much less inclined than in the ancient world to assume that reason, merely from its own resources, could dictate conclusions about the nature of things" (Siedentop 2014, 242). Reason was beginning to hold no longer "the ontologically privileged position it had been accorded by an aristocratic society" (Siedentop 2014, 243). Reason became democratized – it became something one used rather than something to which one had an intrinsic claim or that one possessed. The claims of reason were finally being challenged. However, these same claims are contested far less in contemporary organizational life.

Bachkirova and Cox (2007) point out that most organizations privilege rationality over emotion and that emotion is still viewed as a disruptive influence in workplace decision making. Bachkirova and Cox (2007, 601) observe that there are "critical tensions" between rationality and emotion in organizational life, but they sustain nevertheless that it is impossible to avoid the conclusion that "the experience of the coaching process in the organizational context very often proves to be emotional" (Bachkirova and Cox 2007, 603). Given the centrality of the emotions in the ways we experience and make sense of the world, they are clearly an aspect of any coaching relationship. If organizations are reluctant to acknowledge the impact of the emotions on their employees' capacity for learning or if coaches are unsure of how to address both positive and negative emotion and experience, literature in the form of short stories, novels, or poetry can step in and become the expert guide in navigating such uncharted terrain.

Context: groups, their concerns, and why "The Swimmer"

Throughout one academic year, I worked with two groups of students who were undertaking postgraduate work in coaching. The first group comprised students studying for an MA in coaching who were interested in coaching solutions in their work in a telecommunications company, and the second was made up of doctoral students who were interested in writing better by using my ideas on the link between coaching with emotions and writing clearer prose. I gathered data about reading and using Cheever's "The Swimmer" in the form of interviews and written responses to questions from these two groups. The second group, which consisted of doctoral students, also attended four four-hour workshops in which we examined "The Swimmer" as well as the first chapter of Lampedusa's *The Leopard*, an experience I will recount in the final chapter of this book. Working in the discipline of professional practice both with individuals and with organizations over the past few years has convinced me that fiction has the potential to give people new perspectives on the world around them, a fresh take on others and events, and an ability to connect more intimately at work. My work with these two cohorts of students and the data I collected on my experiences with them enabled me to begin to construct an empirically based defense of the value of reading literary works in coaching education. My background lecturing in American literature made me gravitate to writers such as Melville, Cather, Cheever, Baldwin, and Miller, but I have introduced other groups and individual professional-practice students to writers who explore themes and areas that were directly relevant to my students' disciplines. In the past, I introduced Jack London's *White Fang* about a wolf pack and its hierarchical similarities to the modern canine to a group of dog handlers studying at postgraduate level and Antoine Saint-Exupéry's *Night Flight* about the first hazardous mail posts in South America to a group of aviators working on their postgraduate projects. I have always found the literature relating to work-based learning research inadequate in closing the gap between inquiry and the love of one's profession. Literature seemed to answer students' need for a creative way to fashion their arguments about improving practice or dealing with challenges. Similarly, there is much in coaching literature to be commended, but the fictional narrative approach has a purposeful application in advancing people well beyond the usual training models.

For my work with the two cohorts explored in this chapter, I chose "The Swimmer" because its themes – of loneliness, self-deception, and alienation – seemed ideally matched to individuals who were experiencing significant changes in their personal or working lives. From one-to-one Skype sessions, I learned about tensions at work, floundering marriages, drug and alcohol issues in families, trust issues, and general developmental challenges and emotional blockages. I had not had the opportunity to build up trusting relationships with these postgraduate students, as they were students I saw only for these four seminars and were drawn from all over the university. I was not ever conscious of using a positive psychological approach to coaching with the first two groups (Boniwell, Kauffman, and Silberman 2010), but in retrospect, I believe I drew on its principal tenets, mainly helping students to explore and make sense of their challenges and experiences. Positive psychology interventions are designed to increase personal well-being, as they structure coaching "as an active synthesis of support and challenge, addressing both positive and negative emotion and experience" (Boniwell, Kauffman, and Silberman 2010, 161). My aim was to encourage students to be involved in

"The Swimmer" as a piece of writing to be appraised both emotionally and cognitively. I wanted them to attend to how Cheever guided their emotional responses as well as to explore how his rhetorical devices – irony, metaphor, imagery – are presented.

Jenefer Robinson (2005, 158) is convinced that a careful reading of a text can "educate our emotions." This is a powerful assertion that has an undeniable bearing on the impact of coaching, the results of which I intend to describe further on in this chapter. For now, let me summarize the story and expand on how Cheever's writing can guide all students to become more aware, reflective, and sensitive readers, capable of addressing their conscious and unconscious emotional blockages and helping them to become better communicators, both on and off the page.

"The Swimmer" and John Cheever

John Cheever was one of the most gifted writers in postwar America, publishing his short stories extensively in *The New Yorker* and winning literary awards such as the Pulitzer and the National Medal for Literature. Superficially he had it all: a beautiful wife, three children, a comfortable life in the suburbs, and immense success. Yet the reality was that he was a tortured alcoholic who demeaned and bullied his children, was alienated from his wife, and was deeply conflicted sexually. Two years before his death, he wrote that his family life had been "bankrupt in every way" (Bailey 2009, 6), and seven years before his death, he had gone to AA after decades of dealing with the pain of repressing his homosexuality, enduring full-blown panic attacks, engaging in self-destructive drinking, and allowing himself bouts of gargantuan self-pity. His psychiatrist concluded that "his major personality trait is his narcissism, and underneath it all is tremendous self-doubt" (Bailey 2009, 426). Throughout the torpor of his depressions and his grotesque drink-induced behavior (his drinking gin normally started in the morning), he was considered by his peers a master of prose. William Styron remarked at Cheever's final medal ceremony, "John Cheever's position in literary history is as immovably fixed as one of those huge granite outcroppings which loom over the green lawns and sunlit terraces in the land of his own magic devising" (Bailey 2009, 675).

"The Swimmer" is considered Cheever's greatest story and a "masterpiece of mystery, language and sorrow" (Michael Chabon in Bailey 2009, 318). Thought by many critics to be an analogy for the sorrows of faded youth, the story concerns a middle-aged Neddy Merrill swimming from one suburban pool to the next, encountering episodes from his past. Cheever recalls the writing process: "It was growing cold and quiet. It was turning into winter. Involuntarily. It was a terrible experience writing that story. I was very unhappy. Not only I the narrator, but I, John Cheever, was crushed" (Bailey 2009, 316). At each suburban pool, there is a party, sometimes with responsive bartenders and smiling hostesses and other times with hostile bartenders and vicious hostesses. Neddy's progress turns increasingly difficult as he is scorned as a gate crasher and then spurned by a former mistress. He finally returns home, but the house is dark and empty: "He shouted, pounded on the door, tried to force it with his shoulder, and then, looking in the windows, saw that the place was empty" (Cheever 2010, 788).

The critical reception has abounded in a multitude of interpretations. Similar to the fiction of Willa Cather, Cheever's fiction contains a preoccupation with time and loss. The writers also share a love of classical allusions. The classical allusions in "The Swimmer" have been commented on extensively. Nathan Cervo (1991, 49) perceives that Neddy Merrill is "dead, an earth-bound ghost." His home is Hades, the pools are Stygian and he swims through a pagan underworld. Hal Blythe and Charlie Sweet (1992) discern parallels between Neddy and the Spanish explorer Juan Ponce de Leon: this is an extended historical allusion to a futile journey, a thwarted quest to rediscover one's youth. James Matthews (1992) also detects mythical allusions, this time to *The Odyssey*: here is an archetypal self-indulgent upper middle class man "defeated by an impervious, rapidly changing society as well as by his own illusions" (Matthews 1992, 95). After his exhausting swim and increasingly disconcerting interactions with his suburban pool-owning neighbors and ex-lovers, he returns to his desolate house: he has swum away from his family and, returning, is mystified by their absence. His tragedy is "both personal and cultural – obstinate pride at odds with a society that, like nature, shows no mercy to those who flout its imperatives" (Matthews 1992, 101). Thomas Kennedy (2015) is impressed by Cheever's magnificent prose, reminding the readers of John Keats's phrase "negative capability," which means art that transcends meaning – we may not be able to understand it, but it is nevertheless deeply moving. The story is underscored by craft and artistry – it is mysterious and ambiguous, surrealistic and mythic: "the history of a man's life compared to a summer's day that is just ending" (Kennedy 2015, 15).

The students who, after all, were pragmatic businesspeople in the main, were primarily concerned with how they would coach Neddy Merrill. He was their "guinea pig," someone in their team who presented dysfunctional behavior and was "crying out for help" (as many of them phrased it). Therefore, like with "Bartleby, the Scrivener" and "Neighbor Rosicky," I kept my first set of questions general: How would you coach Neddy Merrill? How could you get your coachee to respond to what ails Cheever's protagonist? With the doctoral students, I concentrated more on how they could use Cheever's technique of metaphor, shifts of points of view, and freshness of style to improve their writing skills. Here is a sample of coaching questions the master's students devised. One student concentrated on goals and told me the following:

> Neddy is living in the past. He is remembering his past and looking for an escape from a bad situation. He has obviously had an affair, lost his youth, lost his job or business and as a result has lost his wife and daughters. I wondered if he was dead and if the swim home was a metaphor for his life. Assuming that he is alive, though, I would be seeking to understand his goals. What is behind this swim? What is really happening in his life? These are the

> major questions I would ask: "Neddy, tell me what made you want to swim home?" "It sounds like a fantastic adventure but tell me more [. . .] what were you looking to achieve with the swimming?" "An act of heroism is sometimes a way of proving that we are still worthy and necessary and needed. Do you want to tell me more about not feeling needed, Neddy?"

These are good "goal-oriented" coaching questions and ones that I would expect from managers concerned about a member of staff. The same student told me that they needed "to be careful as managers who represent large organizations as we are bound by rules and protocol in dealing with certain situations. Sadly the guidelines offered to management are as much about protecting the company from litigation as they are about looking after the well-being of an individual." From the perspective of a coach attempting to manage a coachee's performance when affected by personal problems such as drinking too much, marriage breakdown, or family disintegration, "The Swimmer" seems an obvious text to read and then to discuss. Another student posed a series of questions she called "framing questions." She explained that these questions were designed to target the situation in hand as well as to explore Neddy's options: "You mentioned that your friends were all drinking too much. Do you think that drinking helps you to escape?" "Who can you turn to now in your hour of need?" "Are you ready to face your family and friends and your life's challenges honestly and soberly?" Students reported the story's potential usefulness in broaching sensitive topics such as a colleague's drinking. I asked whether reading and discussing the story was simply adding another layer that acted to move the coach and coachee farther apart – wouldn't it be better to address, say, a drinking problem head on? Students disagreed and, confirming my own intuition, many argued that the extra layer was precisely what made reading and discussing the work so useful: people felt safer discussing the problems of a character rather than their own; there seemed to be less exposure and vulnerability at stake. They argued that the obvious narrative arc of increasing weakness, drunken befuddlement, and physical and spiritual struggle in the story could be accessed to explore goal setting and addressing substance abuse issues. Moreover, in terms of the thorny litigation issues inherent in certain sensitive situations, using a text as a distancing technique could be the kind of protective carapace needed.

Cheever was a raging alcoholic who got sober a mere eight years before his death. Friends and acquaintances commented that reality was too much for him to bear and that he seemed to find no relief from whatever ailed him. After his death, his editor at the *New Yorker*, William Maxwell, observed that Cheever was unable to face himself: "He wanted to understand the world but he didn't want to understand himself" (Bailey 2009, 78). The less obvious, more ambiguous nature of "The Swimmer" offers the opportunity of uncovering a deeper layer of the human psyche through coaching. Cheever understood people and had a particular affinity for writing about "failures," people who were marginalized in society. Hanif Kureishi (in Cheever 2010, vii) makes a crucial point about Cheever's remit: "You might think, turning to the stories, that you would be hard pressed to learn much about a wider America, of black and Hispanic lives, of post-slavery trauma, inequality, political struggle, or poverty. But you do learn about the shabby hard lives of elevator operators, of janitors and the respectable poor." Cheever knows that it is status and work that drives us – perhaps he is the writer fashioned perfectly to address work-based politics, tensions, and complexities? After his brother paid him a visit, he noted the following in his journal:

> We disagree on everything. Any desire, higher than that for warmth and security, seems to have died out in his frame and with that he has cultivated an immense contempt for those poor, sad fools, living on the fringes of society, who have been unable to rent a house in the country, stuff it with antiques, dress their wives attractively, produce beautiful children and come up the gravel drive-way at dusk to love, sherry, supper, wood-fires and the editorials of the *Boston Evening Transcript*.
>
> (Bailey 2009, 88)

Ironically, Cheever appeared to embody such a life, but the reality – as a good coach will know – can be very different. Students were therefore able to use the story especially as an interesting goal-setting exercise in challenging all-too-human traits such as self-pity, denial, and being blocked. A few went beyond the surface, exploring disengagement, melancholy, identity, and the challenges of making sense of one's life. Before turning to a fuller discussion of student engagement with "The Swimmer," I want to investigate two areas: the importance of voice in coaching and the role of memory in coaching. As regards the latter, both Cheever and Saint Augustine offer an enlightening perspective on memory, which can illuminate its role in the coaching.

Voice in coaching

Stephen Greenberg (2014) emphasizes the importance of relationship building with clients. Since the majority of my students are in businesses that are selling services or products, the coaching relationship applies to clients as much as to team members. Greenberg (2014, 1) applies the notion of sales as a metaphor for interpersonal working relations more generally: "professional relationships will always contain an element and degree of selling." Even if someone is not in a formal sales position, the dynamics of the workplace demand that employees sell their ideas to their colleagues. Enhanced communication skills are instrumental both within the workplace, then, as well as with clients in order to foster a trusting relationship with them. Building successful relationships with colleagues and clients is paramount in the business world. Greenberg (2014, 2) summarizes how important sales coaching is in achieving goals:

> Sales coaching and sales training, if presented in an effective and organized manner [. . .] will benefit all who attend. If you are seasoned in your field, a

> refresher course in sales can be invigorating. If you are a successful salesperson, you always have an opportunity to improve on your success [. . .] You professionals, above everyone else, know that effective sales coaching and sales training will improve every salesperson's performance.

My students on the MA in coaching who worked in either direct or indirect selling were unanimous in their agreement that fostering strong and trusting relationships was indispensable in managing teams and clients. They disagreed only with Greenberg's use of the word "training." A sales manager from a successful IT subsidiary remarked, "Coaching is an educational endeavor. It is deep and lasting. Training connotes surface learning."

Alexander Styhre (2008) conducted a year-long study into the kinds of coaching programs that are helpful in developing site managers in the construction industry. His definition of coaching is precise: "a one-on-one interaction process whereby a coach and coachee meet to discuss practical concerns, individual development requirements, and broader matters pertaining to work life, life situations, as well as priorities and aspirations with the objective of making individual leaders more effective in their work roles" (Styhre 2008, 275). Styhre (2008, 276) expresses his concerns about coaching literature, stating that there are very few reports on the outcomes of coaching projects and that there is a pressing need to examine the phenomenon of how valuable coaching is "in epistemological and theoretical terms." He observes that there is a plethora of writing on how to coach, what coaching is and what the characteristics of a successful coach are, but little analytical literature examining the "underlying assumptions and beliefs" (Styhre 2008, 277) of the coaching process. Communication is at the heart of any social system, and it is always vulnerable to breakdown and failure: we misunderstand far more often than understand, and many of us are not as articulate as we could be. Good communication is important because it maintains social institutions and social practices such as trust. Styhre points out that participants on a coaching program must be allowed a voice. Without a voice, there is the danger that "a coachee's more complicated problems will be swept under the carpet, ignored, or dealt with inadequately by executive coaches" (Styhre 2008, 277). In order to resolve conflict in the workplace or in life generally, coachees need to articulate or "emplot" (impose a narrative structure on) their work life experiences. Although Styhre's study does not involve selling in the strict sense of the definition, it emphasizes how important good communication is in the coaching process, a truism that could be applied to any profession.

Good communication is invariably predicated on an awareness of one's voice – being precise and being precise about articulating one's position: "Up to now it has seemed inappropriate to include one's own feelings and story in academic discourse. But since the personal dimension has such a big influence on one's position, perhaps we should turn that convention around and say it is inappropriate to publish an argument or take a position unless you tell your feelings and story" (Elbow 2000, 317). Peter Elbow is commenting on academic discourse, but this comment could be also applied to coaching. If the coachee's voice and her attendant feelings and story are ignored or misunderstood, psychological problems can become exacerbated and organizational and managerial malaise can deepen. Voice can be the quality of text that endows it with authority and power; it is ever present, moreover, in a coaching dialogue, in the narratives that coachees construct around their workplace and life experiences. We build and strengthen our relationships with clear, unadulterated communication, the type of communication that is achieved by a voice informed by a deep knowledge of others and is broad minded, articulate, and unafraid to respond emotionally to a situation. Literature supports us not only in articulating our voices better but also in educating our responses to "real-life" events. Jenefer Robinson makes the point that our emotional responses to literary works function in broadly the same way as our emotions in our daily lives. The capacity of literary works to trigger our emotions goes some way in explaining their value as tools in coaching. When we read "The Swimmer," we may feel anxious on Neddy Merrill's behalf or sympathetic to his dilemma just as we would in real life, but as Robinson argues, there is a distinction between how we respond to life and how we respond to literature. Robinson locates this difference in the varying kinds of cognitive mechanisms we employ to cope with our emotions. In life, we might deny reality if it's unbearable, or we might intellectualize a problem if we don't want to address it. Like in life, we might get anxious or frustrated reading about Neddy, but "literature, like life, often provides us with the coping strategies that we need to deal with its deep and possibly troubling content" (Robinson 2005, 219). Literature offers a different set of coping mechanisms that enable us to face emotionally charged, uncomfortable material that in life we have a tendency simply to avoid: "The formal or structural devices [in a text] allow us to cope with its themes and ultimately to derive pleasure from the very fact that we have successfully coped with a piece of reality" (Robinson 2005, 219). In other words, stories offer us the means to work through material that is difficult to face. A coaching situation often throws up troubling aspects of reality that neither the coach nor the coachee will be willing or prepared to deal with. But literary works offer a set of formal and structural devices that enable us to impose order on a story and to make sense of it. Allowing ourselves to be educated emotionally and cognitively by a literary text is the first step in allowing a coach and coachee to establish a dialogue that refuses to shy away from the thorny issues. A literary text that explores the moral ambiguities that afflict us in our own lives offers a cipher that can be applied to the real-life coaching situation. One of my coaching students remarked after reading "The Swimmer": "The workplace will always have loads of Neddy Merrills who don't know that they are him." The story can therefore be used as an emotional conduit in order to facilitate a frank and productive coaching conversation. This conversation is one that can lead to better outcomes without affecting the comfort and security of the "Neddy Merrill" in the organization, thus minimizing any suggestion of accusation and blame that a straightforward coaching conversation on behavior might produce.

Cheever, Saint Augustine, and memory

In his monumental work on the life and writings of Saint Augustine, Jean Jacques Rousseau and Samuel Beckett, James Olney (1998, 315) states that psychologists have determined that life's mid-point is thirty-seven years old, and thirty-seven is the age that we start to imagine life "not as a heap of snapshot moments but as constituting a connected narrative sequence." In other words, thirty-seven is the age at which reminiscence begins. The role of memory remains relatively unexplored in coaching, but has a central role in narrative, and it follows that, if we are using narrative in coaching, it would be profitable to show how intertwining acts of remembering and narrative remain at the heart of the life-writing practice and should not be ignored in our coaching practice. One of the students' responses to "The Swimmer" as a coaching exercise made me reflect on the crucial role memory plays in exploring the roots of our issues. He stressed how important it was for a manager to understand, empathize with, and counsel his team. Then he touched on memory: "I would try to lead [Neddy] to see how he currently views the world. He sees the world as changing and himself swimming against the tide of change. With my support, he may be able to regain a view of life that is less negative, less demoralizing. He needs to see change as a constant." The student perceives that narrative is serious business. A life is not a record on a chart. Particularly as we grow and mature and reach the age in which our meaningful past becomes a connected narrative sequence, we draw more and more on memory. Jerome Bruner (2003, 93) observes that "through narrative, we construct, re-construct, in some ways reinvent yesterday and tomorrow. Memory and imagination fuse in the process."

Augustine's *Confessions* serve as a reminder of how important memory is in the coaching process. I suggested further reading on St. Augustine (1961) to a coaching student exploring how she could encourage better habits and discourage negative habits in her organization. The world's first autobiographer remembers his habits of theft, of lying, of lustful thoughts. He observes that "we are carried away by custom to our own undoing and it is hard to struggle against the stream" (St Augustine 1961, 36). The student found the reading I had given her from *Confessions* "an epiphany." She told me that she had never thought of habits before as "custom" and believed that the word brought an entirely different perspective to her inquiry. She said that "custom" reminded her of what we are "accustomed" to do – there are also "customs" of a people or of an organization remembered collectively, consciously or unconsciously. She remarked further, "We have certain ingrained habits here which are sometimes not examined and may not be to our best advantages." According to Augustinian understanding, memory has a pivotal role in our identity. Given that identity, its expression and its development are central to coaching, memory too has fundamental role to play in a coaching dialogue: "Memory [. . .] should be the guarantor of identity and continuity of being across time, the only liaison – but an unbroken and fully capable liaison all the same between past experience and present consciousness" (Olney 1998, 6). Coaching is a process of planning future action in light of the past, of reconceptualizing the self in the workplace through reflection on past successes and failures. The role of memory in coaching is a fruitful area of reflection if we meet the challenges of organizational coaching: negative habit formation, the blight of staff not feeling appreciated or valued, or the problems of disaffected and disengaged employees – to name the common issues to which students on the MA program testify and with which they engage in their projects.

Another coaching student told me that his coaching technique would be to eschew any direct or focused questions on "The Swimmer." Because the story is so "multi-layered and open to interpretation," it should "just be given out to read and then to discuss in small groups." He had done simply that with his team and told me that the response was "overwhelming." Team members reported that "the pools were like the ups and downs of the market"; "each job felt like a new pool"; "it [the story] was like getting de-railed at work"; "it hit the mark about where my personal life is going"; "I kept thinking, how can I get there and how can I get back?" He said the best thing about letting his team members react to the story without any "biased guidance" was that they tapped into their memories and imagination. I had selected an excerpt that he gave to the team to focus on:

> It would storm. The stand of cumulus cloud – that city – had risen and darkened, and while he sat there he heard the percussiveness of thunder again. The de Haviland trainer was still circling overhead and it seemed to Ned that he could almost hear the pilot laugh with pleasure in the afternoon; but when there was another peal of thunder he took off for home. A train whistle blew and he wondered what time it had gotten to be. Four? Five? He thought of the provincial station at that hour, where a waiter, his tuxedo concealed by a raincoat, a dwarf with some flowers wrapped in newspaper, and a woman who had been crying would be waiting for the local. It was suddenly growing dark; it was that moment when the pinheaded birds seem to organize their song into some acute and knowledgeable recognition of the storm's approach. Then there was a fine noise of rushing water from the crown of an oak at his back, as if a spigot there had been turned. Then the noise of fountains came from the crowns of all the tall trees. Why did he love storms, what was the meaning of his excitement when the door sprang open and the rain wind fled rudely up the stairs, why had the simple task of shutting the windows of an old house seemed fitting and urgent, why did the first watery notes of a storm wind have for him the unmistakable sound of good news, cheer, glad tidings? Then there was an explosion, a smell of cordite, and rain lashed the Japanese lanterns that Mrs. Levy had bought in Kyoto the year before last, or was it the year before that?
>
> (Cheever 2010, 780)[1]

He theorized that the excerpt triggered people's memories. It seemed that far more than anyone empathizing with the protagonist was their (his individual team members') reaction to Cheever's language: "everyone agreed that he had a way of encapsulating random thoughts which is how our memory works." How can a passage of writing that triggers our memory be notable from a coaching perspective? I would argue that the key elements of this passage in particular – the storm, the cumulus cloud, the plane overhead, dusk falling, birds circling, rain lashing – are observations or memories that are universally experienced. That universal capacity for triggering recollection in any reader who comes into contact with the text creates a powerful and versatile tool for experience-based discussion. Such a passage was able, my student noted, to facilitate group discussion in ways that he had been unable to achieve with other coaching resources. He reported the sense of intimacy fostered in the group by the reading of the passage, as it created a trusting bond and enabled individuals to speak directly and authentically about a shared experience. My student appeared to bear witness to an intimate space in time that bound together memory, language, and emotion. We remember these shapes – of the rain, of the dusk, of the cumulus cloud. Memory has its layers and deposits. St. Augustine wrote of "the great harbour of memory, with its secret, numberless, and indefinable recesses," and asked, "Who has ever reached the bottom of it?" (St Augustine 1961, 216–17). Connecting these shared memories, in remembering for ourselves what a character sees, feels, and smells, we instantly recognize these perceptions and create a coaching conversation that is interactive, open, and sensitive to language.

Cheever's darkness and his journals: parallels between writers and coaches

Cheever's fiction is filled with despair, his characters "adult, full of adult darkness, corruption, and confusion" (Updike 2009). John Updike's (2009) verdict on Cheever's fiction was delivered in a review of Blake Bailey's biography of Cheever and published in *The New Yorker*. Updike (2009) added, "They are desirous, conflicted, alone, adrift. His fiction is filled with despair." Updike quotes from one of Cheever's last stories, "The Leaves, the Lion Fish and the Bear," about two strangers, men, who meet, drink whiskey, and have sex: "How lonely and unnatural man is and how deep and well concealed are his confusions" (Cheever in Updike 2009). Updike identifies the ways that Cheever captures the human predicament, both the general and the particular of experience. It is this blend of the particular and the general in his fiction that opens a realm of exploration for us: since we can never move entirely beyond our physical and perceptual confines, we are grateful to Cheever and writers like him for expanding the world of our imagination beyond the ken of our experience. In doing so, he allows us a more intimate knowledge of each other.

We have seen some of the ways that literary works encourage a process of emotional development in readers and how this emotional education that stories carry out so well can be harnessed in a coaching dialogue in order to explore the uncomfortable aspects of the workplace and life that might otherwise remain unspoken. Stories would appear to lend themselves to coaching as untapped sources of parallel lives that trigger deep reflection in coachees. There are other ways that a writer like Cheever can help coaches though. The kind of learning encouraged by literary works that I want to explore here is what might be termed communicative or linguistic learning.

Beech and Crane (1999) did a survey of team effectiveness considerations, the "soft skills" that lead to measurable enhancement in performance, and found that among the top skills were communication, emotional intelligence, transparency, and the ability to deal with conflict and friction. From Cheever's letters and journals, we learn of his sense of alienation, his divided soul, his desperate need to be part of a group. As early as 1934 when he was just twenty-two, he wrote to a poet acquaintance after attending a football game to articulate his sense of profound separation from others: "The thing I miss most is an ability to identify with a group. When you are lost you are completely lost" (Bailey 2009, 69). Ten years later, he remarked in his journal about a character of his:

> I knew that Laurence [the character] was looking bleakly at the party [. . .] as if in wanting to be brides and football players we exposed the fact that, the light of youth having been put out in us, we had been unable to find other lights to go by, and destitute of faith and principle, had become foolish and sad.
>
> (Bailey 2009, 171)

His letters and journals reveal a despairing man who was unable to connect with others. They also reveal a man with a writerly habit that coaches and coachees should be encouraged to adopt: journaling sharpens one's writing, hones observations, works on techniques, and chronicles the details of feelings and reactions, providing future paths of reacting with greater self-awareness and more productively to people and events. Such prolonged introspection can help us learn about ourselves and others. The space for reflection provided by the elaboration of prose enables quiet reflection on the frailties that afflict us. Self-knowledge is the first stage of self-improvement, and the crafting of stories about our own lives can help us to envisage more clearly and plot the future trajectory we yearn for.

Beech and Crane's (1999) exposition of the skills that lead to measurable enhancements in performance are demonstrated in the stories, journals, and letters of a skilled writer like Cheever. Through the darkness, pain, and alienation, there is always clarity. Cheever communicates his deep understanding of people and their motivations faultlessly – he is a sympathetic chronicler of their souls. He once wrote that he found "no greater pleasure" than in the confirmation "that life itself is a creative process, that one thing is put purposefully upon another, that what is lost in one encounter is replenished in the next and that we possess some power to make sense of what takes place" (Bailey 2009, 210). To me, his observations sound like many coaching manifestos. The ability to deal with conflict and friction is not immediately obvious in the life of an anxiety-prone, lonely, immature alcoholic, but Cheever's powerful insights into the conflicted, fractious lives of others (and into his own) are convincing in their sound judgment and critical sensibility devoid of illusions and misinterpretations. There was a stark disparity between his life and his writing, and there is much in coaching we can learn from the latter. He believed in writing that attempted to make sense of our lives, that had "a voice that appeal[ed] to communal sensibility" (Bailey 2009, 387). His candor was always present in his self-assessments in the pages of his journals. Writing about a young male student admirer when he was teaching in the mid-seventies at the University of Utah, Cheever made the following observation:

> How cruel, unnatural, and black is my love for Z. I seem to mean to prey on Z's youth, to drive Z into a tragic isolation, to deny Z any life at all. Love is to instruct, to show our beloved what we know of the sources of light, and this may be the declaration of a crafty and lecherous old man. I can only hope not.
>
> (Bailey 2009, 549)

He reported that his journal writing was only a way of refreshing his memory, but his voice is suffused with a perspicacious understanding of the pain, sadness, and loneliness of the human condition – the darkness that we would sooner not reveal to the world. This darkness remains under the surface and unexplored during many coaching conversations. Here Cheever described the sorrow he felt when a friend departed:

> The day before yesterday I was saying goodbye to a very dear friend and as I watched him go away it was only, I think, through my grasp of fiction, through narrative and through invention that I could first reproach myself for loving him excessively and then attack psychiatry for adding the element of *prudence* to love – and then to have concluded that *imprudence* is a synonym for love, a conclusion I could not have reached were I not an author of fiction.
>
> (Bailey 2009, 611; original italics)

Coaching others is not only a privilege but an art. Encouraging coaching students to write in their journals, carefully noting their observations about themselves and others, will enhance their writing and support them in their ability perhaps not always to "deal with" conflict and friction but at least to explore such tensions with honesty and attention to detail. Cheever's journal observations, particularly about the ethics of power and manipulation in the teaching relationship, put me in mind of the moral issues in coaching to which I will turn now.

Does morality have a place in coaching?

It is through conversations that humans connect, and conversations that communicate empathy, trust, and respect are the ones we are aiming for in coaching. From more than forty in-depth interviews with postgraduate students from a range of organizations including financial services, telecommunications, retail, and IT, I learned that students yearned for more meaningful dialogue at work. Some organizations were more wedded to the principles of coaching than others. Some of those organizations, however, relied on more prescriptive models of coaching that students believed could be enhanced in more creative ways. My students were almost unanimous in their calls for more imagination in coaching, the kind of imagination that explores the role empathy plays in a coaching relationship, for example. Others were frustrated that narrative coaching did not seem to be taken as seriously as they thought it should be. The instances in which psychotherapists and psychologists insist that their practice has been enhanced by literature are illustrative, for although coaching is not psychotherapy, coaches are well placed to adopt what is useful from its practice in their own.

The acclaimed novelist Mario Vargas-Llosa (2013) writes about the transformative power of literature. For Vargas Llosa, literature is able to stimulate readers' critical faculties and help them to compensate themselves for enduring the difficulty, sometimes even the tragedy of life. In his essay "The Truth of Lies," Vargas-Llosa (2013, 250) writes, "When we read novels, we are not just ourselves but we are also those conjured-up characters into whose midst the novelist transports us. The transportation is a metamorphosis: the asphyxiating enclosure of our real life opens up and we leave it to become others, to live vicariously experiences that novels make our own." It is not difficult to see how the power of literature can connect with therapy. I will explore the ideas of a world-famous therapist in my next chapter, but for now I wish to reiterate how stories of pain and separation in therapy (indeed in any professional context) can be better understood by a deep engagement with literature. Literature broadens our perspectives on life, so it is equally useful in coaching. But where does morality sit in the coaching process? If imagination, emotions, and the affective experience are "controlled by the author and his work," and our own appreciation of a work "may well be enriched by emotions and other affective responses without fear that they might interfere with one's professional responsibilities" (Feagin 2010, 92), then can our moral responses to a text be, if not measured, at least taken into account?[2] And if morality is heightened or enriched by literature, does this have implications in the coaching sphere? Implicit within the coaching construct is the concern for another person's welfare. If we want to connect with another human being, we are demonstrating our concern. The demands upon being authentic in a coaching relationship are well-documented throughout this chapter and book. Those who consider themselves good coaches discuss their concern for their coachees. A student will tell me that there is a big difference in motivation between high-performing and medium-performing salespeople at his organization. His concern is that the medium performers are being held back by something he can identify and help them overcome. Another student will tell me that he is concerned that some of the ethnic-minority members of his organization do not always feel listened to or valued. His concern has motivated him to look at how to enhance the present coaching model at his organization to see if he can build in a way of addressing cultural diversity.

Jesse Prinz (2011, 212) points out that the essence of concern "often seems to involve an element or kind of moral anger," which he believes is important to morality. Empathy is not a precondition for moral judgment, but "emotions are necessary for the development of the capacity to make moral judgments in the first place" (Prinz 2011, 216). Should we consider morality when we are coaching? Prinz relates research that has been done on psychopaths, people who have been diagnosed as lacking empathy. Apparently psychopaths do not differentiate between moral rules and conventional rules. In other words, they display a "profound deficit in moral competence" (Prinz 2011, 216). They may follow conventional, societal rules about what clothing to wear or the salutary effects of bathing daily or eating with utensils instead of their hands when appropriate, for example. Yet the injunctions not to bully people or even not to kill people may not register with them at all. Moral rules that are emotionally grounded resist the psychopath's comprehension. Of course, psychopaths suffer far more than "a general deficit in moral emotions" (Prinz 2011, 217). Psychopaths do not really recognize or feel fear or sadness; they are not touched by the withdrawal of love; they lack guilt and moral anger. Empathy is therefore not necessary for moral judgment, but other emotions are.

The emotions involved in approbation and disapprobation – anger, gratitude, disgust, guilt, pride, shame, admiration – all of these emotions have an impact on us. Prinz explains how our moral emotions function:

> If we anticipate that an action will make us feel guilty, we will be thereby inclined to avoid that action [. . .] A person who judges that stealing is wrong, for example, will be motivated to resist the urge to steal, even when it would be easy and lucrative. Such a person will also be motivated to prevent others from stealing. Those who think stealing is wrong might report a shoplifter to the store clerk even though this intervention carries some risk and no direct reward.
> (Prinz 2011, 219)

He amplifies his argument by then linking good behavior with pride and gratification. Moral emotions – the expression and development of them – are fundamental aspects of how coaches work. Coaching provides an outlet for emotion, even if, as we have seen, emotions are not always readily visible or encouraged.

The moral emotions that Prinz discusses are the reference points used to make sense of our action within the workplace. Literature, in fostering these moral emotions, is instrumental in helping coachees to achieve their goals.

Prinz's conclusion is that emotions associated with approbation and disapprobation appears to have a significant impact on moral motivation. The student who was investigating how to coach middle sales achievers so that they could become higher sales achievers shared the results of what happened after he distributed "The Swimmer" and discussed it in a group of middle-ranking achievers. I asked him specifically about the moral implications both of using the story in this context and of the story itself. He said that no one specifically "judged" Neddy Merrill, but a few salespeople admitted the story was "odd" and made them feel "uncomfortable." When he pressed them for more details, the salespeople commented on "Neddy's fecklessness" and his "cavalier attitude to his family." The student observed that there was a sharp demarcation in the motivations of the high and medium achievers. Medium achievers were concerned with doing well for their families, being busy, and having a full diary. They were also concerned with receiving praise for a job well done. The high achievers wanted to "be the best." My student regarded the high achievers' wanting to "be the best" as being motivated by egocentricity and bravado. It would have been illustrative had my student been able to use the same story with high achievers to see if there was any stark difference in their reaction to the story as a group. Such an experiment might have showed that emotions leading to praise or condemnation have a motivational force and would have demonstrated, therefore, that it is incumbent upon coaches to learn how to coach emotionally. However, the student left the company, and I wasn't able to continue my conversations with him. Yet let's assume that we can indeed coach emotionally. How then would a discussion on Neddy Merrill's swim support strong morality-based coaching practice? "The Swimmer" clearly tapped into the middle achievers' emotion of guilt. They perceived Neddy as a man who abdicated responsibility and neglected his family. I am certainly not suggesting that guilt-tripping employees should be any part of a coaching regime, but it is salutary to acknowledge the role morality plays in our emotions. Morality need not be on any coaching agenda, but coaches should be aware of its existence as a powerful motivational force in human behavior.

Failure in coaching

With so much emphasis on high achievement, objectives, goal setting, great leadership conversations, and increasing business success, it may be difficult to see where failure fits into the picture. Failure is not simply less than high achievement, or meeting one's objectives, being unable to set clear targets, having a less than ideal leadership persona, and not increasing business success. It can often be complete and utter catastrophic disaster: marriages imploding, family members on drugs, stark and increasingly uncomfortable feelings of inadequacy, sadness, and frustration. Feeling like a failure. Does "The Swimmer" hold any answers for those wrestling with a sense of failure? One comment I found particularly poignant from a student was that, after reading the story, he believed that "we are left to choose the character's destiny." Perhaps that sense of choice is the key to a story that appears to offer only hopelessness, struggle, nihilism, and, yes, failure. Neddy fails to connect to his fellow human beings. Whether Neddy is dead or alive, escaping or searching, departing or arriving, not only is his mind blurred but so is his denouement: "looking in at the windows, [he] saw that the place was empty" (Cheever 2010, 788). Neddy is a familiar Cheever character: his misfortunes are due to his weakness. Cheever was fascinated by people who sabotaged their lives, continually acting contrary to their best interests and throwing away what really mattered to them. When he was asked to do university lecturing, one of his assignments was to have students select a series of dissimilar things and "put them into a coherent scheme" (Bailey 2009, 210). He saw life (and, by extension, writing) as a creative process that we have the choice of perverting or embracing – the crucial element is that of choice.

Ernest Becker (1997) discusses this thorny issue of choice. He states that human beings in general lack courage and "lack the strength to bear the superlative" (Becker 1997, 49). We have an acute sense of overwhelming fear and awe when faced with "the crushing and negating miracle of Being" (Becker 1997, 49). In order to support the immense illusion of control, we form defenses that screen us against despair. We need lies, we need defenses, we need goods and toys and things:

> If character is a neurotic defense against despair and you shed that defense, you admit the full flood of despair, the full realization of the true human condition, what men are really afraid of, what they struggle against, and are driven toward and away from. Freud summed it up beautifully when he somewhere remarked that psychoanalysis cured the neurotic misery in order to introduce the patient to the common misery of life.
>
> (Becker 1997, 57)

Becker reminds us that our character is layered: the first two are diurnal layers, what we talk about to get along with others, words that placate, clichés, and our usual role-playing; our third layer is our character defense layer in which lies our emptiness. Underneath this defense layer is our "fear of death layer" where our authentic self lies. We do not need to be adherents to psychoanalytical practice in order to see the validity of Becker's model for understanding the limitations of a coaching paradigm that fails to get beneath the surface of the affable carapace that so often inhibits dialogue. Many people live out their lives never penetrating beyond the first two role-playing layers. Cheever saw psychiatrists but took a dim view of their diagnoses, turning on them with personal venom. One wore "garters [. . .] that had silly clocks printed on them"; he had read now of Cheever's books and used the word "meaningful" fourteen times (Bailey 2009, 393); another "wears a ring" (Bailey 2009, 425). He thought that it was less than helpful to dwell on neurosis – what was important in life was its poetry.

Warren Bennis (1989) produced a study of leadership that focused on a range of successful individuals from the fields of film, television, journalism, information technology, law, politics, medicine, and aviation (not exclusively). He concluded that leaders need to exhibit qualities such as virtue, vision, readiness, and willingness to take risks. His conclusions were supported anecdotally by a series of industry leaders' vignettes illuminating their personal struggles and successes through adversity. He discovered that reflecting on experience, including on failure, was a common theme in his conversations with leaders. He discovers that most ordinary people are paralyzed by fear and immobilized by failure:

> Wordsworth defined poetry as strong emotion recollected in tranquility. That's the time to reflect, in tranquility – and then to resolve. The point is not to be victims of our feelings, jerked this way and that by unresolved emotions, not to be used by your experiences, but to use them and to use them creatively. Just as writers turn experiences from their lives into novels and plays, we can each transform our experiences into grist for our mill. Isak Dinesen said "any sorrow can be borne if we can put it in a story."
>
> (Bennis 1989, 117–18)

Bennis reveals that all of his leaders, no matter the depths of the failure they encountered, manage to reflect on and attempt to understand their experiences. They endeavor to resolve their conflicts positively. You need to admit what you want and recognize what you need: "There is magic in experience, as well as wisdom" (Bennis 1989, 154). Bennis peppers his book with quotations from admired writers. His use of William James, Thomas Carlyle, Mark Twain, Emily Dickinson, Wordsworth, and Dinesen is to demonstrate writers who illustrate the quality of vision he singles out for praise. For Bennis, these are the writers who have quested for human knowledge and who have been able to fashion profound metaphors for this quest and, at times, metaphors for the failure of this quest. "The Swimmer" may not hold any answers to someone wrestling with a sense of failure. Yet reflecting on the hapless watery journey of Neddy may help us to expound on and even comprehend our own internal and external conflicts.

James Baldwin: struggle in coaching

In 1960, John Cheever was invited to appear with the African-American essayist and novelist James Baldwin at a symposium on writing at Berkeley. The general idea was that they would disagree vehemently on everything, thereby providing entertainment. On the surface, they seemed vastly dissimilar in background, but they got on well and apparently failed to provide the political frisson required (Bailey 2009). Baldwin shared with Cheever, despite the vast disparities in the nature of their narrative projects, a common feeling of being a stranger struggling with aspects of an identity. In Baldwin's case, his sense of exclusion was all pervasive: "Be it also remembered that America was a British colony, that I was born in the English language, have a British name, and speak as the descendent of the slave of a subject" (Baldwin 1961,16). Baldwin's essays are stark and angry portrayals not only of the failure of race relations in America but also of Baldwin's failures to square his homosexuality with his powerful Christian morality and to reconcile Christianity's claims to be based on love when Christian nations enslaved others. Baldwin's essays are timely reminders – especially in the coaching arena – of how important it is to reflect on our choices and not to succumb to failure:

> We are never free not to choose, and this eternal condition means a great burden of individual responsibility, not only for her or himself, but for everyone's life. Although the authentic act is one in which the individual is not acting as part of a collective or crowd, the choice still involves all [. . .] Baldwin has the world in mind as he attempts to create a future he wants, by never succumbing to destructive emotions. Though time and place were not kind to African Americans, racism according to existential thought is theirs, meaning that they and all people are responsible for it and must act in consequence of it. Baldwin's choice realizes the inevitability of choice and his is a mirror for all.
> (Lapenson 2013, 201)

We are always free to choose. Indeed, organizational coaching is predicated on the idea that we can choose to effect a break with prior habits and conduct. In fact, we can never escape the constant freedom of choice. Moreover, we have much to learn about failure from Baldwin's practice of intense reflection and self-examination. Writing about the death of his father in his essay "Notes of a Native Son," he observed, "He had lived and died in an intolerable bitterness of spirit and it frightened me, as we drove him to the graveyard through those unquiet, ruined streets, to see how powerful and overflowing this bitterness could be and to realize that this bitterness now was mine" (Baldwin 1955, 88). Much of Baldwin's work centers on the questioning of identity, an identity that frustrated and eluded him. His own struggle with identity offers a powerful lens for self-analysis in the context of a coaching dialogue, as I discovered when I introduced one of my students to his work.

Cheever and Baldwin were writing contemporaries and there was also mutual respect between them, but, as far as I am aware, scant recognition of how alike they were. Both were sexually conflicted, grappling with the difficulties of being human and perpetually examining the intense despair, anguish, and isolation that affected their lives. They occupied radically different milieux. Cheever made the suburbs the habitus of his feelings, habits, introspection, and observation. Baldwin, or as he called himself, the "bastard of the West" in *Notes of a Native Son* (Baldwin 1955, 6), concerned himself more with the white-black American racial psyche. His perspective was at times that of an exile (in Paris) and his sense of place was urban America: the American empire was his "cultural collision" (Baldwin 1955, 54) and his confrontation issues of inequality, citizenship and power.

One of my coaching students at a large American financial services company wanted to interrogate race and diversity in his coaching project and subsequent practice. He avowed that his company was "progressive" and that there were "people of color" in senior positions, but he thought that "there was always room for improvement." He believed that his inquiry could strengthen the organization's coaching program. I suggested that he read Baldwin's essay "Notes of a Native Son" to ascertain whether the bleak portrayals of white and black relations in postwar America could support ideas around a coaching conversation about race. Was Baldwin's essay still relevant more than seventy years later? Could Baldwin's ideas serve as a guide to the landscape of racial politics in America if indeed it was still relevant? Would it be less uncomfortable to use Baldwin's writing as a prism through which race could be discussed meaningfully as a way of facilitating the more difficult conversations around inequality, unfairness, and intolerance, the same workplace tensions that can otherwise be difficult to broach? Before using the essay in a coaching scenario, the student read it and answered my questions about whether Baldwin's reminiscences about the strained relationship with his father, his family's life in Harlem, and his fraught encounters with white America could support someone struggling with racial issues in the workplace. I will relate his response here:

> I am not certain that I have experienced the same level of overt racism that Baldwin lived through. However, as an African-American, I have experienced enough in the area of racism to identify with the struggle he passionately describes. I think the most important thing to do in discussing issues of race, culture or diversity is to invite coachees or clients to an open discussion of their thoughts and feelings to gain a deeper insight into their perspectives. Part of this discussion would consist of my opening up about the personal struggles I have had in this area. Baldwin's essay helped me to appreciate the sense of pride and respect that resides in all of us and fuels our desire to be acknowledged, accepted and valued. The essay also helped me to appreciate the serious consequences that can result when a person feels alienated, isolated or ostracized from society – or an organization. These consequences can be in the form of a deep-seated frustration or anger or rebellion. It is important for us as leaders to do our best to ensure that every member of our team feels respected, valued and appreciated so that they are motivated to positively contribute to the cause for which we are all enlisted.

The student added that reading and discussing "Notes of a Native Son" was a "creative way to help people express themselves productively." I had been concerned that the political import of a writer like Baldwin's work might be deemed irrelevant, since Baldwin was relating events from 1943:

> Perhaps the most revealing news item, out of the steady parade of reports of muggings, stabbings, shootings, assaults, gang wars, and accusations of

> police brutality, is the item concerning six Negro girls who set upon a white girl in the subway because, as they all too accurately put it, she was stepping on their toes. Indeed she was, all over the nation.
>
> (Baldwin 1955, 99)

The work turned out to be as relevant and urgent today as it was all those decades ago. As my student remarked:

> I am fortunate to live in a time where people are more tolerant than in the past. Nonetheless, I am not naive to the undercurrent of divisiveness and discomfort that still has a grip on our society. The pain and struggles that Baldwin describes are still with us. I do believe, however, that Baldwin's dialogue challenges us to look within ourselves to see who we are in relation to the issues he raises.

Although I have always been careful to make a clear distinction between coaching and counseling or coaching and therapy, it is undeniable that integrating writing into coaching has its therapeutic benefits. I have been thus far discussing verbal coaching, but there is strong and compelling evidence that writing about significant issues gives access to our emotions and stimulates our reflective capabilities. The distinguished social psychologist James Pennebaker (2016) has researched emotional inhibition and the benefits of detailing one's emotional experiences. In a recent interview with Molly H. Moran (2013, 3), Pennebaker discussed his psychological experiments that made him reach the conclusion that "writing about a traumatic experience was associated with improvements in health" and that writing was beneficial if you think about something too much: "You're almost forced to bring about structure in what you are saying. You are not going to be distracted. You are in a room by yourself focusing on the topic" (Moran 2013, 3). His work has cross-over implications in coaching. There was no doubt in any coaching student's mind that "Notes of a Native Son" was the personal account of racial trauma. The incident in which Baldwin hurls a mug of water at a waitress who has just told him, "We don't serve Negroes here" then ducks while the glass shatters against the mirror and Baldwin rushes out into the street is clearly traumatic: "I lived it over and over again, the way one relives an automobile accident after it has happened and one finds oneself alone and safe. I could not get over two facts, both equally difficult to grasp, and one was that I could have been murdered. But the other was that I had been ready to commit murder" (Baldwin 1955, 97).

The essay is permeated with trauma. Baldwin's writing is the very embodiment of self-examination as he demonstrates "the necessity of social or collective forms of interrogation" (Schlosser 2012, 488). My student designed one specific coaching question to promote discussions on culture and diversity that Baldwin's writing encapsulates: "Do you believe that race and ethnicity are important to discuss in the pursuit of understanding how we can become more powerful and effective coaches?" To my student, the glass incident represented a starting point for discussions on race, morality, and trauma. He said that Baldwin's dialogue "constantly challenges us to look within ourselves. Is it right to rebel against something you deem wicked? Is it right to lash out against an establishment you deem oppressive?" He agreed with Pennebaker that writing about an incident such as Baldwin's would be beneficial. After all, Baldwin needed to write about it himself. Pennebaker's findings could of course be particularly useful in long-distance coaching, a topic I will explore in the final chapter.

Final thoughts

In this chapter, I have tried to capture the beauty and mystery of works of art such as Cheever's meditation on melancholy, self-deception, and the temporal; St. Augustine's conception of time and memory; and Baldwin's fiery and impassioned struggle against the immolation of racial prejudice. I have enlisted biographers, novelists, philosophers, psychologists, historians, and academic experts on coaching to illuminate my argument that reading works of art helps us to learn about other human beings, an axiom that lies at the heart of the coaching relationship. I have discussed the importance of keeping a coaching journal, the critical tensions between rationality and emotion in the workplace, the role of voice in the coaching dialogue, the implications of morality in the coaching sphere, and addressing struggle and failure. Most of all, though, I have allowed my students' voices to guide my ideas on what coaching can learn from literature: the exposition of their experiences from reading and sharing Cheever's and Baldwin's images, symbols, and eloquent prose become the final judgment on the efficacy of my pedagogical beliefs. These images, symbols, and prose remind us of how coaching can be used to explore our own possibilities, which are, at the risk of sounding hyperbolic, limitless. Inherent in my literary approach is pragmatism. This is the pragmatism that Elaine Cox (2013) explains as the quality coaches need when they use whatever techniques and tools they deem useful. The pragmatic model centers on understanding the client's experiences: it "begins and ends with the client's experience" (Cox 2013, 2), which is an evocative way of reflecting on what coaching should be.

Coaching draws on a range of disciplines, but supporting the client or coachee to make explicit the implicit and to comprehend their experiences is the central activity that underpins the transformative process we call coaching. At the heart of coaching, Cox sees an interrogation of how we "meet the fullness of [clients'] experiential dilemmas, stand back and observe that experience through the use of a reflective space, and then work in a critical, rational way with reflective material in order to transform it into learning" (Cox 2013, 160). The reflective space that Cox perceives to be central to the transformative potential of coaching is, to my mind, meaningfully accessed and realized through the reading and discussion of literature. This chapter has sought to show how digging deeply into a coachee's beliefs and values can be effected by a discussion of a literary work; simply allowing coachees to react to a text can be a strategy for mutual discourse, privileging the centrality of language in the coaching relationship. If our own stories are a good way of exploring ourselves, our acts, and our work and life events (Drake 2010), then commenting on how resonant a story is to our own life is not only useful in a coaching dialogue but frees us also from uncomfortable or exaggerated personal narratives that can veer into more therapeutic domains and prevent coaches from being supporting yet detached participants in the process.

Cox (2013, 39) points out that, for some, telling the story of events is "natural and helpful"; for others, it could be perceived as obtrusive. She observes that many coaches work in a "Gestalt way," staying in the present (Cox 2013, 39). Literature provides a mirror image of our stories that illuminates our own lives through reflection or refraction and thereby obviates the need to confront them head-on. Using literature in coaching provides a cipher for self-exploration while minimizing the potential to do harm. The coachee can use the story, the essay, the poem, the novel as a conduit for his or her story, thereby revealing obliquely what needs to be revealed. "The Swimmer," with its strange undercurrents of desire, pain, loss, discomfort, and wonder, is an ideal text to work with the complexity that underlies human relationships and that simmers below the surface of the coaching dialogue.

Notes

1 From "The Swimmer" by John Cheever, published by Jonathan Cape. Reprinted by permission of The Random House Group Ltd. ©John Cheever 1979.
2 Although Feagin is referring specifically to literary critics in her discussion of the fear that the emotions can impinge on our professional responsibilities, we can extrapolate to professional organizations in general, which tend to display the same anxieties about emotion that Feagin diagnoses in the academy.

References

Aristotle. 1991. *The Art of Rhetoric*. Translated by Hugh Lawson-Tancred. London: Penguin.

Bachkirova, Tatiana, and Elaine Cox. 2007. "Coaching With Emotion in Organisations: Investigation of Personal Theories." *Leadership and Organization Development Journal* 28 (7): 600–12.

Bailey, Blake. 2009. *Cheever: A Life*. London: Picador.

Baldwin, James. 1955. *Notes of a Native Son*. Boston: Beacon Press.

Baldwin, James. 1961. *Nobody Knows My Name*. New York: Vintage.

Becker, Ernest. 1997. *The Denial of Death*. New York: Free Press. First published in 1973 by Simon and Schuster.

Beech, Nic, and Oliver Crane. 1999. "High Performance Teams and a Climate of Community." *Team Performance Management: An International Journal* 5 (3): 87–102.

Bennis, Warren. 1989. *On Becoming a Leader*. Reading: Addison-Wesley.

Blythe, Hal, and Charlie Sweet. 1992. "Cheever's Dark Knight of the Soul: The Failed Quest of Neddy Merrill." *Studies in Short Fiction* 29 (3): 347–52.

Boniwell, Ilona, Carol Kauffman, and Jordan Silberman. 2010. "The Positive Psychology Approach to Coaching." In *The Complete Handbook of Coaching*, edited by Elaine Cox, Tatiana Bachkirova, and David Ashley Clutterbuck, 158–71. 2nd edn. London: Sage.

Bruner, Jerome. 2003. *Making Stories: Law, Literature, Life*. Cambridge, MA: Harvard University Press.

Cervo, Nathan. 1991. "Cheever's the Swimmer." *The Explicator* 50 (1): 49–50.

Cheever, John. 2010. *Collected Stories*. Introduction by Hanif Kureishi. London: Vintage.

Cox, Elaine. 2013. *Coaching Understood: A Pragmatic Inquiry Into the Coaching Process*. London: Sage.

Drake, David. 2010. "Narrative Coaching." In *The Complete Handbook of Coaching*, edited by Elaine Cox, Tatiana Bachkirova, and David Ashley Clutterbuck, 120–31. 2nd edn. London: Sage.

Elbow, Peter. 2000. *Everyone Can Write: Essays Toward a Hopeful Theory of Writing and Teaching Writing*. Oxford: Oxford University Press.

Feagin, Susan. 2010. "Giving Emotions Their Due." *British Journal of Aesthetics* 50 (1): 89–92.

Goldie, Peter. 2000. *The Emotions: A Philosophical Exploration*. Oxford: Oxford University Press.

Greenberg, Stephen. 2014. "Let's Talk About Relationships." *Orientation News* 23 (6): 1–3.

Kennedy, Thomas. 2015. "Negative Capability and John Cheever's 'The Swimmer'." *South Carolina Review* 48 (1): 9–15.

Lapenson, Bruce. 2013. "Race and Existential Commitment in James Baldwin." *Philosophy and Literature* 37 (1): 199–209.

Matthews, James. 1992. "Peter Rugg and Cheever's Swimmer: Archetypal Missing Men." *Studies in Short Fiction* 29 (1): 95–101.

Moran, Molly Hurley. 2013 "Writing and Healing From Trauma: An Interview With James Pennebaker." *Composition Forum* 28: 1–10.

Olney, James. 1998. *Memory and Narrative: The Weave of Life-Writing*. Chicago: University of Chicago Press.

Pennebaker, James. 2016. "Award for Distinguished Contribution to the Applications of Psychology: James A Pennebaker." *American Psychologist* 71 (8): 681–3.

Prinz, Jesse. 2011. "Is Empathy Necessary for Morality?" In *Empathy: Philosophical and Psychological Perspectives*, edited by Amy Coplan and Peter Goldie, 211–29. Oxford: Oxford University Press.

Robinson, Jenefer. 2005. *Deeper than Reason: Emotion and Its Role in Literature, Music, and Art*. Oxford: Oxford University Press.

Saint Augustine. 1961. *Confessions*. Translated by R.S. Pine-Coffin. London: Penguin.

Schlosser, Alden. 2012. "Socrates in a Different Key: James Baldwin and Race in America." *Political Research Quarterly* 66 (3): 487–99.

Siedentop, Larry. 2014. *Inventing the Individual: The Origins of Western Liberalism*. London: Penguin.

Styhre, Alexander. 2008. "Coaching as Second-Order Observations: Learning From Site Managers in the Construction Industry." *Leadership and Organization Development Journal* 29 (3): 275–90.

Updike, John. 2009. "Basically Decent: A Big Biography of John Cheever." *The New Yorker*, March 9, Review of *Cheever: A Life* by Blake Bailey. www.newyorker.com/magazine/2009/03/09/basically-decent

Vargas-Llosa, Mario. 2013. "The Truth of Lies." In *Making Waves: Essays 1962–63*, edited and translated by John King. London: Faber and Faber.

Chapter 4

Sales coaching, dysfunction, and family

Arthur Miller's *Death of a Salesman*

Born in 1915 in Harlem to Polish immigrants of Jewish descent, Arthur Miller knew that the pressure to conform is a constant. Miller's tumultuous life – from Manhattan to Brooklyn and from the University of Michigan to becoming one of the most successful playwrights in American history – is an instructive one for coaches. Miller's trajectory is the story of a man who never forgot his roots. He used the dynamics of his own family and his upbringing to capture the idiosyncrasies of human communication. True to his principles, he refused to give evidence to the notorious House of Un-American Activities Committee and was punished for declining to inform on his friends. Miller lived a colorful life: he was married to Marilyn Monroe and was particularly interested in exploring how human beings can be part of the world in which they live and yet remote from it at the same time. His work is motivated by a desire to illuminate how we can be ourselves, whoever we are and whatever that might mean, in a pressurized, conformist, and at times treacherous society, workplace, and family.

Two of Miller's uncles were salesmen, one of whom, Manny, was a model for Miller's protagonist Willy Loman in *Death of a Salesman*. Like Willy's in the play, Manny's patch was New England. In his autobiography, *Timebends* (1987), Miller reminisces about the potential for fantasy this kind of job held: "He was not in some dull salaried job where you could never hope to make a killing. Hope was his food and drink, and the need to project hopeful culminations for a selling trip helped, I suppose, to make life unreal" (Miller 1987, 126). Willy Loman's rich fantasy life, in which the audience contemplates a tapestry of the protagonist's wild emotional swings, his distorted past, and his extravagantly unrealistic future dreams, offers a window onto the extreme range of personalities we may encounter in organizational coaching. We can use Willy Loman's family dynamics to explore the dead hand of conformity in office life. *Death of a Salesman* is a play about work: the work to put a roof over one's family; the work of bringing up children; the work of keeping a family from disintegrating. Willy Loman's family functions as a potent metaphor for workplace dynamics, where the strain of interpersonal relationships, the contested hierarchies of management structures, and the perils of miscommunication serve to mirror and amplify the tensions within the family unit.

This chapter will briefly trace the history of the salesman, the forces at work in the commercial traveler's existence, and the origins of *Death of a Salesman*, including Miller's philosophy with respect to success, money, and morality. My coaching students who decided to use the play and the 1985 film version (Schlöndorff 1985) with their coachees found that Miller's work served as an effective springboard for discussing workplace themes. I will report on how they used Miller's play with their colleagues to support coaching dialogue, and I will provide detailed feedback gathered from my interviews with a number of students, interviews that help to build up a thick description of the potential benefits of using a play such as Miller's in the context of organizational coaching. The students I worked with on integrating Miller's play into their coaching practice were from a global telecommunications corporation, one that was at the time experiencing market difficulties, and a large US–based insurance company. I also used Miller's play with a student who had recently completed a coaching module and was interested in pursuing further study in the field by undertaking a master's degree in coaching. This last student worked for a UK–based sales solution firm. The range of responses reported on in this chapter help to gauge the efficacy of using *Death of a Salesman* in a sales coaching conversation. How can Miller's masterpiece support coaches and their coachees in discussing emotionally charged themes such as success, money, and morality as both parties resist the stifling influence of corporate conformism? How can we acquire a deeper understanding of a poignant life like Willy's and then apply our response to understand our own lives a bit better? This chapter seeks an answer to these questions, using the students' testimony as a guiding thread. I will explore how our emotional responses to Willy and the Loman family are not only relevant to the field of coaching but can, moreover, have a significant impact on the practice of sales coaching. I will argue, furthermore, that one of the useful aspects of engaging with literature lies in the role literature can play in keeping coaches and coachees from messy and potentially embarrassing encounters.

This chapter develops the idea broached in preceding chapters that literary works can serve as a proxy in difficult coaching conversations. We will see how, by using a literary text as a touchstone to explore a character's emotional predicaments, we don't feel compelled to confront the person sitting across from us. Our emotional responses to literary characters such as Willy and the other members of his family we encounter in the play are triggered by the act of reading or watching, and these same responses can subsequently be used to channel the discussion of personal issues in an impersonal framework. As we discuss the Loman family in a coaching dialogue, we are often actually discussing ourselves. The identity of the coach and coachee lurk behind the primary object of their discourse, and the literary work functions as a framing mechanism that allows the participants in the dialogue to confront the embarrassing, humiliating, and painful issues that tend to remain below the surface in more direct coaching techniques. The practice of the oblique reference that is facilitated by the use of a text like Miller's has the benefit of providing a degree of security to the more vulnerable among us. Coaching participants are able to gain a fuller emotional understanding of the flesh-and-blood people we are through an emotional appraisal of a fictional character. Discussing Willy's dysfunction sometimes feels far safer than discussing our own.

This chapter also opens up new avenues through which to consider the benefits of using literary works in organizational coaching. It explores the ways in which engaging with fiction have greater emotional and cognitive benefits than reading the usual self-help and self-styled inspirational books on coaching and leadership. While these kinds of texts have an undoubtedly important role in supporting coaching, literary works, we will see, can have a more significant impact on how we relate to other people. The simple exercise of analyzing the degree of dysfunction exhibited by a literary character such as Willy can have an immensely powerful effect on our awareness of the complex, contradictory, and mysterious nature of what it means to be human. It is this human element, so obviously important in coaching and so readily cultivated by literary fiction, that can become lost when as coaches we confine ourselves to case studies and secondhand accounts of leadership in action.

Coaching challenges and why Willy?

When Arthur Miller was at the University of Michigan (1934–38), he became immersed in the plays of Henrik Ibsen. He was attracted to the social power of Ibsen's works, particularly their willingness to challenge the orthodoxies of the past and to address the hypocrisies of society. He perceived the works as anti-capitalist and found "a sense of indignation about the given, a rejection of social hypocrisies, in tune with his own rigorous rebelliousness" (Bigsby 2008, 106). Miller detected a strong connection between Ibsen's spirit and that of the ancient Greek dramatists. Both Ibsen and the Greeks saw that the chaos, ruin, and malaise of the present were invariably rooted in the transgressions of the past. Ibsen seemed to Miller a revolutionary who wanted to supplant Victorian society with one tolerant of freedom and intolerant of denial, repression, and false values. Ibsen's play *A Doll's House* showcased a family riven by falsity, hypocrisy, and stifling convention and conformity. For Miller, playwriting and the theater represented a galvanizing force, one akin to radical journalism, the kind of experience that would provoke the type of social change he believed was necessary to create a better American society from the moribund fossil he saw: "the play was not like a little isolated cell where things went on disconnected from the city around us, but was one cell among the myriad, part of the sound and the anxiety and the almost universal frustration of life at that time" (Miller 2015, 360). Here Miller is commenting on Clifford Odet's output in general, but he was equally galvanized into playwriting by the works of Eugene O'Neill, who in *The Iceman Cometh*, *Desire under the Elms*, and *Morning Becomes Electra* created families who symbolized everything that was wrong in society – the family as the microcosm of societal tensions. These playwrights who influenced Miller during his university years reinforced not only Miller's strong sense of moral and political engagement but also his conviction that the private and the public world were inextricably linked. Miller's most famous family, the Lomans, immortalized in *Death of a Salesman*, is a family that yearns for "the golden glitter of a dream" (Bigsby 2008, 327). Miller's work was also heavily influenced by the Great Depression and leftist politics. The Great Depression was not simply a financial catastrophe but an event that caused him to take on the mantle of a public intellectual. The powerful currents of these times of little means and, to his mind, the cataclysmic failure of the capitalist system tempered his radicalism and sharpened his lifelong interest in the plight of the individual and the choices he or she makes, choices that reveal an individual's spirit: "I knew the Depression was only incidentally a matter of money. Rather, it was a moral catastrophe, a violent revelation of the hypocrisies behind the facade of American society [. . .] when at the same time the old order has also melted and the old authority has shown its incompetence and hollowness, the way to maturity is radicalism" (Miller 1987, 115).

In his works and particularly in *Death of a Salesman*, Miller explored class conflict and the deleterious effects of the capitalist system, yet his characters are not symbolic husks that represent the passivity of victims. Instead they are fleshed-out individuals who are beholden to an all-powerful, ruthless machine. Miller was, above all, a responsible playwright who conceived his practice as one that would connect to the people: he wanted to use his art as a vehicle for contact with the masses. Drama was real language to Miller – dialogic and emotional: "with drama you pick up the real language. It was thrilling to write that" (Miller in Bigsby 2008, 112). Miller's plays reveal a sense of the absurd, a world in which meaning is elusive and aging and failure will break a man's spirit. His early writing uses language to reflect the confusion, distress, and complexity of a life without meaning.

The Hollywood production of *Death of a Salesman* (Schlöndorff 1985), which I used with my coaching students, has an absurdist quality that recalls the work of Samuel Beckett. Beckett, like Miller, had rejected traditional narrative conventions because he believed that such formal conventions could never accommodate "the mess" of the modern world (Olney 1998, 12). Miller shares with Beckett the desire to say something meaningful about human nature and about man's existence in the crushingly absurd chaos of contemporary society, full of alienated individuals lacking a unifying social vision and enmeshed in what Miller saw as a never-ending and absurd race to glean reward and advantage. This race for social advantage, for wealth, prestige, and reputation, is embodied in Miller's play by the aspiring salesman. Miller uses the salesman as a symbol for unbridled ambition, and it is this symbol that can be harnessed as a pregnant locus of meaning in coaching dialogue. Miller's character, we will see, is able to speak to aspiring members of the world of contemporary business, for the hopes and fears articulated by Willy Loman are the very desires and anxieties harbored by coachees. In seeing aspects of their own personality and situation reflected and amplified in Miller's character, coachees, we will see, are able to come to a better understanding of what their work means to them and the path by which they are able to reach their goals.

A detailed discussion of how Miller's play was used by one of my students to enhance his inquiry into how to develop coaching in his organization helps to illustrate the play's potential as a tool for enhancing coaching dialogue. One of my sales coaching students' projects began as an investigation into the key motivational traits of top and middle sales performers at his organization, with the expressed objective of identifying the best ways to coach both groups. Andy's inquiry was initially predicated on the leadership lessons put forward by two books: *Leading on the Edge: Leadership Lessons from the Limits of Human Endurance, the Extraordinary Saga of Shackleton's Antarctic Exhibition* (Perkins et al. 2000) and Weisinger's and Pawliw-Fry's *Performing Under Pressure: The Science of Doing Best When It Matters Most* (2015). The first book traces the 1914 trans-Antarctic expedition of Sir Ernest Shackleton and traces the philosophy behind Shackleton's goal to achieve the first overland crossing of the Antarctic. The authors claim that an examination of those who endured horrific conditions and mobilized others to survive or even triumph over those conditions can yield lessons about teamwork and self-sacrifice as well as how to flourish in the teeth of adversity. The challenges today's leaders face may not involve physical survival but rather the challenges of competition, uncertainty, and disruption. Nevertheless, the authors contend that Shackleton's philosophy of setting a personal example, never surrendering, and engendering an atmosphere of camaraderie and teamwork can guide a leader to success. The story of Shackleton's Endurance expedition can help leaders deal with the human reactions to adverse situations and can become a blueprint for leadership for the modern stressed-out executive. The narrative of this 300-mile trek across a frozen, inhospitable terrain amounts in the end to a self-help, motivational tract for those wishing to improve their leadership skills. The second book, *Performing under Pressure* (Weisinger and Pawliw-Fry 2015), claims that, contrary to popular belief, pressure is not a stimulant to success but an enemy of success that undermines performance. Pressure, according to Weisinger and Pawliw-Fry, adversely affects our thinking, decision making, memory, and attention because of a perpetual feeling of anxiety that overwhelms our system: only those who have learned to minimize and control pressure are able to perform at their best. Both books have admirable aims, and Andy was able to use these texts in his project to capture the relevance both of the story of Shackleton's Endurance and of the physiological and psychological complexion of stress and pressure as they relate to the field of organizational coaching. Both books emerged in the initial stages of Andy's project as good vehicles for explaining leadership. Andy's project was billed as a case study showing how the texts could be used as a source of paradigms that could subsequently be emulated by coachees in his organization. But the problem that emerged when Andy attempted to use these two leadership texts in his coaching sessions was that he discovered they were overly prescriptive. Neither is marketed as a coaching text, but these two books were the core texts used in the coaching program at this organization. Andy used the texts to compile a scale of leadership qualities and devised an exercise in which his coachees in the organization would map their own motivations against the scale of ideal leadership qualities. But his inquiry into the motivational traits of top and middle performers yielded a rather obvious if worrying finding. Andy discovered a disconnect between the motivations of the paradigmatic leaders he had compiled from his reading and the self-avowed motivations of his top- and middle-performing coachees in the organization. The core theme that emerged again and again in his coaching sessions as a motivational driver was, unsurprisingly, "money." As he put it, "money was highlighted as the top motivator for every participant within the study." But rather than interrogate this disconnect between the motivations of the exemplary leaders and those of his colleagues in the organization, Andy insisted on using his scale as an action plan for his coachees. He disregarded what they were telling him about how and why they were motivated to succeed and insisted on providing them with series of lists and urgent bullet points that might transform them into the leaders profiled in the leadership manuals. It was only when I encouraged Andy to take a different approach to his coaching sessions that he began to see the value of allowing his colleagues to open up. Descriptions of leadership and action plans for enhanced success would get him only so far: the coaching sessions, by his own admission, had turned into "a monologue in which I would reel off the important bits and they would sit there jotting it all down." I suggested Andy use an excerpt from the film version of *Death of a Salesman* in his coaching sessions as an innovative, perhaps rather unorthodox way of exploring what his coachees truly thought about their jobs. What happened was a transformation that was reflected in Andy's written work too: description and prescription were substituted by interrogation. Andy was able to get inside the skin of his coachees and give them a space to tell their stories, a space that had been stifled by an overreliance on an expository mode of coaching practice. Before, Andy had simply skimmed the surface of what motivated his colleagues. "Money" tended to be their default, bravado-driven response that helped to erect a barrier to intimacy. His coachees had felt no inclination to delve into their personal reasons for joining the company or their background that had motivated them: by claiming that money was the only thing that interested them, they could evade the kind of deep personal reflection that a discussion based on Miller's play elicited. Before watching the play, their responses had been almost robotic in their unanimity: money represented a means to maintain a good lifestyle; a comfortable future for their family; financial security; a psychological safety net. Money was what drove these top sales performers to set good examples for their team, to take risks, to handle pressure effectively, to make plans for dealing with adversity, to deal with changing environments. But was money really all there was to it? *Death of a Salesman*, with its subtle portrayal of the conflicting psychological undercurrents that shape human action, was able to encourage Andy's coachees to mine beneath the surface of their simplistic response that money was what drove them. The deep reflection triggered by their watching the play provided, as we shall see, an unparalleled richness to the coaching sessions.

Death of a Salesman is particularly well equipped to speak to the world of contemporary business. Its themes of success, failure, the death of the American dream, the price of conformity, and the conflicted nature of the relationship between American society and the salesman are ones that Andy found his colleagues could relate to. Deeply steeped in and influenced by Greek tragedy, Arthur Miller identified the poignant paradox of his Everyman, Willy Loman. Historian Tim Spears (1995, 7) points out that "in selling product and self, the salesman proved humanly fallible, yet he constantly tried to create himself anew and became something more." Miller's Willy Loman was situated firmly in the cultural myth of the continually traveling salesman who epitomized the transient, continuously moving nature of the American people in the late eighteenth and early nineteenth centuries: everywhere was movement, and movement, by definition, was a good thing that meant progress. Progress meant expansion. Expansion meant growth. Growth meant money. Willy was impervious to the scale of rapid change in American business. His hero, Singleman, is a salesman in his eighties whom Willy reminisces about meeting him when he was a young man. Singleman is so remarkable for the young Willy because he was seemingly able to do what Willy is trying and failing to do as he approaches old age: to conduct face-to-face, personality- and relationship-based selling in the era of mass commercial culture. Ultimately, Miller's play is an existential one concerning a loss of self. In Willy's obsession with being upwardly mobile, in assimilating his dreams of success with the iconic American cultural dream, with urging his sons to be "well liked" over everything else, he sacrifices his soul: "death of a salesman" becomes "the loss of self implicit in the dynamics of commercial travelling" (Spears 1995, 117). Willy's loss of selfhood manifests itself in his confused visions, his communicating with long-dead relatives and friends, his betrayal of his long-suffering wife, and his confusion or rather conflation of home and business. Andy found that the 1985 production with Dustin Hoffman and John Malkovich brought the play alive in ways that offered a richer experience than a simple reading.

Willy Loman and students' reaction to him

Before I turn to Andy's (and other students') reactions to *Death of a Salesman*, I think it would be helpful to provide a summary of the play and to expand on the historical context broached in the previous section. *Death of a Salesman* (1949) is the story of a late-middle-aged man Willy Loman who cannot connect with his sons and neglects his wife. In the 1985 version Andy used with his coachees, Dustin Hoffman plays Willy as a shuffling, shambolic, broken man who veers from mumbling self-pity to aggressive, obnoxious shouting in an instant. He is a salesman from an unnamed New York borough, most likely Brooklyn, who is tired of driving all the time back and forth from his New England patch. His grown-up sons, Biff, a one-time high school football star and now maudlin failure and Happy, a shallow, spendthrift womanizer, live with their parents in a cramped, wood-peeling tenement house. Willy's wife, Linda, unaware of his womanizing activities while in New England, is a passive-aggressive stocking-darner, forever colluding in her husband's delusions and self-deceptions and admonishing her sons to worship him as a provider and a successful and sociable personality, which is the image he projects of himself when he is not screaming inane verbiage at his older son, Biff, or muttering darkly at strangers or begging and alternatively threatening the boss who fires him. Throughout the play, there are intimations that Willy has contemplated suicide. Biff confronts him with a rubber hose that could be attached to a car's exhaust pipe. The tone of the play, despite the nagging and petty concerns of the characters, is elegiac. Willy's death, off stage, by suicide is transcendent and moving. In the end, a play about cultural values in decline and an Everyman crushed between the Scylla and Charybdis of an uncaring universe and his own distorted, self-absorbed psyche haunts viewers (and readers) with its unflinching analysis of family. Although the setting of the Great Depression and its attendant issues of labor rights, political radicalization, and social class struggle may seem light years away from the hyperconnected twenty-first-century business model, *Death of a Salesman* still has much to say about power relations, faith, conformity, family, and love. In many ways it is the ideal text to use in a coaching conversation, particularly with people working in sales.

As a writer, Arthur Miller listened to, reveled in, and assimilated the stories he heard all of his life into his artistic creations. Two such stories told by relatives might have contained the kernel of *Death of a Salesman.* His mother told him the story of a Depression-era relative who became successful but obsessively paranoid and ended up hanging himself in a barn. Miller learned as well about a relative who was successful and one day dropped dead at the beach. After being unsuccessfully resuscitated by a hunchback doctor, the dead man was transported by the doctor in his car back to his family's house. Apparently the family screamed hysterically at the doctor, horrified by his hunchback. Miller started to question the arbitrariness of fate, the capricious nature of success, the absurdity of death, the meaninglessness of life (Bigsby 2008). Jeffrey Mason (2014) is convinced that Miller was shaped by the Depression, leftist politics, the labor movement, and class conflict. *Death of a Salesman* reveals those undercurrents and more: Miller perceived that "reputation and image trump deeds and transactions" (Mason 2014, 336) and that the choices we make reveal the spirit of our souls.

So why did Miller choose a salesman to convey these heady ideas? The choice was certainly not arbitrary. Tim Spears (1995) explains that the salesman was a kind of cultural middleman, a creature of American historical consciousness, an emblem of US links to the past and future modern business success. His father had been in the garment industry and had, during a particularly fallow period, begged money from his Broadway playwright son. Willy Loman is the center of a tragedy "which elevated a discarded salesman to the centre not only of his universe, but of ours" (Bigsby 2008, 322). Willy is an idealist, a true believer, a desperate egotist, and a relentless searcher. Harold Pinter went to see the London production in 1949 and commented

> Jewish people took it very much to heart, the whole idea of selling and going down the drain, of life falling apart. It touched a real vein in the Jewish

> community in London. They were keen to see it and make it their own but at the same time not all of them approved of it because it was a question of defeat. They found it very worrying.
>
> (Bigsby 2008, 337)

Jeffrey Mason (2014, 336–7) calls Willy "the lonely man of his time [who] places his faith in essence and so cannot see that he moves in a world where only actions and accomplishments count." In a coaching dialogue, Willy is a character within whom we can project a range of meanings and interpretations. The play's long-standing success suggests its ability to encompass a diversity of cultural, political, and psychological interpretations.

The interviews I conducted with my students who had used Miller's play in their coaching sessions build up a picture of the ways that it was able to capture their coachees' and indeed their own imagination. The play emerged as a tool for enhancing introspective dialogue particularly because of the ways it encouraged self-reflection in both coach and coachee. Many of the coaches gave their colleagues the choice of reading the play or watching the film version. Most plumped for the second option. Andy told me that before engaging with *Death of a Salesman*, he had been convinced that money was the greatest motivator for both high and middle producers. The only difference was that money represented a means to enjoy a comfortable lifestyle for middle producers and symbolized security and even power for the top producers. It seemed that for the middle producers, money was the means for immediate gratification. For top producers, it was an existential shift in their conception of life: it meant never having to rely on anyone else. Watching and reading the play had an effect on Andy's thinking about coaching. He said,

> I started to think about my own life and what had been driving me to be a top producer. I realized that it wasn't money so much but a sense of autonomy I derive from mastering my craft and consistently achieving the top spot. Money is simply a given. Miller understood that it is mastery over one's fate that motivates some people and if we coach all of our producers to improve their skills and embrace mastery over their profession, their sense of autonomy will give them the kind of validation that leads to success. The paradox for me is that a play about failure in family, business and self-knowledge can be used as a touchstone for discussions on winning, being the best and competitive goal setting.

Andy's discovery of the value of Miller's play in emphasizing the crucial role autonomy plays in our lives and the empowerment that such an emphasis on autonomy could give his coachees also chimed with the feedback that my other coaching students reported from their own use of the play.

Anton worked for a large global telecommunications firm and despaired that coaching was not part of what he called "the company's DNA." He believed that the company's recent downturn and seemingly unstoppable descent were due to the lack of using "dream-based propositions" in its strategy. He told me that he saw his company's apparently intractable problems clearly: "They need to work out what dreams they have which would impact on the lives of their customers. How do they want to have a positive change? They need to base their incubation business on dream based propositions." Anton cited Elon Musk as a successful businessman who used dream-based propositions as a starting point. According to Anton, the Tesla motor vehicle was not a goal in itself and was not based on customer demand but was conceived by the dream of providing sustainable energy production: "When a company or individual has a strong idea of how he wants to change the world, there needs to be a belief, a dream that there is a better way to do something." The problem with his company, as he saw it, was that neither dream-based propositions nor coaching was encouraged. Anton responded to the challenge of using Miller's play in coaching sessions with members of his team with enthusiasm. He thought that an innovative coaching session structured around the play would model the kind of dream-based solutions he believed the company should be investing in.

In a series of interviews I conducted with Anton that were scheduled at the end of each of his coaching sessions, I was able to gauge the impact of *Death of a Salesman* on the reflection-based discussions he had been having with his team. Anton reported that the play was an excellent vehicle to use when discussing morality. He was convinced that morality played an essential role in dream-based propositions and was therefore an important component in his coaching discussions. Anton believed that the reluctance of senior management to experiment with dream-based propositions was rooted in fear. Micromanagement and mistrust, he believed, are their moral guides: "In terms of morality, I am personally quite a believer of living with high moral standards for my personal piece of mind as well as for the principle to do good and to receive good. In the way I coach and manage people, I reflect that by always sharing with people what my values are. Morality is the key to life." I asked him what he and his team thought was wrong with Willy. He told me that people answered the following: "Willy has no sense of reality and is dishonest"; "He is not self-aware"; "He lives his life in a negative spiral which typically leads, at work at least, to hidden agendas, dispersed teams, lack of focus, distrust and micro-managing"; "No one in the play has identified the values by which they want to live"; "Willy puts unnecessary pressure on others and is verbally and physically abusive towards his family"; "He takes suffering to an art form." That last comment, to my mind, captures Miller's creative intentions. All of the dishonesty and subterfuge that Anton and his team detected in the Loman family ties in with Miller's insistence that healthy relationships are predicated on honest introspection. The comment on suffering made me reflect on Miller's time in analysis, an exercise he deemed useful but repetitive, thinking that psychiatry's emphasis on neutralizing suffering was counterproductive. Suffering was valuable and even necessary for creativity (Miller 1987). What emerged from Anton's feedback about his coaching sessions was how useful Miller's play had been in encouraging his team to reflect on the qualities that inhibit productive working relations. Anton observed that his coaching sessions before had been structured around to-do lists for self-improvement. What had been missing was a frank discussion of his team members' frailties. Willy Loman provided an opportunity for his colleagues to perceive the worst imaginable traits in a working environment amplified. Willy was a lesson in what not to do, how not to behave. One of Anton's colleagues reported that seeing Willy in action had reminded her of how she had behaved on a recent occasion – in an admittedly exaggerated form – and had opened her eyes to the impact of her conduct on those around her. Anton remarked that his colleague's self-critical admission was unprecedented in its honesty. In his coaching sessions, he had never witnessed a colleague being so frank about her perceived personal weaknesses. Miller's play was clearly tapping into a previously unexplored well of openness in this particular coachee. He remarked that she had been "cagey" and unwilling to engage in the sessions before and that their discussion after watching the play was the "first time she seemed really tuned in."

Another of Anton's coachees said that what he found particularly useful about the play is that it shows the way our acts can have unintended consequences for those around us. He observed that "Willy caused more sufferance than he himself experienced" and that a "recognition of how this happened could help managers in the organization to have a deeper understanding of how their language influenced and actually inhibited the creativity of junior colleagues."

The following exchange encapsulates what Anton and his team identified as Willy's negative spiral, his lack of self-awareness, his ambivalent moral code, his self-inflicted pain:

Willy: Oh, I'll knock 'em dead next week. I'll go to Hartford. I'm very well liked in Hartford. You know, the trouble is, Linda, people don't seem to take to me.

(*They move onto the forestage.*)

Linda: Oh, don't be foolish.

Willy: I know it when I walk in. They seem to laugh at me.

Linda: Why? Why would they laugh at you? Don't talk that way, Willy.

(*Willy moves to the edge of the stage. Linda goes into the kitchen and starts to darn stockings.*)

Willy: I don't know the reason for it, but they just pass me by. I'm not noticed.

Linda: But you're doing wonderful, dear. You're making seventy to a hundred dollars a week.

Willy: But I gotta be at it ten, twelve hours a day. Other men – I don't know – they do it easier. I don't know why – I can't stop myself – I talk too much. A man oughta come in with a few words. One thing about Charley. He's a man of few words, and they respect him.

Linda: You don't talk too much, you're just lively.

Willy (smiling):	Well, I figure, what the hell, life is short, a couple of jokes. *(To himself.)* I joke too much *(The smile goes.)*
Linda:	Why? You're . . .
Willy:	I'm fat. I'm very – foolish to look at, Linda. I didn't tell you, but Christmas time I happened to be calling on F. H. Stewarts, and a salesman I know, as I was going in to see the buyer I heard him say something about – walrus. And I – I cracked him right across the face. I won't take that. I simply will not take that. But they do laugh at me. I know that.
Linda:	Darling . . .
Willy:	I gotta overcome it. I know I gotta overcome it. I'm not dressing to advantage, maybe.
Linda:	Willy, darling, you're the handsomest man in the world . . .
Willy:	Oh, no, Linda.
Linda:	To me you are. *(Slight pause.)* The handsomest.
	(*From the darkness is heard the laughter of a woman. Willy doesn't turn to it, but it continues through Linda's lines.*)
Linda:	And the boys, Willy. Few men are idolized by their children the way you are.
	(*Music is heard as behind a scrim, to the left of the house; The Woman, dimly seen, is dressing.*)
Willy (with great feeling):	You're the best there is, Linda, you're a pal, you know that? On the road – on the road I want to grab you sometimes and just kiss the life outa you.
	(*The laughter is loud now, and he moves into a brightening area at the left, where The Woman has come from behind the scrim and is standing, putting on her hat, looking into a "mirror" and laughing.*)
Willy:	Cause I get so lonely – especially when business is bad and there's nobody to talk to. I get the feeling that I'll never sell anything again, that I won't make a living for you, or a business, a business for the boys.
	(Miller 2015, 2340–1)[1]

His gargantuan and frankly rebarbative self-pity and his wife Linda's collusion highlight the pathos of the human condition, that of suffering. The greatest challenge for all of us is how to live a meaningful life, and Anton and his team were able to identify Willy's problem of not being able to live a meaningful life. When we discuss "values," "morality," "self-awareness," "distrust," and "suffering" and we read or hear Willy's plaintive phrases – "people don't seem to take to me," "I talk too much," "life is short" – we are discussing the human soul and its incessant search for meaningfulness amidst the appointments, the meetings, the e-mails, the end-of-year reports, the flotsam, jetsam, and detritus of our working lives. We all suffer, and maybe, as Miller suggests, *need* to suffer, but that suffering also needs to be transformative – it needs to provide a depth and heft to the structure of our lives. It needs to support us in leading a life worth living.

Willy's tragedy does not lie in his suffering but in his obstinate determination to cower in a cave of his own unenlightened making. The prolific author and psychiatrist Irving Yalom (2013) believes we all – despite outward success – suffer from the pain of existence. People want to be loved, to be respected, to be healthy, to be young again, to accomplish something lasting. Coaching is not therapy, and as coaches, we are not equipped to address deep seated and even dangerous obsessions and issues, but we must be attentive to the fact that in coaching, although everyone's story unfolds differently, the stories have "roots stretching down to the bedrock of existence" (Yalom 2013, 4). To be alive is to suffer, and our responsibility to our clients, our team members, and our students is to support them in accepting a steady and lucid gaze at reality and in rejecting false certainties, neat solutions, and treacherous assumptions.

I asked Anton if he and his team had any ideas on how to coach Willy. Anton was unequivocal:

> I may sympathize with Willy's feeling of dependence on a broken economic system and his struggle to support his family, but any coaching I would do for him would depend on his own path to self-awareness. I would coach on self-awareness and on the management of expectations. Only when people realise who they are is there then a basis on which the coach and coachee can build a plan on how they can take the next steps in life.

He and his team devised some preliminary questions they thought could promote beneficial change in Willy's worldview:

> How do you see yourself? Why?
> How do you think others see you? How do you know?
> What does the value of honesty mean to you?
> Do you live by the value of honesty?
> Is there something you would like to change about yourself?
> What do you think others would like to change about you?

Anton mentioned that he thought Willy encapsulated the rigid traits of fear and lack of risk taking that encapsulated his senior management's reluctance to embrace the concept of dream propositions in his company. Anton's colleague from the same coaching cohort, Spencer, made an astute observation. He deemed Willy a "lost cause" and "uncoachable" for the following reasons:

> Willy is in the early stages of dementia (a lot of the play has him talking to his long lost brother). My limited knowledge of people experiencing dementia is

> that their focus is on past events and people and there is little to no attention paid to the present and even less to the future. Even if we rule out dementia, Willy wouldn't accept coaching. He wouldn't accept an offer of a job from his neighbor – he felt it was failure to accept help. Of course he is immersed in feelings of failure and all he has are memories. I would suggest that Willy has reached the time in his life when coaching couldn't give him what he wanted. He is too far gone into his illusions and fantasy life. On the other hand, Biff would make an ideal coaching candidate. He has the character to examine his failings and a future in which he could explore how we could increase his confidence and self-knowledge.

Can some people resist coaching? Are there some people who remain, as Spencer puts it, "uncoachable"? That idea is an intriguing one that I will follow up in an upcoming section, but before I turn to coaching – or not coaching – dysfunctional characters, I would like to make a valuable detour into the realms of emotion.

Our emotional response to Willy

Emotions may not equate to evaluative judgments, but they do include some kind of judgment: an appraisal is necessary for an emotion. Jenefer Robinson (2005, 26) makes the point that "whatever the evaluations in an emotion are, they are evaluations of what we want, what we care about, what our interests are." How can reading or watching a performance of *Death of a Salesman* teach us about the role of emotions in coaching? Anton, his team members, and Spencer worked at a global telecommunications company that gave a perfunctory nod to coaching – there was no formalized coaching program, although coaching was encouraged among most teams by most leaders. Of course, the company supported the students' postgraduate coaching projects, which would indicate it had a vested interest in seeing coaching strategies used to ameliorate workplace performance, among other coaching benefits inherent to performance enhancement such as finding positive intrinsic motivation, building self-efficacy, and expanding mindful awareness. Anton, his team members, and Spencer demonstrated cognitive sophistication in evaluating Willy and his family. These students had a visceral emotional response to Willy, especially, bearing out Robinson's observation that in ordinary life, we tend to weigh an emotional experience by applying a generalized label to it – "I was really angry," "I was jealous," "I was disgusted" – but that a work of art will "encourage us to reflect upon our emotions in a careful and detailed way" (Robinson 2005, 79). The careful and detailed reflection on people and situations is a vital component of good decision making. The emotions of course play a fundamental and often unexamined role in the processes by which we make decisions. Decision making in the prevailing folk psychology of the business world tends to be thought of erroneously as a purely rational act. A play like Miller's, in encouraging coachees to reflect on emotions and on their own emotions elicited by watching it, can help to cultivate a culture of attentiveness to and awareness of the emotions in the workplace. Such a cultural shift in the visibility of emotions is a way of making decision making more transparent and ultimately more accountable to relevant stakeholders. When the emotions are unspoken, they are able to influence decisions without ultimately being interrogated and weighted. The company that neglects the role of emotions is in effect hindering its capacity to make self-aware decisions.

Another of my coaching students, Eric, is a vice president of sales for a Fortune 100 company that has a substantial coaching program, which uses a range of personality and behavioral assessment tools in its performance coaching strategies. I have discussed the use of DISC in Chapter 1 and will detail my thoughts on Personalisis in my discussion of *The Leopard* in the next chapter. Predictably enough, the coaching program used at Eric's company avoids any references to emotions, but both Eric and the other students with whom I work from the company are cognizant of the role emotions play in the workplace. Work is part of life, not an emotionally hived off aspect of it. Those strong feelings of anger, regret, envy, despair, and pride, feelings that are showcased in *Death of a Salesman* and evident in most family life, have a tendency to spill over or seep into the workplace. If, as Robinson (2005) suggests, our emotions help us to understand a fictional character, then knowing how the emotions actually function will enable us to understand ourselves and each other with more accuracy. If a company like Eric's is anxious to avoid stirring up powerful or even unpleasant emotions in a coaching conversation and about veering into possibly litigious therapeutic territory, there are other productive ways of bringing the emotions to the surface of a coaching dialogue. In previous chapters, I have discussed the ways in which literary works in coaching sessions can function as stand-ins that enable coaches to address delicate issues without immediately approaching them directly. A literary work can help to elicit personal reflection from a coachee that can be used to guide a potentially transformative workplace intervention. Robinson's (2005, 102) "'reader-response' theory of interpretation that treats our emotional responses to a novel or play as important data in arriving at an interpretation," offers a defense of the significance of the emotions in cognitive processes, and shows how our unexamined physiological responses to external stimuli are instrumental in how we make sense of the world. Novels can step in, Robinson (2005) suggests, as a sentimental education. They can expand the circle of empathy, training us to be alert to others' feelings and to see the world from their perspective. Literary texts like Miller's can bring a sentimental education to the realm of organizational coaching. If we accept that emotions will influence our thoughts and beliefs and that our emotional responses help us to understand a text, they are also an essential source of data for comprehending other people, like our team members or colleagues. Instead of asking tricky or uncomfortable questions directly and maybe receiving elusive or overly emotional responses, we can instead engage with literature. Instead of directly responding to our frustrated and unhappy colleagues in an encounter likely to throw up the kind of messy emotions Eric's organization is keen to avoid, we can respond to Willy Loman. If we want to help the unhappy hero, and if we, as sensitively responding readers, feel frustrated that we cannot help him, "we are in a good position to try to discover *why* we respond emotionally as we do" (Robinson 2005, 111). Being engaged in this type of deep reflection encourages us to look at the origins of our response, improving the coaching experience and keeping that necessary distance between coach and coachee. Using *Death of a Salesman* as a touchstone for conversations about failure, money, autonomy, and family helped Andy, Anton, and Eric to avoid potentially confrontational discussions with underperforming colleagues. Eric, in a session that mirrored Andy's success with using the play as a spur for self-reflection with a female colleague, reported that after using *Death of a Salesman* as a basis for a performance appraisal with one of his coachees, his coachee spontaneously opened up about his own family life and how his unhappy home life may have been distracting him at work. Together, Eric and his coachee had a discussion about how they could plan some adjustments to his work schedule to free up some time for the coachee to get to grips with his problems at home. Eric mentioned that perhaps without the stimulus of Miller's play, his coachee might not have opened up about the real difficulties that were affecting his performance and that he therefore would not have been able to help him find a solution. The text, then, whether it is Miller's play, Cheever's short story, Cather's novella, can be a stimulus, receptacle, or proxy for a range of powerful emotions that cannot readily find another outlet in a repressive working environment. The emotional education, which in Robinson's (2005) analysis is integral to the value of literary works, constitutes a powerful argument for the benefits of integrating literary texts into coaching practice.

Fiction as an alternative to self-help

Family dynamics are important, as Eric's anecdote of how he was able to help a struggling colleague makes plain. If we return to the excerpt that highlights the exchange between Willy and Linda, Willy pities himself, alternating between denigrating his appearance and character – "I'm fat," "I'm very foolish to look at," "I talk too much," "I'm not noticed" – and a false, barbaric bravado: "I cracked him right across the face," "I simply will not take that," "I want to grab you sometimes and just kiss the life outta you." Linda's role is that of a cajoling colluder: she takes the typical compliant attitude to her dominant abuser ("But you're doing wonderful, dear"; "you're just lively"; "you're the handsomest man in the world"; "few men are idolized by their children the way you are"). It is a dance of pity-soaked assertion and submissive denial that is generally heard between an exhausted, frantic parent and a spoiled adolescent desperately seeking assurance within a mutually reinforcing bond.

When I meet my postgraduate coaching students, most of them are already well acquainted with self-help and instruction books generally aligned to coaching or the field of psychology. My task is to encourage them to immerse themselves in more academic literature that is appropriate for the task of research, in part owing to the rigor of the peer-review process and also because of the level of complexity in works written for an academic audience as opposed to a more generalized, nonspecialist reading public. If students find some academic reading particularly challenging, I urge them to persist in their efforts – after all, no pain, no gain. Academic journal articles, I find, make for far stronger research in coaching than the popular best-selling books to which students tend to gravitate. Popular nonfiction on appreciation, valuing, leadership, stress, team building, and a host of topics addressing "corporate issues" makes for less analytical and less trenchant research that tends only to touch the surface of a given theme and deal with generalities. I am certainly not advocating doing away with such nonspecialist works for students in coaching, because they sometimes help students along the path of getting a solid grasp on their subject matter and substantiating their observations and opinions with validated academic theory, especially in their early stages of their academic careers. Popular reading has a place in coaching research, and many of its intuitions can in fact be supplemented or strengthened by integrating into coaching the kind of literary works I describe here.

Manfred Kets de Vries's output is an example of the well written, intellectually sound, and academically rigorous research in leadership development and organizational change that can be helpfully combined with the literary fictional coaching perspective I am advocating here. In his 2016 book that purports to help coaches to be more effective by presenting several profiles of toxic executives and then offering expert advice on working with these difficult people, Kets de Vries sets out a series of insightful categories of "toxic executives" that bear a number of striking commonalities with the characters in *Death of a Salesman.* A few illustrative cases should help to clarify exactly how literary works constitute such a rich source of the diverse and sometimes extreme personalities we encounter in organizations and, in turn, how we can utilize these works as an experiential archive of coaching practice.

Kets de Vries (2016, 7) profiles Simon, the quintessential narcissist, who is typical of the narcissistic personality in being "driven by grandiose fantasies about themselves [who] are selfish, inconsiderate, require excessive attention [and] have a sense of entitlement." Simon lives in a "binary world" in which he perceives people as being either out to get him or on his side. Doris is a detached executive who is avoidant with "a great capacity for rationalization" (Kets de Vries 2016, 18). The detached are also experts at deluding themselves and are socially inhibited and have rock-bottom self-esteem. Don, the paranoid executive, feels perennially threatened, distorts information, and engages in delusional thinking. Don has trust issues, feelings of inadequacy, and a dysfunctional outlook. When Kets de Vries meets him, the psychologist recognizes "an undertone of hostility, stubbornness, and sarcasm in the way he talked [. . .] he also seemed depressed. In spite of putting a positive spin on things, I think he knew things weren't going the way they should" (Kets de Vries 2016, 27). The bipolar or cyclomythic executive is "dominated by soaring highs and melancholy lows" (Kets de Vries 2016, 32). Frank has embarked on a number of affairs, is reluctant to admit his behavior is unacceptable, and exhibits "emotional and behavioral volatility" that is starting to impact negatively on the firm (Kets de Vries 2016, 32). Arnold, the psychopathic executive, has no sense of responsibility toward others, is blind to his shortcomings, and always deflects issues when confronted. Arnold is a habitual liar who is full of empty promises. The passive-aggressive executive has little self-confidence and is more often than not seething with anger but, like Mary, is unable to express that anger openly. Mary agrees to requests, but she expresses resentment by making excuses, being forgetful, and procrastinating. She is superficially compliant and well-meaning but bottles up her feelings. In fact, she consistently lacks insight into her own feelings. Accustomed to avoiding responsibility, she is unable to acknowledge her strengths and has a poor self-image and extremely low confidence. There is a lot of Simon, the narcissist; Doris, the detached; Don, the paranoid; and Frank, the bipolar or cyclomythic executive in Willy Loman. We can hear Simon's selfishness, Doris's delusion, Don's dysfunction, and Frank's behavioral volatility in the following exchange between Willy and his neighbor Charley:

Willy: Did you see the ceiling I put up in the living room?
Charley: Yes, that's a piece of work. To put up a ceiling is a mystery to me. How do you do it?
Willy: What's the difference?
Charley: Well, talk about it.
Willy: You gonna put up a ceiling?
Charley: How could I put up a ceiling?
Willy: Then why the hell are you bothering me for?
Charley: You're insulted again.
Willy: A man who cannot handle tools is not a man. You're disgusting.
(Miller 2007, 2344)

Willy Loman exhibits many of the destructive and unpleasant personality characteristics of Simon, Doris, Don, and Frank but little of the verbal dexterity and slick articulacy that I suspect Kets de Vries's clients possess. Willy is meant to be inarticulate, a man who struggles to express himself, to make himself understood. Arthur Miller wanted his play to be radical and innovative. The other characters are meant to be perplexed by the final day of a man they never understood. Miller "wanted to take his audience on an internal journey through the mind, memoirs, fears, anxieties of his central character, locating these in the context of those he encounters both in fact and in imagination" (Bigsby 2008, 319). The play is poetic, experimental, nonlinear and, of course, deeply personal to the playwright. It is about family. Here is Happy giving his brother Biff advice after Biff made a mess of a longed-for interview that would have led to a job to help the family:

Happy: Say you have a lunch date with Oliver tomorrow.
Biff: So what do I do tomorrow?
Happy: You leave the house tomorrow and come back at night and say Oliver is thinking it over. And he thinks it over for a couple of weeks, and gradually it fades away and nobody's the worse.

Biff: But it'll go on forever!
Happy: Dad is never so happy as when he is looking forward to something.

(Miller 2007, 2375)

We can detect the essence of Kets de Vries's Arnold in Miller's Happy. Like Arnold, Happy lacks responsibility, undermines others with subtle innuendo, and tells people what they want to hear. For Happy and Arnold, the ends invariably justify the means. Like Kets de Vries's Mary, Willy's wife, Linda, bottles her emotions. Willy has been planting seeds in inhospitable urban soil in the dead of the night in the backyard, while Linda accuses her sons of abandoning their father physically and emotionally. Willy enters the house:

Linda (to Willy): Did you plant, dear?
Biff: (at the door, to Linda): All right, we had it out. I'm going and I'm not writing anymore.
Linda: (going to Willy in the kitchen): I think that's the best way, dear. 'Cause there's no drawing it out, you'll never get along.

(Miller 2007, 2386)

Kets de Vries's advice to passive-aggressive Mary could easily be applied to Linda: "I need to help her realize how her passive-aggressive behavior was affecting others negatively. She had to find better ways to control her anger and anxiety and to learn to express her feelings more directly" (Kets de Vries 2016, 56).

Biff, the most articulate and direct character in Miller's play, seems refreshingly free of obvious neuroses and does not easily fit into any of Kets de Vries's toxic executive categories. Although he had once been a football star, a great golden hope and more popular than Willy could ever dream of being, he had walked in on one of his father's assignations at a Boston hotel and had been seemingly scarred since. This particular father–son dynamic is as emotionally fraught as tainted with betrayal. The play of course is very personal. Miller's father had been in sales and had been ruined during the Depression: the relationship between the four characters is not that far removed from those in Miller's early life. Like Biff, Miller had even flunked mathematics – twice (Bigsby 2008). Kets de Vries, like Miller, does not shy away from delving into the family dynamics of his toxic personalities. Kets de Vries recognizes that the anger children feel for their parents can manifest itself in the adult workplace. He perceives that strained relationships at work have their roots in our dysfunctional patterns of thinking, nurtured and reinforced by specific unhealthy family dynamics. He pragmatically points out the fact that in order to help clients get a sense of pleasure in and control over their lives, they need to explore their long-buried feelings and motives and reflect on the fact that our personal histories impact on how we think and act. With passive-aggressive Mary, Kets de Vries decided to discuss her family dynamics to help her to "understand the reasons why she was the person she was [and to help her] identify events that triggered certain insecurities, fears, and anxieties" (Kets de Vries 2016, 57).

Ultimately, it is the role of a coach to understand how the irrational and the unconscious affect our behavior. We can read about Mary and learn a great deal about how to close the gap between desired and actual behaviors. There is a wealth of professional insight and therapeutic wisdom proffered as Kets de Vries puts Mary, Don, Frank, and the others under his probing, forensic, and yet sympathetic gaze. And yet there is a sense in Kets de Vries's work that Mary, Don, Frank, and alike are one dimensional. They are categories that become the receptacles for dysfunctional traits. There is also something slightly supercilious about tying up human beings with their manifest complexities, contradictions, and mysteries into neatly labeled neuroses and presenting them as case studies. To my mind, one of the most powerful, entertaining, and humane ways of recognizing that what people say and what people do can be radically different is through the means of fiction. The largest part of human behavior is unconscious, the gargantuan iceberg under the water line, which a writer like Arthur Miller can actually bring to the surface. The medium of literary fiction can function as a catalogue of life's idiosyncratic personality traits much like Kets de Vries's case studies. It offers a universe of strange and remote beings, beings that are infinitely different from us and yet at the same time made to feel so similar. In a literary work like Miller's, we see the world from a character's perspective, and the work fosters our acquaintance with them in ways that we sometimes feel as if we know them. The difference between Kets de Vries's neurotic people and Arthur Miller's is that Miller humanizes his. Through his writing craft, Miller gives us a means to empathize with them. Long after we've forgotten Simon, Doris, Don, and Frank, there will always be Willy Loman shouting out his contradictory, fractious messages, bullying his sons and wife, pitifully stumbling to oblivion, but always surviving in our imagination. Arthur Miller has dramatized a "toxic" executive, and it is the dramatization that allows us to enter the world of someone like Willy imaginatively. Willy is "Everyman," and I suspect that not only do we recognize Willy, we also recognize facets of Willy in ourselves.

"Uncoachable" Willy and resistance to coaching

Is Willy, as one of my coaching students, Spencer, put it, uncoachable? Are there people who resist coaching? Howard Guttman (2007, 14) defines coachability as "the willingness to enter one's discomfort zone to change behavior." For Guttman, this precise ability is a marker of success, and encouraging it should not be left to professional coaches: the leader of the organization or team needs to get the less-than-ideally-performing members to close the gap between what they are doing and what needs to be done. There are cases of executives who resist coaching because they refuse to acknowledge their shortcomings. Guttman points out that executives resist what he terms "reinventing themselves" and the concomitant rising to meet ever greater challenges. Guttman argues that these executives shy away from or avoid their discomfort zone because they are unclear about the benefits of confronting their negative learned behaviors or perhaps are distrustful about the rationale for changing their behaviors. Guttman devises a series of questions designed to ascertain whether a team member is coachable. Three of the eight seem applicable to Miller's protagonist, Willy: Do they defend the status quo? Do they cling to self-limiting stories about themselves? Are they stuck in the past? Willy might seem the perfect candidate for Guttman's final analysis scenario, in which an individual who cannot let go of an unproductive story needs to exit the company.

In their analysis of the field of sales performance, Shannahan, Shannahan, and Bush (2013) emphasize the qualities of trust, respect, flexibility, adaptability, and openness as the markers of a coachable individual. The authors advance the following proposition: "Salespeople who exhibit higher degrees of achievement, motivation, agreeableness, and conscientiousness will be more coachable than those who exhibit lower degrees of these personality traits" (Shannahan, Shannahan, and Bush 2013, 414). Shannahan, Shannahan, and Bush's proposition suggests that some people are more coachable than others. The ingredient needed to move people to being more rather than less coachable is transformational leadership. However, the authors sustain that if a salesperson's coachability is low, transformational leadership will have little effect on his or her performance. They conclude that in spite of an empowering and inspirational leader, an individual who is not willing to be coached will resist coaching. Spencer may have been right, then, when he used Willy as an example of someone who is not coachable. Precisely because he is not trusting, respectful, open, and flexible, Willy may simply not be coachable. Or, if we conceive of Willy as one of those toxic executives in charge of coaching others, no matter how coachable these team members are, they will "find themselves in the situation of a leadership style that does not elicit their coachability" (Shannahan, Shannahan, and Bush 2013, 417). But in using fictional characters to enhance coaching practice in organizations, the question is not so simplistic as how to coach a given character or the extent to which an irascible and seemingly intractable character may be coachable or not. The question to my mind is not whether Willy is coachable or how we could coach him. The question rather should be phrased like this: how can we use Willy to examine the nature and reality of coaching and *Death of a Salesman* as a rich alternative to the self-help books in order to explore the roots and manifestation of individual unhappiness at work? Willy, as we have seen from the testimonies of my coaching students who exposed their coachees to *Death of a Salesman* in their organizations, functions as a cipher for coaching discussions. He can stimulate self-exploration and deep introspection. He can be used as a proxy to initiate difficult conversations. He exhibits facets of the personalities we encounter in the workplace and indeed aspects of ourselves. Willy is, moreover, a character with the weight of a past as well as a present. We learn to know him through his own words and through those with whom he interacts, such that our perspective on Willy is as far-reaching and comprehensive as if we ourselves had been acquainted with this fictional character in person. We see Willy's flaws in all their ugly glory, but we also have infinite forgiveness and compassion for him. Our emotional engagement with Willy is a sentimental education, bringing our emotions to the center-stage of the coaching discussion.

One final example of the versatility of Miller's play in contributing to the practice of organizational coaching will help to illustrate precisely how varied and far reaching the applications of literary fiction truly are. One of my students completed a coaching module and had the choice of finishing the master's program with a postgraduate certification or continuing to complete his master's by investigating a coaching solution to his work challenges. Barry had informal and formal experience in coaching but was concerned that he was unable, in his words, to "foster the coachee's ability to resolve their challenges." Barry remained unconvinced that coaching, as it was practiced at his organization, a medium-sized, UK–based sales solution company, was even effective. His company had adopted what he called a solutions-focused approach to coaching as it "applies to a sales environment." The model, as he described it, consisted of setting out a fictional problem for the coachee, asking the coachee to give his perspective on the problem, and then the coach would "guide" the coachee to come up with a solution. The problems with such an approach to coaching are self-evident. The idea that the coach is simply the locus of wisdom that can be emulated by the coachee in a one-size-fits-all approach stifles the kind of transformational self-development that coaches can inspire by allowing coachees the intellectual space to come up with innovative solutions themselves. I persuaded Barry to use Arthur Miller's play as inspiration to try to improve his organization's coaching model. Barry saw that his organization's approach had a "firm foundation in adult learning theory," and although in his view it has repeatedly "failed to help his coachees," he was determined to find innovative ways of improving it. He claimed that part of the problem with coaching in general was a widespread resistance to it "across the sales industry."

Part of the trouble with the coaching culture in Barry's company is undoubtedly related to the fact that it is perceived as a means of providing solutions to problems. Robert Goldberg (2005) has identified a resistance to coaching that occurs when a company conceptualizes coaching as a problem-fix. Goldberg provides a case study of a client who appeared to be resistant to coaching because he needed to "preserve his image as a strong capable person." Goldberg's client didn't want to show any vulnerability, which the admission of needing new skills would confirm (Goldberg 2005, 11). Goldberg takes the reader through his strategies – attempting to develop chemistry through a shared language, framing feedback around modulating rather than shifting behavior, describing his own personal reactions to the client – in order to effect "the power of authentic helping relationships to transform leadership performance" (Goldberg 2005, 15). Goldberg recognizes that, like clients, coaches can be resistant to change and resistant specifically to the changes brought about by coaching. He admits that despite "strong, friendly" relations with clients, his detachment had hampered the coaching relationship. It wasn't until he disclosed to his client the anger he felt about his client's behavior at a meeting that he became "authentic."

Barry was one of the few students who detected that it was his discomfiture as a coach that created a less-than-ideal coaching experience. He described his problem as "wanting to be liked" and admitted that he was fueled by the fear that if he wasn't liked, he would lose a contract: "I did my best to get clients to like me and continue to share positive feedback on our experience with their leaders." He admitted that in four years of coaching, his desire to be liked was "the single biggest mistake" he made in his coaching practice and that it had prevented him from engaging in deeper coaching conversations that could have led to "more significant transformations in my coachees." Goldberg underscores the vital component in coaching as being authentic with others, of being sure about our intentions: leadership is not simply a matter of technique but one of intentions. Barry echoed such convictions, telling me that he had become overwhelmed by fear – the fear of always trying to prove himself valuable, competent, qualified, likable. After reading *Death of a Salesman*, Barry became increasingly aware of his own personality traits that were impacting negatively on his ability to coach. He saw himself reflected in Miller's protagonist, particularly in Willy's obsession with being "well liked." Barry quoted part of the play when we had a discussion about how he might improve his coaching technique at the organization: "Willy: I'll get him a job selling. He could be big in no time. My God! Remember how they used to follow him around in high school? When he smiled at one of them their faces lit up. When he walked down the street . . ." (Miller 2007, 2330). In the passage that captured Barry's imagination, striking a chord with his own self-perception, Willy is reminiscing about his son Biff and is using this desired (and most likely distorted image) of his son for his own self-aggrandizement through his association with his own flesh and blood. Willy gives an idealized snapshot of someone who is charming and well liked. But the scene is undercut with the irony of a diminished figure singing the praises of someone else as his only claim to recognition. Barry felt that Willy was someone he could relate to: he had talked about wanting to impress his clients with what he was saying. Our all-too-human desire to be believed, to be entertaining, to be *liked* creates problems, as Barry discovered. He particularly highlighted one behavior that had been sabotaging his coaching endeavors: sharing too much of his personal life. Instead of primarily listening, Barry opted to share his experiences, believing that this openness about what happened to him was creating an atmosphere of trust. Perhaps unconsciously, he was trying to entertain and to be creative. Seeing Willy on the screen was a deeply troubling experience for him, Barry admitted. He saw so much of himself in the character and was almost embarrassed by the uncanny resemblances he had found.

Arthur Miller was familiar with underhand sales tactics as a means to survival in the Great Depression. In the crescendo of the culminating lines of the play, Biff pronounces a troubling verdict on his father. After living for so long in a charade of self-deception and feeding his father's delusions, Biff's verdict is designed to remove the scales of illusion from everybody's eyes:

Biff: I am not a leader of man, Willy, and neither are you. You were never anything but a hard-working drummer [salesman] who landed in the ash can like all the rest of them! I'm one dollar an hour, Willy! I tried seven states and couldn't raise it. A buck an hour! Do you gather my meaning? I'm not bringing home any prizes any more, and you're going to stop waiting for me to bring them home!

(Miller 2007, 2388)

Barry commented on Biff's revelation as "the only guilt-free moment in the play." Would using the *Death of a Salesman* as a touchstone help people to overcome their "resistance to coaching"? Barry had evidently been moved by what he had seen. When he reflected on his own coaching practice in the context of Miller's play, he was able to see how his own conduct had hindered some of his work with the coachees in his organization. Barry thought that the play's theme of "being liked at all costs" could appeal to people involved in sales coaching. To him, "the play illustrates people misunderstanding each other, not listening to each other, not facing reality, and instead believing in fantasy. Of course, sometimes there is an air of unreality in the selling process."

Robert Goldberg realized that he wasn't being authentic with his client – he had wanted to be seen as the fount of wisdom rather than as someone with real feelings. The value of engaging with *Death of a Salesman* from the perspective of a coach is that we can become aware of our own resistance to coaching. When we perceive with clarity the ways that our behavior impacts on those around us, in an introspective movement that the play encourages in spectators, we are on the path to uncovering a more authentic coaching practice that takes account of our own limitations. Barry ultimately envisaged his master's project as a bid to redesign coaching in his organization around plays like Miller's. The experience of reading and watching the play had illuminated his own practice as a coach, and he was convinced it could have a similar effect on his colleagues. For Barry, the power of a play like Miller's was found to some extent in the characters' raw, vulnerable, and at times uncontrollable emotions. Barry focused on the emotion of guilt in the play because of his own guilt in recognizing that he eschewed what was really happening with his clients and instead opted to offer advice to bolster his ego and to be thought of as a fount of wisdom. Barry was not unique. I found that sales coaches in general had a particular response to *Death of a Salesman*. Unsurprisingly, because of the sales theme, their response is visceral, direct, and very emotional. Success, money, morality, and conformism are themes that surface again and again. Yet alienation, guilt, and anger are there as well. After Biff confronts Willy with their respective inadequacies in a passionate, heartfelt speech, Willy responds without reflection, "You vengeful, spiteful mut!" (Miller 2007, 2388). Visceral, direct, and very emotional. And by its very example of a total lack of introspection, Willy's statement has the effect of encouraging our own. Willy's blindness to himself is so obvious that we are forced to question our own self-awareness.

Miller's insistence on voice

Roger Scruton (2010, 186) reminds us that there is a style of writing that will always be considered "profound." It can be utter gibberish, but as long as it is subversive and unintelligible, the work will be praised (Scruton 2010, 186). Scruton is exaggerating for effect, but there is a grain of truth here in that so many students resist reading the academic articles we as educators implore them to read. They instead cling to their arsenal of best-selling business and coaching-related books, their hackneyed and simplistic models and formulas for success, which they so rarely have the confidence to question or at least problematize. Students need guidance in evaluating what makes rigorous research, reasoned argument, falsifiable methods. They need help to be able to separate the wheat from the chaff. Students need to be encouraged to trust their judgment that something that they are reading that is dense and difficult to follow is probably not worth pursuing. Ideas may be complex, but the way they are rendered must be clear and straightforward: coherent and cogent prose is the holy grail for students to read, and, in turn, to produce. *Death of a Salesman* is not narrative prose, but there are still lessons for the attentive student to learn from Miller's use of voice and his style of writing. First of all, the play is innovative in form – it is structurally experimental, especially in its depiction of time as nonlinear. To demonstrate how we perceive reality, how time circles around in our thinking, how simultaneity is nearly always present in our minds, Miller decided that he would "take his audience on an internal journey through the mind, memories, fears, anxieties of his central character, locating these entities in the context of those people he encounters both in fact and in imagination" (Bigsby 2008, 319). This experimental technique is a relevant one for examining our own coaching techniques.

We should encourage our students to experiment with form and with time. At times, they are able to recognize that going with the flow of a conversation, following its meandering streams and tributaries, creates a much more effective coaching space than one dictated by preset questions and almost anticipated responses. There is a rhythm to the play, especially to Willy's troubled mind, that can remind those involved in coaching that a less constricted, more fluid structure to the give and take of conversation is likely to elicit more information and engender more intimacy and trust. There is no extraneous fat in the play. Words are there to convey meaning; they are not there for decorative effect. Even though the characters are not educated or articulate, their struggle is never verbose but precise. The dialogue is crafted for dramatic effect.

Because Miller started out in radio, he was accustomed to how important it was to get one's message across succinctly. In a 2003 interview, he described the importance of being able to write with an eye on brevity – learning how to condense material was crucial: "Less is better. Why? It's very simple. It's like dreams. Dreams are very brief and some of them you never forget because they are very discrete. Nothing is wasted. No dream has got excessive material. It all counts" (Bigsby 2008, 211). From Melville, the whaler, to Cather, the journalist, Cheever, the magazine writer, and now to Miller, who worked for years in warehouses, American writers have been known to want to validate their work by appealing to their endurance of a lived experience. Work and its attendant sorrows and drama are never far from their core themes. The lived experience of writers such as Arthur Miller can provide a rich and satisfying way of entering a coaching conversation. Miller never lost sight of the value of both personal and collective responsibility, which, to my mind, is the cornerstone of what coaching is all about.

Final thoughts

I started this chapter by stating that Arthur Miller used family dynamics to examine how human beings communicate: he explored how we can remain separate yet be part of the world. We have seen some of the ways in which *Death of a Salesman* might be included on the reading list for a coaching curriculum and why. Miller's careful exposition of his characters' emotions accounts for a good deal of the value that can be derived from the play as a stimulus for coaching discussions. As readers, we are able to trace the emotional processes exhibited by the characters, and we have seen why this is important in coaching. Good decision making encompasses an emotional component: we may use rational strategies, but we also appraise and re-appraise situations emotionally. A work such as *Death of a Salesman* encourages us to reflect on our emotions: from such works of art, we learn how to be attentive to human emotions.

Emotions are so vital to our understanding and experiencing our world that natural scientists are keen to investigate which other creatures share similar appraisals of their environment. The octopus, for example and perhaps surprisingly, is said to express itself eloquently. Sy Montgomery (2015, 83) has been studying octopuses and has concluded that, like humans, they possess the ability to "ascribe thoughts to others [which is] a sophisticated cognitive skill, known as 'theory of mind.'" I mention the octopus because this self-awareness, this ability to differentiate between what we think and what others think, is such an essential aspect of coaching. The reason Barry's coaching interventions were unsatisfactory was because of his overreliance on giving advice. He was unable to "get into the head" of his clients and wasn't tapping into the knowledge that the other individual had. Kets de Vries's toxic executives uniformly resist empathy, while Sy Montgomery (2015, 123) relates that the neuroscientist Antonio Demasio has claimed that anemones, who have no brains and the smallest trace of a nervous system, demonstrate emotions such as "joy and sadness." My excursion into the animal kingdom is germane to my argument. If naturalists are not only curious about the inner experiences of these sea creatures but also convinced that they possess a "separate, holy, mysterious, private theater" in their minds (Montgomery 2015,

112), then we coaches need to be equally attuned to the minds of our coachees, for it is surely the extent of our curiousness about and dexterity in mapping others' minds that makes us human. In literary works, we have a powerful tool for exploring the intimacy of our fellow beings, and coaches would do well to realize the potential of this tool in their practices.

In my work as an educator in corporate coaching and in corporate sales coaching, I see too often people wanting to play it safe, relying on simplistic models and conforming to the tried and tested practices that don't rock the corporate boat. Such models will struggle to capture what Montgomery (2005, 112) refers to as "separate, holy, mysterious, private theater" that resides in each of our coachees and clients. Coaching to a conformist and even rigid corporate model will inevitably yield less-than-ideal results: skimming the surface of each other's consciousness will always be a mean substitute for the treasures of literary exploration.

Note

1 From "Act One" from DEATH OF A SALESMAN by Arthur Miller, copyright 1949, renewed @ 1977 by Arthur Miller. Used by permission of Viking Books, an imprint of Penguin Publishing Group, a division of Penguin Random House LLC. All rights reserved.

References

Bigsby, Christopher. 2008. *Arthur Miller: 1915–1962*. London: Weidenfeld and Nicolson.

Goldberg, Robert A. 2005. "Resistance to Coaching." *Organization Development Journal* 23 (1): 9–16.

Guttman, Howard. 2007. "Coachability." *Leadership Excellence* 24 (6): 14.

Kets de Vries, Manfred. 2016. *You Will Meet a Tall, Dark Stranger: Executive Coaching Challenges*. London: Palgrave Macmillan.

Mason, Jeffrey D. 2014. "Arthur Miller: A Radical Politics of the Soul." In *The Oxford Handbook of American Drama*, edited by Jeffrey Richards and Heather Nathans, 322–39. Oxford: Oxford University Press.

Miller, Arthur. 1987. *Timebends: A Life*. New York: Grove.

Miller, Arthur. 2007. "*Death of a Salesman*." In *The Norton Anthology of American Literature*, edited by Nina Baym. Literature since 1945, vol. E. New York: W. W. Norton.

Miller, Arthur. 2015. *The Collected Essays of Arthur Miller*. London: Bloomsbury.

Montgomery, Sy. 2015. *The Soul of an Octopus: A Surprising Exploration Into the Wonder of Consciousness*. London: Simon and Schuster.

Olney, James. 1998. *Memory and Narrative: The Weave of Life-Writing*. Chicago: University of Chicago Press.

Perkins, Dennis, Margaret Holtman, Paul Kessler, and Catherine McCarthy. 2000. *Leading at the Edge: Leadership Lessons From the Extraordinary Saga of Shackleton's Antarctic Expedition*. New York: Amacom.

Robinson, Jenefer. 2005. *Deeper than Reason: Emotion and Its Role in Literature, Music, and Art*. Oxford: Oxford University Press.

Schlöndorff, Volker. 1985. *DVD. Death of a Salesman*. Performed by Dustin Hoffman, Kate Reid, John Malkovich, and Stephen Lang and directed by Volker Schlöndorff. Produced by Roxbury and Punch and distributed by CBS.

Scruton, R. 2010. *The Uses of Pessimism and the Danger of False Hope*. London: Atlantic.

Shannahan, Kirby, Rachelle Shannahan, and Alan Bush. 2013. "Salesperson Coachability: What It Is and Why It Matters." *Journal of Business and Industrial Marketing* 28 (5): 411–20.

Spears, Timothy. 1995. *100 Years on the Road: The Traveling Salesman in American Culture*. New Haven: Yale University Press.

Weisinger, Hendrie, and JP Pawliw-Fry. 2015. *Performing Under Pressure: The Science of Doing Your Best When It Matters Most*. New York: Crown Business.

Yalom, Irvin. 2013. *Love's Executioner and Other Tales of Psychotherapy*. London: Penguin.

Chapter 5

Coaching and writing

Giuseppe Tomasi di Lampedusa's *The Leopard*[1]

Giuseppe Tomasi di Lampedusa's *The Leopard* (*Il Gattopardo*) is widely considered one of the most important works of twentieth-century Italian fiction. It is a deeply political novel, exquisitely written, and a great work of art in any language. Political readings of the novel have emphasized how it is a work of historical fiction. David Quint (2010), for example, suggests that the novel encapsulates the love/hate relationship directed at the aristocracy in the process of being dislodged from power during the nineteenth-century Risorgimento, or Italian unification. Steven Smith (2010, 30) discerns Lampedusa's concern with the transition from the aristocratic to the bourgeois world and questions whether Lampedusa was a "reactionary lamenting the decline of the traditional ruling class" or simply a skeptic, mistrustful of reform. There is no avoiding what John Gilbert (1966, 32) memorably calls a "descent into bestiality" and "material putrescence" represented by Lampedusa's account of the replacement of the aristocratic families by the unrefined and ill-mannered bourgeoisie. Yet *The Leopard* is much more than a recording of the events of the Risorgimento from the eyes of a member of a dying society. Smith (2010, 34) reminds the reader that history and context are crucial to understanding the novel, and the revolutionary and political upheaval form a "backdrop" to the principal characters, but it is the prince of Salina Don Fabrizio's contemplations of history, meditations on change, and judgment on others that provide us with the means to understand the complex sympathies and subtle emotions of another. Through Lampedusa's skillful artistry, we witness a life that different from our own. It is Lampedusa's talent in relating the prince's resentfulness, reservations, anxieties, and disgusts – his ability to "paint in miniature," as Smith (2010, 34) avows – that will help coaching students better understand the complexities of experience, and, in David Nolan's (1966, 410) words, to then "translate obscure feelings into exact language."

My aim in this chapter is to demonstrate how *The Leopard* can be fruitfully incorporated into a coaching conversation. I will draw on the novel itself, on the critical reception of the novel, and on Lampedusa's *Letters from London and Europe*. I will begin with a synopsis of the novel and will proceed to situate Lampedusa in his historical and literary context. I will then touch upon the key themes of the novel, discussing the ways in which my coaching students responded to these themes, and illustrating how my students' responses offer evidence of the role a novel like Lampedusa's can play in enhancing the empathy of coaches and their coachees. I will also discuss long-distance or virtual coaching and the topic of emotional intelligence, relaying the stories of how my students used *The Leopard* to facilitate a coaching dialogue in this increasingly common scenario.

The Leopard elicits strong feelings in students. In this chapter, I will discuss some of the problems that an innovative coaching paradigm that integrates literary works into coaching practice can come up against. I will show how some students resist engaging with complex prose such as Lampedusa's and will confront the apparent contradictions in responses to using literature in coaching. Two of my students admitted they found Lampedusa's story "unreadable," while other students were adamant that the novel was not only compelling and pleasurable to read but that they saw clearly its potential as a coaching resource. My objective was to train my coaching students to see the potential of literary works in their practice. One of my students was particularly successful and reported that he had used the novel with three of his coachees in his organization, who had read *The Leopard* and had subsequently used the novel as a springboard for discussion on "flawed leadership" and the "inevitability of change." Based on the success of his coaching encounters, my student described the novel as the "ideal coaching resource." He found the novel particularly poignant as well in its reminder of how "we are mere mortals, not on this earth for long." *The Leopard* is a model text to coach to the changing reality in all of our lives. As I will describe in this chapter, it is also a particularly apt tool for reflecting on writing in coaching and for addressing writing challenges. It is no surprise that its complex prose pushes away people who are unaccustomed to reading or those individuals who do not readily see the value of reading in getting to grips with their own experience. In this chapter, I will set out the benefits of overcoming an initial resistance to literary works such as Lampedusa's, illustrating how an exposure to such writing can have a tangible impact on the ways that coachees narrativize their own experience. For those who learn to welcome an encounter with beautiful, textured, allusive descriptions, Lampedusa's novel is a master class in reflecting on and improving their own writing practice. Admittedly, *The Leopard* is perhaps not a coaching tool for everyone. It is more suited to those who have the time and inclination to reflect on their reading. The novel is not a source of quick-fix solutions; it offers a space for contemplation of our own lives and work, our own adaptation to the world in flux that surrounds us. It is a novel that encourages us to take a step back from the hubbub and noise of our busy day-to-day routines. In a coaching dialogue, it can act as a particularly powerful stimulus for the introspection and emotional education I have been arguing is so integral to improving the practice of organizational coaching.

As an illustration of the kind of creativity promoted by the reading of Lampedusa, I will give the example of my own writing and coaching ideas that were initiated by my reading Lampedusa's letters. In this discussion I will analyze writing blocks and show how similar they are to coaching blocks. I will contrast these ideas with an evaluation of the coaching tool Personalisis, which is used in many organizations as a means of helping people to learn about how they communicate and how they want to be communicated with. I was told by an advocate of this tool that "corporate America likes structure." That may be so, but corporate America presumably must also like the robotic, prescriptive, uncritical thinking, which this type of tool is in danger of fostering. I will demonstrate how we can use *The Leopard* as an alternative in corporate coaching or, for those without the time or desire to read it, how we can use the ideas inherent in the novel as a blueprint for corporate coaching practice, based on a reading of *The Leopard* and of Lampedusa's letters. My analysis ultimately suggests ways we can use the creative process to engage more fruitfully with coaching and how the creative process can be used to substantiate our ideas on working and living more productively.

The story of Lampedusa and *The Leopard*

Giuseppe Tomasi di Lampedusa was a Sicilian nobleman born in Palermo in 1896. He was an avid traveler who roamed Europe, particularly England and Paris, and wrote hundreds of letters about his travels to his beloved cousins, letters I will turn to when I discuss my theory of writing and coaching in the final part of this chapter. He died in Rome in 1957, having published nothing in his lifetime but bequeathing short stories, letters, an incomplete novel, and *The Leopard*, which was published posthumously in 1958.

The story opens with the final line of the Hail Mary: "*Nunc et in hora mortis nostrae*. Amen" (Lampedusa 2007, 1). The prince of Salina, Don Fabrizio, has recited the Rosary with his family, a tradition representing order, continuity, and a contemplation on life, death, and the future. The tradition and all it represents in Don Fabrizio's family distills the essence of the novel in microcosmic form. The sublime nature of the divinities – Andromeda, Jove, Mars, Venus – frescoed onto the ceiling, is evoked as the narrator wryly observes, "Beneath this Palermitan Olympus the mortals of the Salina family were also dropping speedily from mystic spheres" (Lampedusa 2007, 2). It is 1860, and outside the palace rages the Risorgimento, a movement that would end the Bourbon monarchy and replace the ruling aristocratic class, rending their way of life obsolescent and leaving them at the mercy of the demands and imperatives of the nouveaux riches in a new order that would also threaten the Church's position and authority.

The prince, Don Fabrizio, is a proud Sicilian, a leopard, "a crossbreed of lion and panther" who predicts that the new order coming into being will see jackals and hyenas replace the aristocratic leopards and lions (O'Mara 2008, 639). Before dinner, as his family disperses after prayers, he recalls the corpse of a young soldier lying in his garden, killed by the rebels, "his face covered in blood and vomit, crawling with ants, his nails dug into the soil; a pile of purplish intestines had formed a puddle under his bandoleers" (Lampedusa 2007, 5). The dead soldier is symbolic of the catastrophic change that will engulf Sicily and the prince's world, disturbing his inner calm, his self-possession, his regal composure, and making him one who is no longer honored and feared but a disillusioned man overcome by the futility of any endeavor. Everything in Don Fabrizio's world seems flawed, temporal, subject to change. The soldier's corpse in his garden is also an omen, and the reader enters the prince's reminiscences, sometimes morbid, at times lustful, disdainful, even self-pitying. We are forever reminded that in a novel about political upheaval and change, the prince's meditations on death, and more specifically, the death of a way of life, lie at the center of the novel. Here the paintings in his villa are described:

> The wealth of centuries had been transmuted into ornament, luxury, pleasure; no more; the abolition of feudal rights had swept away duties with privileges; wealth, like old wine, had let the dregs of greed, even of care and prudence, fall to the bottom of the barrel, preserving only verve and colour. And thus eventually it cancelled itself out, this wealth which had achieved its own object was now composed only of essential oils – and like essential oils soon evaporated.
>
> (Lampedusa 2007, 21)

The pictures of the estates of the house of Salina are being sold off. The anxious prince, highly dismissive, even of his own family who he perspicaciously regards as sclerotic and moribund, has faith only in his nephew Tancredi, who will marry the beautiful and rich but low-born and vulgar Angelica. Tancredi will survive the onslaught of change and even prosper. The charming and self-interested Tancredi voices the famous lines from *The Leopard* (lines that were immortalized in Visconti's 1963 prize-winning celluloid version): "If we want things to stay as they are, things will have to change" (Lampedusa 2007, 19). Eminently practical, even Machiavellian in his survival instincts, Tancredi, like the prince, Don Fabrizio, knows that one ruling class will replace another, but unlike the prince, he is not sadly meditative about what a flat, ugly, tradition-less future awaits him.

The critical reception of Lampedusa's novel can be divided broadly into two different camps, or at least an attempt to straddle the two: there is a focus either on Lampedusa's politics or Lampedusa's literary themes. There is no denying the political backdrop to the book. Before Lampedusa died, he wrote to his friend Enrico Merlo, entrusting him with the manuscript. He explained that *The Leopard* was the story of Prince Lampedusa, his great-grandfather Giulio Fabrizio, a Sicilian nobleman, and of his family. He imagines the story will be interesting because it details a reaction to a "moment of crisis" (Lampedusa 2007, xi). He mentions the family's degeneration and remarks "Sicily is Sicily – 1860, earlier. Forever" (Lampedusa 2007, xii).

David Nolan (1966, 404) perceives the novel as an exploration of social revolution which "shrouded in national myth, lies at the root of modern society." As history, *The Leopard* reveals the details of human action. Yet the novel is also fictional, so it is concerned with the enigma of human nature. In the vein of the celebrated novelists of the nineteenth century, Lampedusa's concern is with disentangling "the complexities of experience" and with "translat[ing]" how people feel into "precise language" (Nolan 1966, 410). Nolan's point about translation captures the rationale underlying the choice of *The Leopard* as a coaching text. The novel's lucidity, deep reflection, and captured moments of entangled emotions make it a particularly fruitful resource for the kind of coaching practice I have delineated in these chapters. *The Leopard* gives expression to a compelling insight that is especially relevant to the business world: the centrality of the emotions in how we respond to change. One of the greatest impediments to successful change and dealing with change – which is what the novel addresses – is an inability to capture what we are feeling, to put into exact words those conflicting, subtle, and baffling emotions we experience, particularly in the maelstrom of change. Don Fabrizio has to face the unpalatable truth of change – a changing society, a change to his power, a change to his status, and the change from his vitality and vigor to decrepitude and finally death.

In Lampedusa's novel, the theme of change is articulated with reference to myths. Amid the political dimensions of Lampedusa's artistic canvas, John Gilbert (1966) perceives how Lampedusa uses myth as a particularly apt metaphor for change. For Gilbert (1966, 22), all of the statues, paintings, and frescoes of the gods in the villas of the House of Salina represent "the replacement of theogony by another." In a political sense Sicily descents into gross materialism, and in a mythic sense the Salinas and other aristocratic families are no longer immune to the effects of time and social change: like the gods of old, these divine beings like the Salinas had only an illusion of power. Don Fabrizio, knowing that his ancien régime is being superseded, decides to champion his nephew Tancredi's marriage to Angelica as well as invest all of his emotional energies into this upcoming union. His wife and children can be swept aside just like the mores and traditions of society: "The Salina princesses, mother and daughters, clearly reveal the weaknesses and inhibitions of the ancient régime's nobility. Hemmed in by century-old traditions, unable to accept the demands of the modern world, they cling to their religion, which by the end of the novel, has become superstition and idolatry" (Gilbert 1966, 28).

One of the prince's daughters, Concetta, is in love with Tancredi, but the prince dismisses her feelings and pushes Tancredi closer to Angelica. Don Fabrizio is enchanted by Angelica's beauty: when they dance at the ball, which is the centerpiece of the novel, his thoughts are flooded by memories of his own youth. The last chapter, set in 1910, long after the prince and princess and even Tancredi have died, reveal the Salina sisters who, although visited at times by a still-vigorous and politically involved Angelica, live in "an inferno of mummified memories" (Lampedusa 2007, 201). Alone, embittered, widowed or never married, the sisters sit watching over the relics of saints, waiting for the Cardinal of Palermo to inspect the bones and pronounce on their authenticity.

In its dramatization of the decrepit state of stasis that can ensue when individuals fail to react to changing circumstances, *The Leopard* gave my coaching students food for thought. A number were working on projects that explored how coaching in their organizations could better equip their colleagues to deal with change. A number of their businesses were still seeking to reposition themselves in the changing economic climate inaugurated by the 2008 financial crisis. They were shoring up parts of their business, closing down others, and generally responding to the paradigm shift that had swept over the world economy. They were convinced that coaching could be used to help their colleagues enact the kinds of behavioral shift that were being advocated by the upper management of their companies, and some of them were able to see in *The Leopard* powerful warning of the detrimental impact of failing to change with the times.

It is the attention Lampedusa pays to depicting the psychology of his characters that means these characters and the details of their innermost thoughts can be transported into a coaching dialogue as a means of examining a number of different models for how human beings respond to a world in flux. We see not only how Lampedusa's characters act but, more importantly, the thought process that guides these actions. We are able to weigh up the rationality, morality, and justification of their choices and in seeing the world as they see it, can understand the psychological and behavioral limitations that impinge on our ability to act. Eduardo Saccone (1991) compares Lampedusa to Shakespeare, commenting on his lack of religiosity, his universal compassion, and his ability to peel away the skin of the human psyche. Scene after scene, Lampedusa regards his characters from a distance that enables readers to look at themselves more closely: "[Lampedusa] offer[s] a comment or commentary moral, delightful or merely mischievous through his mirror or picture upon life" (Nolan 1966, 410). Like Shakespeare, Lampedusa provides profound meditations upon life, meditations with which students of coaching can engage productively. In the next section, I will draw out the main themes students discerned in their reading and explore how these coaching students reacted to the challenge of using *The Leopard* in their own coaching practices.

Themes, student reaction, and empathy

The first theme that my coaching students invariably identified in this mediation on history is that of transition, the transition from one world to another, the change from one class to another, the upheaval of a regime and its substitution by another. Some of the students were perceptive in their analyses of how Lampedusa's theme of the decay of the Italian aristocracy could be compared to the profound change in their own organizations. A group of coaching students from a global telecommunications company that had suffered falling share prices, diminishing markets, and an exodus of talent to its competitors were divided in their opinion of the novel and its efficacy in opening up a coaching conversation. These students were expected to write a 12,000-word investigatory postgraduate project that explored challenges at their organization to which they offered recommendations for improved practice.

I provided the students with a brief background of Lampedusa and the concerns that precipitated his writing of this novel that was published after his death. This particular group of students was engaged in long-distance coaching, so my choice of literature was guided by the length of the text. I reasoned that someone who had to cover a large geographical area, for example, perhaps having few face-to-face coaching sessions, would have the time to engage with a novel rather than a short story. I also reasoned that employees who were undergoing disruptive and dramatic organizational change may find that Sicily's resistance to modernization and the prince's skepticism and mistrust of reform (Lansing 1978) might resonate with their challenges. Four of this group of students read this story, three males and one female, and were divided pretty much down the middle in their judgment of the efficacy of using this novel (or excerpts of it) in long-distance coaching. Their experiences make for an interesting insight into the challenges of organizational coaching and particularly the challenges of using an innovative pedagogy like my own within organizations that have tried and tested procedures for coaching practice and are resistant to trying anything unconventional.

Diego had reported a specific coaching problem and thought that using *The Leopard* might help in resolving the issue. A member of his team who was located in the head office over 100 miles from where he was at the time had complained to Diego that she felt the MD was "undermining" her in front of colleagues. Diego asked her what kind of outcome she wanted in this situation, and she replied that she wanted an open, honest, mutually supportive relationship with her MD. She realized that the company had undergone seismic operational shifts and that morale in general was low. She thought her MD was under enormous pressure and was "taking out his frustration" on her. During a series of Skype sessions, Diego had used solution-focused questions in his quest to make her goal as specific, clear, and targeted as possible. He had asked her to prepare a draft of how she could challenge her MD to see how his behavior was undermining her confidence and making her feel less than valued. Diego and she discussed questions she had designed for her MD, questions she then recognized were "awkward." She admitted that she was not comfortable talking to the MD yet and did not feel as though the questions were supporting her in her desire to have a mutually transparent conversation about their lack of communication. Diego had an inspiration: he had loved *The Leopard* and decided to share chapter 1 with his coachee. He suspected that the practical steps they were undertaking were not sufficient and what was called for was a way of developing her psychological skills.

I asked Diego what in chapter one of *The Leopard* could support a conversation about change and a way of helping his coachee address her feelings of being undermined. His response is illuminating:

> The whole chapter is about fear and my coachee was obviously afraid to confront her MD about her perception of being undermined, of being made to feel insignificant and not valued. I vaguely knew her MD and thought he was acting out his own fears toward the momentous changes our organisation is going through. On the one hand, this first chapter encapsulates the concept of constancy. At the beginning the Prince and his family recite the Rosary – the

> idea of routine and order is symbolized by the calmness of prayer – "For half an hour the steady voice of the Prince had recalled the Sorrowful and Glorious Mysteries; for half an hour other voices had interwoven a lilting hum from which, now and again, would chime some unlikely word; love, virginity, death" (Lampedusa 2007, 1). On page 2, the frescoes are personified: "They knew that for the next twenty-three and a half hours, they would be lords of the villa again." Everything is order and timelessness. On the other hand, the chapter introduces discordance – the Prince's fear that all this constancy would be undermined by societal change. There are textual hints that the Prince is irritated – "poor Prince Fabrizio lived in perpetual discontent under his Jove-like frown" (Lampedusa 2007, 4) and also that he blames others around him, which in my opinion is an obvious manifestation of fear. Change, more than anything, produces fear.

His coachee read the chapter after Diego told her that he would be seeing her in two weeks for a face-to-face discussion based on her reading. Diego said that reading the chapter had offered her, in his words, "a kind of psychological courage." She found obvious similarities between the stance that her MD had toward change and that of the prince. She particularly was struck by the prince sitting next to his wife, regarding her, and then jumping up to go to see his mistress. In the scene by which Diego's coachee was struck, the princess strokes the prince's hand, a gesture "which loosed a whole chain of reactions in him; irritation at being pitied, then a surge of sensuality, not however directed at she who had aroused it" (Lampedusa 2007, 11). Diego's coachee had said that the story spoke to her about fear and that fear could reveal itself in irritation, in running away, in undermining others. She had never thought of the MD as a fearful man before: she had seen his behavior as rooted in strength and arrogance. Now she suspected he was fearful of change. She felt equal to discussing his behavior with him – like the prince, he was hiding his head in the sand.

Did Diego's intervention work?

A month later, she left the company, saying that she finally felt the courage to freelance. Had she spoken to the MD? Yes. He had admitted he was under a lot of pressure and recognized that he might not have been as aware of his tone of voice and his attitude as he should have been.

Would Diego use the story or chapter again with coachees?

> Absolutely. *The Leopard* delineates the moods and mindset of a character in turmoil. Just in the first chapter we are confronted with leadership in transition: "I'm just a poor weak creature," he thought as his heavy steps crunched the dirty gravel. "I'm weak and without support" (Lampedusa 2007, 16). The Prince's reflections alone are worth engaging with from an organisational point of view. We can all ask ourselves what is driving an emotion. In my coachee's case, she detected only the observable behaviour. It was only when she drew the connection between organisational and societal flux, did she

> start to go beyond the observable behaviour and make those helpful connections for herself.

I thought that Diego's success in using the novel in his coaching practice might have something to do with his own passion for the book. It perhaps was not so much a case of Lampedusa being able to interact with Diego's coachee and give her the advice she was yearning for. To see literary fiction as a source of answers about how we live our lives is too simplistic to account for the psychological forces at work in the coaching sessions Diego described to me. I am certain that had Diego been using a story by John Cheever or a novella by Willa Cather or Herman Melville's "Bartleby" or indeed any other fictional work, he might have achieved equally convincing results with his coachee. What the literary work had been able to achieve in Diego's coaching, which his prior, more formulaic methods had not, was to enable both him and his coachee to take a step back from the workplace scenario at hand. When Diego asked his coachee to read a chapter from *The Leopard*, he was, in effect, recommending that she put some distance between her and her current workplace problems. She had been overly absorbed and wrapped up in her relationship with her manager; it had been plaguing her at work and out of work. She needed an escape from it. Lampedusa happened to provide that escape. The Italian writer had offered a historical and literary context to her current woes, had shown her that there was a world outside of the office politics that absorbed her at the time, that her own problems were not unique but were the very same that afflicted people from all walks of life, throughout human history. Lampedusa gave Diego's coachee the confidence to confront her workplace problems by enabling her momentarily to inhabit a space that was emotionally detached from her current troubles. It was the perspective she gained from contemplating another's life – through the medium of the fictional work – that allowed her to face her own with equanimity.

Two other students, James and Fiona, reported that the novel would "not work" in a coaching discussion about organizational change mainly because the novel was a "struggle" to read. James told me that for

> over two months I picked up the book and started reading and could never finish it. The story did not flow. Within the story there are details that are not relevant. For example on page 31 Lampedusa writes "At the end of the meal appeared a rum jelly." Even though much of my coaching is remote and novels would be fine to trigger a conversation about organisational change and how to adapt to it, this novel is way too dense for my busy team.

Fiona as well thought the writing "confusing" and that it was "too much of a leap to discuss in a business sense."

Lampedusa observed that Sicilians do not want to change because they all see themselves as perfect. I asked James and Fiona if perhaps at least as far as that observation was concerned, the Italian author and the situation he depicts might be able to resonate with some aspects of modern organizational life. They had slightly different takes. James commented: "Organisations find comfort in maintaining the status quo. They believe their processes and structure are perfect and they resist change. Organisations need to offer opportunities for employees to move to different parts of the organisation so people don't get trapped in the safety of doing things as they've always been doing." James was unwittingly echoing the wisdom of Lampedusa's novel. But what he was unable to see was why the novel should be used to tell him things he already knew. James was wedded to a utilitarian view of the function of the written word. To his mind, words were significant only to the extent that they conveyed information. What he was unwilling to be open to was the idea that how ideas are constructed is sometimes of equal importance to what they tell us. The significance of *The Leopard* is not what the novel tells us about change but how it does so, the ways it shows the inner lives of characters reacting to change and gives us an insight into the barriers that other people, who are different from us, may face. James was unconvinced.

From a trawl through Amazon reviews of *The Leopard*, I noted a very mixed bag of reactions to the novel, with many readers calling it a "beautiful, moving masterpiece" (and variations on that theme) and others finding it, as James and Fiona did, "difficult to access." Ultimately, coaches must decide what will work for them. I remain convinced that, in Diego's case, as I have already mentioned, it was his own positive reaction to the novel that paved the way for his success in using the work in a coaching session. If he hadn't been inspired by *The Leopard* and had nevertheless felt obliged to use it with his coachee, I am certain that the result would not have been the same. In Anne Perschel's (2010) investigation into coaching people to achieve maximum engagement at work, she found that one of the major barriers to experiencing deep and fulfilling engagement at work is the responsibility of dealing with a plethora of tasks and roles within an atmosphere of constant interruptions. We need to be able to achieve focused attention if we are going to achieve anything. Fiona made an important point about brain functioning at work in her reaction to *The Leopard*:

> This kind of writing needs the kind of attention I frankly don't have the time to give. I don't think reading it would facilitate our coaching process because we are not able to give the work the kind of concentration and focus it deserves. Our industry is looking for short-term solutions and we are always racing against time. Perhaps unlike the Sicilians, organisations don't see themselves as perfect but don't have the time to do anything about their flaws.

Perschel argues that those who are able to work on ways to help them express themselves, who are not solely attempting to meet other people's expectations, can gain more satisfaction from their work. Diego's coachee found that reading the first chapter of *The Leopard* and focusing on its themes of leadership and change supported her in gathering the courage to leave the company. According to Diego, coaching through *The Leopard* provided her with the impetus to grow: using the lens of the narrator observing the Salina family in its disorder, decay, and lack of leadership confirmed to her that her talents lay elsewhere, that she wasn't being engaged and motivated. Through her empathy with Don Fabrizio and his family, she was able to feel their emotions, namely those of fear, and she was able to subsequently act positively in her own life. It could be argued that intimate knowledge of the prince's experience provoked her desire to alter her own position. It is clear that empathy can be a "route to the experience of emotions not previously felt" (Matravers 2011, 28). It is acknowledged that there are different routes to empathy, but my concern here is with the nurturing of an empathetic response through a specific medium: literature. Murray Smith (2011, 100) defines empathy "as a kind of imagining, perceiving or more generally experiencing events, in contrast to *impersonal* or *acentral* imagining, where we imagine that certain events have taken or are taking place, but without imagining that we perceive or experience them. In centrally imagining a situation, we mentally *simulate* experiencing it." Diego and his coachee discovered that to imagine what it is like to be someone else is a valuable exercise. Moreover, in the coaching context, in which the development self-knowledge and knowledge of others is paramount, a training in practice of empathy, an empathy that is nurtured and refined "through its engagement with the narrative arts" (Smith 2011, 111), is immensely valuable.

Another of my students, Alex, found *The Leopard* powerful because of its intense engagement with what he perceived as the "twin themes of change and death." He said that

> Through the Prince's eyes we see a multitude of change happening both in the political and social domains. The description of the decaying rooms encapsulates themes of not only change but death, the latter saturating the novel. The message is that life change is inevitable and it is best to embrace it as a natural process. Like the Prince, we all have thoughts of mortality and our life ebbing away akin to grains of sand in an hourglass. Maybe we miss a trick in coaching when we don't acknowledge death as universal to the human condition.

The theme we avoid

In the 1963 Visconti film version of *The Leopard*, there is a scene in which all of the members of the Salina family at Mass are lined up like a row of corpses. It is evident that the director wanted to emphasize the living death and imminent collapse of this aristocratic family and others like it. Lampedusa himself emphasized the theme of death echoed in the opening words of the novel, the final line of the Hail Mary that implores the mother of God to pray for us sinners "now and at the hour of our death" (Lampedusa 2007, 1). The visual impression in Visconti's film is indeed haunting. *The Leopard* offers readers the experience of an impending death. Alex, who was persuaded that the novel could be read as a coaching tool, pointed out the number of passages relating to death, observing how Lampedusa helps us to comprehend the paradoxical nature of human existence: in life we are always in the shadow of death. Alex highlighted a passage in which Don Fabrizio contemplates young people at the ball and in which Lampedusa details the unpalatable truth of what we all must face:

> The two young people drew away, other couples passed, less handsome, each submerged in their passing blindness. Don Fabrizio felt his heart thaw; his disgust gave way to compassion for all these ephemeral beings out to enjoy the tiny ray of light granted them between two shades, before the cradle, after the last spasms. How can one inveigh against those sure to die? [. . .] Nothing could be decently hated except eternity.
>
> (Lampedusa 2007, 172–3)

The theme of death, in its patent relevance to all mankind, has a place in coaching. Ernest Becker (1997), in his philosophical Pulitzer Prize–winning *Denial of Death*, claims that the source of all human motivation is the need to deny the terror of death. Our greatest fear is suppressed in our overwhelming need to possess the semblance of being in command of ourselves and our destiny. We demand illusions, no matter how dangerous and ultimately self-defeating, and both individuals and groups are forever hungry for heroes who symbolize immortality:

> People create the reality they need to discover themselves. The implications of [this] are perhaps not immediately evident, but they are immense for a theory of transference. If transference represents the natural heroic striving for a "beyond" that gives self-validation and if people need this validation in order to live, then the psychoanalytic view of transference as simply unreal projection is destroyed. Projection is necessary and desirable for self-fulfilment. Otherwise man is overwhelmed by his loneliness and separation and negated by the very burden of his own life.
>
> (Becker 1997, 158)

Lampedusa, widely read and incidentally married to a psychoanalyst, was manifestly no stranger to the human condition and its denials, transferences, and projections. David Nolan (1966) differentiates history from fiction in making his case that *The Leopard* is above all a work of fiction: history may reveal human nature in the course of exploring past events, but literary fiction concerns itself foremost with mystery and enigma. The narrative, in its quest to explore the mysteries of existence, touches upon what Nolan (1966, 408) discerns as the counterpart to death: the eternal problem of living for a purpose. Don Fabrizio either meditates on or confronts death during the course of the novel. The following passage describing the aftermath of Don Fabrizio's shooting a rabbit is a particularly evocative metaphor for the human condition:

> It was a wild rabbit; its humble dun-coloured coat had been unable to save it. Horrible wounds lacerated snout and chest. Don Fabrizio found himself

> stared at by big black eyes soon overlaid by a glaucous veil; they were looking at him with no reproval, but full of tortured amazement at the whole ordering of things; the velvety ears were already cold, the vigorous paws contracting in rhythm, still living symbol of useless flight; the animal had died tortured by anxious hopes of salvation, imagining it could escape when it was already caught, just like so many human beings.
>
> (Lampedusa 2007, 76)

Lampedusa is capable of that most wondrous of translations, vital in the best of coaching interactions: he allows us to empathize with his characters and allows us to enter their own empathetic responses to others, both human and animal. If our behavioral and psychological motivation can be characterized and explained by our denial of death, *The Leopard* is replete with passages on this theme that reach far beyond any clichéd, familiar imagery, allowing us to bypass tired stereotypes and generic ideas in order to permit us to connect with each other through the means of literary coaching. In recognizing the prominence of the theme of death in Lampedusa's work, my coaching student Alex had discovered a potentially rewarding instrument to use in his own coaching.

Alex's project: virtual coaching and emotional intelligence

Alex was interested in how emotional intelligence could be given a more prominent role in coaching. His hypothesis was that a more productive, happy, and fulfilling working life could be achieved by putting emotions at the forefront of coaching. He explained,

> Our organisation needs to find ways of overcoming inefficiency and low morale caused by high levels of stress. As I am responsible for a large geographical area and my team is dispersed far and wide, I do a lot of coaching on Skype or even by phone. My project is an investigation of how and which emotions dominate my respondents' or team members' working lives and how these emotions affect productivity.

He added that his telephone and Skype interviews were difficult because of a lack of immediacy and the danger of misinterpretation. He concluded that if we extrapolate from the challenges that arise when conducting long-distance interviews, long-distance coaching is even harder. In the process of supervising Alex's project, I encouraged him to see if literature might help to stimulate a willingness in his respondents and team members to discuss emotions. He had explained that perhaps because of the virtual medium in which his discussions had taken place, he found it difficult to, in his words, "read" his colleagues. He had diagnosed in them a reticence to discuss emotions. A number of his colleagues had told him they were convinced that personal feelings tended to be absent in a reason-driven workplace in which it was necessary to erect a barrier to prevent unwanted emotions from "contaminating" decisions and "creating a touchy-feely atmosphere that could stifle productivity." Alex explained to me that a certain hostility to emotions had been a recurrent theme in his discussions with his colleagues and that it had been this apparent hostility that had inspired him to investigate emotions in the working environment in the first place. I wanted Alex to see if getting his colleagues to read *The Leopard* might be a starting point for a more frank discussion of emotions. Lampedusa's meticulous depiction of his characters' psychological states could, I suspected, be a potent ingredient to galvanize Alex's discussions. Alex decided to share chapter 1 of *The Leopard* with his team and leave them with two questions for discussion. He decided that the conventional interview approach would not give him the rich qualitative data he wanted and was curious whether reading the chapter would support his team in accessing, understanding, and discussing their own emotions. Alex's research project was predicated on the assumption that those individuals who could analyze and recognize emotional complexity could understand themselves better and that self-understanding is a high-order skill potentially beneficial to an organization. He asked his team what emotions were evoked in reading the chapter and if they could draw any parallels between Lampedusa's descriptions of the political and social challenges to the aristocratic Salina family and their own organization.

The team response to the reading exercise echoed the mixed results I had obtained in my own endeavor to use *The Leopard* with my coaching students. Some of Alex's respondents enjoyed the reading, others were neutral, and about a third found it obscure and difficult. Nevertheless, whether they had enjoyed the reading or not, their responses modeled the emotional responsiveness Alex was seeking to stimulate in his team. Emotional adjectives ranged from "bored," "confused," "mystified," and "exhausted" at one end of the scale to "fascinated," "intrigued," and "mesmerized" at the other. All of his team, however, could discern parallels between what was happening to the family and what was happening to their organization. What surprised Alex somewhat was a unanimous desire on the part of his respondents to focus on the concept of "family." Team members used expressions such as "familial support," "belonging to a close knitted group," "being recognised and respected as ourselves – as a working group, like a family." His team said that they saw the same frustration, despair, and sadness expressed by Don Fabrizio as they saw at work. Alex told me that his individual follow-up Skype conversations to discuss the questions he had designed on the Lampedusa chapter had been richer and more satisfying than any of his previous coaching sessions. He attributed this phenomenon to team members being eager to open up about their emotional state in a guided manner: "The chapter offers safe boundaries. People can discuss their dissatisfaction, anger, sadness and use strong emotions, and they are at less risk of exposing themselves when the discussion is filtered through a literary lens."

The topic of "family" surfacing so frequently in Alex's discussions can be illuminated by Veronika Koubova and Aaron Buchko's (2013) study of emotional intelligence. Koubova and Buchko (2013, 703) theorize that "family and personal life dominate work life in terms of EI development." The implication of Koubova and Buchko's study is that our emotional skills are already developed at home by parents and care givers. The more we learn at an early age, the better equipped we are to deal with a range of emotional situations at work. What Koubova and Buchko draw out is how much more important "personal-life interactions" are to work-related ones. High EI influences well-being, and EI is "an important predictor for maintaining and promoting one's mental, social, and physical health" (Koubova and Buchko 2013, 708). The authors conclude that happier employees need to be able to reconcile their work and family roles: EI can be improved by nurturing strong and productive cognitive and emotional communication in the workplace. If it is essential for managers to understand the emotions of others in the workplace, then there need to be models of motivating and inspiring others, of fostering EI and coaching skills. In order to unlearn unhealthy emotional habits, there needs to be the time to do so: "organizations should aim not only at providing more EI learning opportunities for managers and employees, but also assure that these opportunities are long-term and continuous rather than brief and short term in order to be effective" (Koubova and Buchko 2013, 713).

Alex was aware that the implementation of a quick-fix model such as GROW, for example, was not going to create a foundation for the open and frank discussion that encompasses people's emotional needs. He wanted a different perspective. Encouraging his team to read fiction allowed them to explore their emotions, an exploration that is part of a transformative process of learning. In previous chapters, I have explored in detail the mechanisms by which fiction promotes empathy and helps us to relate our own experiences to those of other people. There has, moreover, been anecdotal research in this area that supports the paradigm shift in coaching practice for which I am arguing. Patricia Leavy (2013, 20), for example, uses fiction to disrupt stereotypes and is interested in transforming learning through challenging assumptions: "Through the pleasure and at times the pain of confronting emotionally charged truths, the process of reading fiction can be transformative." The reading of fiction can be transformative in other ways too. It can also transform the way coachees express themselves. By encouraging individuals to reflect on the mechanics of prose construction, an exposure to literary works, can, under proper guidance, improve their communication skills. Such an improvement is not simply a fortuitous by-product of using literary works in coaching practice. It can actually be instrumental in ameliorating the quality of coachees' self-reflection.

Writing challenges and metaphor

With a colleague, I ran a series of seminars aimed at improving the writing skills of doctoral-level students. We entitled the series "Lessons from Coaching" and explained in the promotional blurb (that went out to doctoral students across our university) that we intended to look at how an author "manipulates emotions" in order to glean lessons on improving writing skills for drafting doctoral dissertations and projects. Large groups of between twenty and thirty students attended the seminars; some of the students were doing doctoral work in coaching, and all of them were there to learn how to reflect on their writing and ultimately craft their work better. Among the key challenges in doctoral writing – framing the research, establishing a niche, deciding on the personal pronoun that should guide the writing – developing a strong, persuasive voice infused with one's own values and principles is paramount. In the seminars I decided to build on my recent success with Diego and Alex, among others, in using *The Leopard* as a stimulus for emotional reflection in coaching. I wanted to see how Lampedusa's text could be used in the cognate area of improving writing skills by encouraging students to develop a personal voice in their writing and as a means of conveying their authority as researchers through carefully crafted prose. Perhaps because the majority of doctoral students are in the position of grappling with large datasets and substantial reading – often of dense academic prose that can sometimes seem impenetrable to those outside of the discipline – the first chapter of the Lampedusa novel I used in the seminars was received with a total absence of complaints about its length, level of difficulty, or applicability. The overarching question I wanted to explore with the students was the following: How does Lampedusa manipulate his readers' emotions in order to engender a sympathetic imagination? Its corollary was: How can we apply what Lampedusa does to doctoral-level writing?

Before my colleague and I met the students, we distributed the chapter via a virtual learning platform and asked the students to come to the seminar prepared to discuss the text. By an overwhelming margin, the majority of students who attended the seminar – most of whom were working in disciplines outside of the humanities and therefore had limited training in textual analysis – engaged productively with the text. Under careful guidance in close reading, they were soon able to identify the ways in which Lampedusa's meticulous language, particularly his figures of speech such as metaphor, created an emotional landscape in which fear, fear of aging, fear of change, loss of faith, loss of face, and impending destruction and death loomed. Some of the doctoral students in the field of coaching readily recognized the chapter's pertinence to twenty-first-century organizational life. One student found striking parallels between "a world blind to rapid changes" in nineteenth-century Sicily and "a world wedded to mainstream thinking" at her organization:

> In the chapter we detect Don Fabrizio's dismay at the prospect of a future dominated by a new social class. I think many of us in corporate America are going to be in for a similar feeling of dismay when robotics and automation take over. The elite are always those that control the narrative and most of us are distracted by organisational tools and day to day data dump. When we read something as thoughtfully constructed as *The Leopard* we are able to stand back and look at ourselves more closely. Entering into a world other than our own can help us to see and hopefully discuss what is happening right under our noses.

Another student examining coaching strategies in UK organizations reported that the chapter would be an ideal basis for exploring how sclerotic industries are replaced by more agile ones:

> The British manufacturing industry post second world war is a perfect example where there was a culture of self-satisfaction, complacency and limited vision. Possibly there was an underlying selfishness in the major players. They had made their money, created their comfort zone and cared little for the future. I do think that in the twenty-first century the structure of companies (responsible to shareholders) does not allow for such complacency. As Lampedusa foreshadows the contrast between the moribund Salina family and the ever-practical Tancredi, the successful organisation embraces change. With such an expanding global market and the speed at which technology is being updated, it is not possible to survive without making changes – all of Lampedusa's powerful images contrast decaying immortality (frescoes of the gods) with the need for change and the willingness to embrace it (the lithograph of Garibaldi and Tancredi's restless action).

The student's commentary models exactly how a careful reading of the Lampedusa chapter can support the forging of coaching ideas on stasis and change and, at the same time, provide lessons on crafting our written work. In terms of Lampedusa's figures of speech, students felt his use of metaphor intoxicating, and they were enthusiastic about the idea that they had "permission" to use metaphor in academic work. In a book that discusses writing in academia, *Pathways through Writing Blocks in the Academic Environment*, Kate Evans (2013) examines the difficult process of setting down words to convey precisely what we want to convey. Evans investigates the elements that create writing blocks, claiming that such elements are weighted with emotion. Among her practical advice on writing, such as examining the emotional experiences that prevent us from writing clearly and reminding us that writing is a skill that can be developed, practiced, and nurtured, Evans makes the point that using metaphor is central to the creative process.

The doctoral students found that Lampedusa "manipulates" the reader in two ways: through the use of metaphor and by providing a character's subjective experiences, thoughts, and impressions in a precise and careful manner. I will discuss the second practice in my next section, and here I will stay with the key role metaphor plays in getting an audience's attention. Evans (2013, 104) is clear that metaphor is omnipresent in the English language (obviously in Italian as well) and defines it as "the use of a tangible image to explore more ephemeral experience." It is a vital means of conveying how we see the world, and it is the key to unlocking others' worlds. We need metaphor because our minds are always searching for comparisons in order to describe a complex object, idea, or phenomenon. One of the most striking metaphors most students commented on was the rum jelly served at the end of the Salina family's meal (if you recall, this was the rum jelly my coaching student James thought an "irrelevant detail"):

> It was rather threatening at first, shaped like a tower with bastions and battlements and smooth slippery walls impossible to scale, garrisoned by red and green cherries and pistachio nuts; but into its transparent and quivering flanks a spoon plunged with astounding ease. By the time the amber-coloured fortress reached Francesco Paolo, the sixteen-year old son who was served last, it consisted only of shattered walls and hunks of wobbly ruin. Exhilarated by the aroma of rum and the delicate flavour of the multi-coloured garrison, the Prince enjoyed the rapid demolishing of the fortress beneath the assault of his family's appetite.
>
> (Lampedusa 2007, 31)

Lampedusa could very well have reminded the reader that the Salina family's villa and, by extension, entire way of life, is being threatened by the new order in society and politics. He could have also reminded us that the Salina family's very foundations are weak and unstable. He might have brought to our attention that Garibaldi's new flag of red, white, and green would supplant the lily-white crest of the Salinas. There is also the matter of the ill-favored son of Don Fabrizio being served last, once the pudding had been all but decimated: this natural heir would be passed over financially and emotionally by his father, who favored the more politically astute and emotionally savvy nephew, Tancredi. Finally, the sensual prince, louche and solipsistic, is enjoying the spectacle of the ruined pudding. Lampedusa achieves a subtle expression of all these underlying facets of the family's experience simply through an aptly crafted literary image. The demolished pudding is a metaphor for the wider changes being wrought on the family's way of life. As Evans (2013, 112) points out, metaphors are superb writing tools because they are "layered." We use them in order to appeal to the reader's different senses. They make an impact on the reader. Because they "tend to percolate into all human communications," we need to be aware of their power in academic (and in all) writing (Evans 2013, 113). If writers need a heightened awareness of their capabilities, they could do no better than begin to examine how metaphors are constructed and the effects they have. Lampedusa's work abounds in these kinds of layered, potent images, ripe for picking apart by astute students keen to discover how writing achieves its effects.

The students in the seminar soon learned how their writing could be improved by using metaphor. Such a layered and descriptive way of giving a great deal of information in a compact and creative way, they realized, is the ideal means of engaging the reader. Students also picked up on the metaphor of time and how central its concept is to the meaning of the novel. Time is conveyed most strikingly by Lampedusa's use of the image of the sun:

> Under the leaven of the strong sun everything seemed weightless; the sea in the background was a dash of pure colour; the mountains which had seemed so alarmingly full of men during the night now looked like masses of vapour on the point of dissolving, and grim Palermo itself lay crouching quietly

> around its monasteries like a flock of sheep around their shepherds. Even the foreign warships anchored in the harbour in case of trouble spread no fear in the majestic calm. The sun, still far from its blazing zenith of that morning of the 13th of May, was showing itself the true ruler of Sicily; the crude brash sun, the drugging sun, which annulled every will, kept all things in servile immobility, cradled in violence and arbitrary dreams.
>
> (Lampedusa 2007, 27)

There is simply no need for the author to detail how any of the characters *feels* at this time nor to tell the reader that the characters are creatures as ephemeral as the events of this particular day in the month of May. The sun takes on the mantle of the significance of time – an inexorable, brutal, uncaring, and unforgiving existence to which everything on earth is subjected.

Students were able to discuss specific metaphors they could use in their theses in order to make their writing have a greater impact. A coaching student working as a head teacher in a secondary school likened her staff to "apine members of a smashed hive." There was little need to elaborate on such a striking image that conjured up teachers who wanted to cooperate, collaborate, and create a workable environment for their students in contrast to a school system – monolithic and damaged – that prevented such productive activity. The head teacher had expressed her frustration with what she termed "the usual conventions of coaching" and was keen to explore how using literature such as *The Leopard* might help her to engage with her staff, reeling from constant bombardment from "change initiatives," in more useful and emotionally satisfying coaching conversations. She made the point that the authentic voice – the precise, creative, persuasive voice we need to develop for the doctorate, for this high level of academic writing – varies little from the authentic voice we need to develop in our coaching conversations. She suggested that having coachees explore an emotional disturbance or block by using metaphor could be a way of explaining complexity and a means, ultimately, by which people could find deeper meaning in their work.

The head teacher's intuition of the intrinsic link between writing and coaching leads me to the cornerstone of this chapter: my theory that writing, like coaching, is relational. As writing is a means of discovery, so is coaching. In drawing out the similarities between writing and coaching, I hope to demonstrate how writing can inform coaching and coaching, writing.

Personalisis

A student from a coaching program in a large American insurance company with which I had been working shared her "Personalisis Summary" with me. Like DISC, which I discussed in my first chapter on "Bartleby, the Scrivener," Personalisis claims to be a scientific management tool that explains how one thinks, feels, and acts under pressure. It purports to offer a snapshot of your personality and is designed to support people in their communication with others. The idea is that a person answers a questionnaire that will in turn indicate aspects of his or her personality broken into different dimensions: instinctive, rational, positive, and negative behaviors. I read Lily's Personalisis Summary and underlined specific statements that surprised, confused and, in some cases, astounded me. Lily had been one of my postgraduate coaching project students over two terms, and I felt that I knew her both as a professional and, to a certain extent, on a personal basis. We had spoken on Skype frequently, and she had expressed frustration with various elements of her organization's coaching program, mainly that not one of the tools they relied on such as DISC and Personalisis encompassed the emotional aspects of coaching which she thought should be emphasized. She told me that she found Personalisis "adequate," and when I individually asked the other members of this coaching cohort what they thought of it, their responses ranged from highly complimentary ("it keeps us focused on our challenges"; "it is highly individualized"; "it confirms what someone may already know about their motivation, learning roles and decision making") to neutral ("it's neither good nor bad; it's simply a tool"; "it's about structure"; "it's supposed to represent how you communicate and interact with others – maybe so . . ."). I underlined the following phrases in Lily's ten-page report:

- "Lily should not choose roles that require spending time in introspection or bookish pursuits";
- "Feeling threatened, Lily is unable to be objective and fails to listen";
- "Lily is impatient with long discussions";
- "She is frustrated by constant change, disorganisation and bureaucratic policies";
- "She does not respond well to those who are over-controlling and restrictive."

These statements did not just run contrary to my experience of Lily both as a member of the group and also as an individual whom I had gotten to know; Lily was completely unrecognizable in this report. I was dismayed that this purportedly "scientific tool" had got it so wrong in this case. The report was in danger of sounding like robotic nonsense that mostly stated the obvious. On the few occasions it ventured beyond vague generalities and tried to say something specific about a person, it seemed utterly misguided. Lily was an excellent scholar who enjoyed reading and, with my support, broadened her enquiry to explore a wealth of philosophical texts. She always listened patiently to others in her group and provided reflective, intelligent responses in group discussions. I had always experienced Lily as courteous and infinitely patient, listening carefully even to the most rambling and discursive contributions made by her colleagues and invariably responding with tact and appropriate questions. The report was right in its assertion that Lily was not enamored of disorganization, but she was no more frustrated by an atmosphere of constant change and bureaucratic chaos than was any other conscientious member of an organization. To the part about "not responding well" I penciled in next to it, "sounds like canine obedience school." I also highlighted a few phrases that struck me as particularly spurious:

- "Personalisis is based on an energy model of personality";
- "Under *functional* stress, we are concerned about maintaining power or control" (my italics);
- "If you feel good about yourself, you have a sense of mastery";
- "If you meet the expectations of the person with whom you are dealing, you set the stage for a static-free response."

I fully accept that, as one of my students told me, "corporate America likes structure," and I can see that, like horoscopes, the Personalisis tool is appealing in its focus on the individual quirks and strengths of one's personality and performance. However, the reports it generates are compartmentalized and highly speculative: there is no nuance, no gradation. This pigeon-holing people into their "preferred styles of communication," "motivational needs," and "communication expectations" does not aid communication; it stops it dead in its tracks. If Lily took its advice "not [to] choose roles that require time in introspective or bookish pursuits" not only would she have decided not to embark on her postgraduate course in coaching, she would not have been open to any of its opportunities for learning and self-development. If she had taken too much heed of its admonishment to "keep clear of duties that demand listening or engaging in free-floating dialogue," she would have been unable to produce her ultimately enriching research, which entailed wide reading, reflective and reflexive engagement with the inquiry process, penetrating questions to interview respondents, and the subsequent analysis of their answers with insight and evaluative finesse. Lily's research culminated in a project that set its sights on reshaping practice in her organization for the better. Had she followed Personalisis and not her own intuition, her organization would have been the poorer for it.

One of the most glaring omissions in Lily's Personalisis report – a report that ostensibly concerned communication – was any mention of writing. In higher education, we have little difficulty in accepting that working in an academic environment necessitates a familiarity and fluency with solid writing skills. In the corporate world, there is far less widespread recognition of need for those same writing skills, although they are integral to organizational life. Those who draft unclear reports or send confusing e-mails – however excellent Personalisis deems their "communication approaches" – will encounter a degree of frustration in corporate life. If coaching is a de facto corporate tool for supporting change, focusing on positive outcomes, and facilitating clear communication, then it must encompass models of good writing. Lampedusa's *The Leopard* and the author's epistolary style showcased in *Letters from London and Europe* provide salutary lessons in the all-important objective of improving communication. In the letters we find the embryo of Lampedusa's subsequent novel. They show his development as an artist and therefore model the evolutionary stages in perfecting writerly craft.

Venustry of style

Between 1925 and 1930 Lampedusa traveled throughout Europe, and his subsequent correspondence to his cousins was collected in *Letters from London and Europe* (Lampedusa 2010). The author's detailed descriptions of landscapes, people, encounters, and himself profiles a style of writing that is detached yet intimate, ambitious yet circumspect, introspective, penetrating, and wry. Lampedusa has a sharp eye for human comedy, which is a helpful quality to have in coaching. In this 1928 letter describing a ball he attended at the French Embassy in London, he mordantly analyzes the aristocrats present:

> Madame l'Ambassadeur receives the guests at the top of the staircase. [. . .] Below, the footman pounds out the names: "His Highness the Prince von Bismarck," a skinny little bespectacled shrimp, far removed from the bull-like power of his formidable grandfather, "the Count and the Countess von Blücher," "His Grace the Duke of Wellington" – a momentous trio of names ironically brought together by Fate, one after the other, under this French roof. Diminished and subdued, the national disasters of France kiss bony pomp. His Excellency smiles behind his beard; he is desperately trying to find witticisms that are at the same time full of bonhomie, profundity and dignity; he invokes the protection of his master Talleyrand; he cannot find it; he clears his throat.
>
> (Lampedusa 2010, 108)

What the letter shows us is Lampedusa's innate skill for capturing the little idiosyncrasies that distinguish individuals from one another. He is able to capture what makes us tick, and it is this same intuition that he will later perfect in *The Leopard*. The act of taking two texts by a single author, written at different moments in his or her life, and setting the two in contrast as a means of gauging chronological development can be a valuable tool for illustrating how communication is not an innate skill but instead can be developed with effort and attention. When I showed my doctoral students in the writing seminar an excerpt of this earlier letter by Lampedusa, they were, at first, unable to recognize the masterful linguistic craftsman of the novel in this earlier snapshot of Lampedusa's developing craft. They found the narrator of the embassy letter "cruel" and "inhumane." How could this possibly be the same author who in *The Leopard* has such a warm, poignant, and forgiving gaze on his characters? But the students at the same time were able to see how Lampedusa would later build on and perfect certain techniques present in the letters. For example, with Don Fabrizio in *The Leopard*, he will exercise this same anatomy of the inner being. The emergent process of imagining a mind other than his own is detailed throughout these letters. What the exercise showed the students ultimately, though, is that our development as writers is not static but dynamic. We can evolve as authors through practice and reflection on the more and less successful aspects of our self-expression.

In a letter of 14 July 1928, Lampedusa reminds his cousin that he has described to him dog races, dinners, talking films, and contemplations on everything from "the situation in Egypt" to "the new safety razors." He rebukes him for his tardiness of replies to his own correspondence, "all of which reveal in their content the customary sagacity of his spirit, while in their form they sparkle with every venustry of style" (Lampedusa 2007, 115). Poring through English dictionaries both online and in book form, I found the word "venustry" elusive. Finally, consulting an Italian dictionary, I found "venustro," which means "beautiful or comely." I realized that the translator had produced an apt neologism for Lampedusa's ability to provide delightful sketches that penetrated the essence of their subjects. I hypothesized that if a masterpiece of character analysis was preceded by small epistolary sketches aiming to describe a person or thing in minute detail, a coaching scenario could be strengthened by brief sketches as well – there was a link between the brief sketches and the final piece of work in the writing process.

There are connections between writing and coaching, connections that are not just obvious but unavoidable. Taking four obvious connections can illuminate how, like Lampedusa, we coaches and coachees can begin "sketching" our observations about ourselves and others before we start the actual coaching conversations. Both writing and coaching are skills that can be developed. Both are creative acts that rely on a great deal of reflective practice. Both contain blocks or frustrations that are telling us something important about ourselves. These blocks are, to my mind, triggered by our emotions. Far too often, we turn to neat, prescriptive boxes and models to guide us in the coaching process. Equally, we search for a specific, helpful template in crafting our writing. Extrapolating directly from lessons and advice on improving writing skills, coaching students will find startling commonality between writing and coaching. When we are blocked in our coaching – unsure of what questions to ask, reticent to explore an issue at greater depth, unclear about an avenue to go down – it is valuable to reflect on how we can overcome writing blocks. How do we move from a jumble of ideas to a clear narrative thread that our reader can easily follow? We are all familiar with the truism that all writers have to apply themselves to their writing. Giuseppe Tomasi di Lampedusa, writing his observations on his travels daily with precision and detail, supplies us with the link between writing and coaching that has been hitherto unexamined.

I will draw my discussion on Lampedusa to a close with a characteristic sketch from the letters. Watching a cat cross a London street near Piccadilly, he writes,

> It was marvellous to see the cat begin a kind of dance, a series of leaps, tumbles and somersaults, in an effort to avoid the darting vehicles. A dog would have been despatched ten times over. After a couple of minutes of elegant acrobatics which made everyone pause on the pavement, it gave up.
>
> After disappearing through the window from where it began its progress, the cat was applauded by the audience watching from the pavement, and

> Lampedusa mused that he had "never before seen a cat abandon its intention [which] filled him with immense delight."
>
> (Lampedusa 2010, 107)

We too need to take delight in the resolution to abandon the intention of finding a straightforward, easy solution to either coaching or writing. Human beings are mysterious; their personalities and behavior can confound neat explanations. By making notes of our daily observations, by making the study of ourselves and others our habit, we can become more careful and attentive coaches and writers. By relinquishing our desire for certainties and our insistence on discovering a model that explains the gamut of human behavior (and feline for that matter), we can become more sensitive and therefore more effective coaches. Literary works hold up a mirror to our souls. Read them, discuss them, analyze them: they will become one of the most indispensable and vital coaching tools you could ever wish for.

Final remarks on *The Leopard* and prefatory remarks on Shakespeare

I chose *The Leopard* for my coaching students because I found it a splendid, valuable work of literature and also because I recalled reading about its use in change-management scenarios. P. Khalil Saucier and Tryon Woods (2014) draw on the novel as they consider the 2013 island of Lampedusa boat victim case as a manifestation of the accumulated violence against black people globally. Scenes of police violence meted out on survivors in the wake of the vessel capsizing and with the subsequent loss of 366 of its 500 migrants from Eritrea and Somalia have made the island of Lampedusa a symbol of "Italian decadence and sloth in the midst of an unethical social order and its inevitable comeuppance" (Khalil Saucier and Woods 2014, 56). The authors are struck by the similarity between Tancredi's urging his uncle to switch allegiance to Garibaldi and the insurgents and the inescapable paradigm shift globally. Like the indolent and decadent Sicilian aristocracy in Lampedusa's novel, Europe itself is a "twilight civilization" seeking to stop the transformation of its lands into "a home for all human beings" (Khalil Saucier and Woods 2014, 56). The global movement from south to north, compelled by social and political upheaval, must – like some of Lampedusa's more enlightened aristocrats grasping the enormous mid-nineteenth-century cultural sea change – be understood as a given: this is *the* era of global mass migration.

Lampedusa's novel has been used as a symbol for change and resistance to it in a multitude of other research contexts. An article reflecting on management accounting change and calling for "an understanding of the multiplicity of the nature of management accounting systems which makes them appear always different but inevitably the same" draws on Tancredi's observations on change and stability in *The Leopard* (Busco, Quattrone, and Riccaboni 2007). In an article examining the distinction between social influence and persuasion, Jorge Correia Jesuino (2008, 108) examines the vital social context that he argues is always "behind the scenes" in the persuasion of an individual's behavior and attitudes. Correia Jesuino reminds us that experiments on persuasion demonstrate that it operates indirectly and, more often than not, subliminally. Quoting the famous dictum from Tancredi, "if we want things to stay as they are, things will have to change," Correia Jesuino argues that social influence is aimed at social change rather than social control. Persuasion "in the enlightened sense of redirecting humans onto the right track seems to lose ground to the myriad of social influence processes that constantly impinge on and affect our conduct" (Correia Jesuino 2008, 117). In a study of "corporate heritage" – identities, institutions, and cultures – John Balmer (2011) notes that marketing scholars link a brand's worth to its heritage. Balmer connects the very notion of heritage with Tancredi's dictum as the essence of paradox: heritage is a paradox because its concern is modernity – it "implies a consciousness of our place outside – or beyond – history" (Balmer 2011, 1386). Lampedusa's thesis reveals the very paradox of corporate heritage identities in that although identity may be the same, the meanings we give corporate heritage identities can change.

The Leopard lends itself to discussions in a range of fields and disciplines when the concept of change is explored. Tancredi's riddling proposition has the power to capture the imagination of writers grappling with the concept of change. In discussions of the fast pace of change in medicine, marketing, society, at least a passing familiarity with Tancredi's dictum has become a fashionable truth that lends a certain elegance and sophistication to an argument. In coaching, my recommendation is to move beyond Tancredi's pithy observation in discussions on change. In this chapter, we have seen the results of encouraging students of coaching, coaches, and coachees to engage with Don Fabrizio's meditations in order to understand the complexities of human experience. I am well aware that the novel will not appeal to every reader, but, used judiciously – whether selecting a chapter or a section of the novel – it can yield rich coaching dividends when exploring themes of flawed leadership and the unavoidable nature of change.

Returning to the concept of leadership within the coaching context, I would argue that thinking about responsible consequences, modeling conscientious and dependable behavior, and creating more good than harm are at the forefront of leadership qualities. Neither Don Fabrizio nor Tancredi (nor even the off-stage Garibaldi) could ever be thought of as modeling sound ethical leadership. In fact, in a typical postmodern vein to the novel, there is an absence of leadership, a void where there needs to be authority, a preoccupation with death instead of an embrace of life. The novel of course can be read as a treatise on survival, and all leaders need to know how to survive. At the risk of sounding obvious, even obtuse, I will observe that leaders are also human, and the novel concerns itself with the enigma of human nature and what people "feel" when faced with an onslaught of emotion.

As I have argued in this chapter, one of the greatest obstacles to dealing with change is the inability to capture what we are feeling, to put into exact words those conflicting emotions we experience when faced with the kind of change brought about by powerful situational forces. I have demonstrated how coaching students found value in using *The Leopard* in different coaching scenarios. I have also discussed some students who found the work a "struggle." There will inevitably be a range of reactions to the novel, as there are to any work of literature or indeed to any model of coaching. Nevertheless, an engagement with Lampedusa's figures of speech, especially metaphor, can provide lessons on crafting written work, lessons that are beneficial ultimately to all students.

The key to using literary works with coaching students, I have found, is variety. There will always be a writer to whom students can relate, a snippet of prose or a few lines of poetry that can inspire discussion and trigger productive thoughts and emotions. In my final seminar with the doctoral students who attended the course on coaching and writing, I decided to use a passage from Shakespeare's *The Tempest*. Lampedusa's detailed observations on landscape, people, parties, antiques, and animals have been likened to the observational prowess of Shakespeare (Saccone 1991). Shakespeare seemed a natural progression for the class and an opportunity to look at themes of power and manipulation in the context of coaching. Like all skilled writers, Shakespeare manipulates his audience's emotions through language. His work exhibits a mastery over language to achieve certain effects and constitutes a master class for students reflecting on language in order to improve their own use of it. In terms of examining power and manipulation, we could do no better than to examine Prospero, the magus and arch-manipulator in the play. I selected for analysis Prospero's speech at the end of the play:

> You do look, my son, in a moved sort,
> As if you were dismayed. Be cheerful, sir.
> Our revels now are ended. These our actors,
> As I foretold you, were all spirits, and
> Are melted into air, into thin air;
> And like the baseless fabric of this vision,
> The cloud-capped towers, the gorgeous palaces,
> The solemn temples, the great globe itself,
> Yea, all which it inherit, shall dissolve;
> And, like this insubstantial pageant faded,
> Leave not a rack behind. We are such stuff
> As dreams are made on, and our little life
> Is rounded with a sleep. Sir, I am vexed.
> Bear with my weakness. My old brain is troubled.
> Be not disturbed with my infirmity.
> If you be pleased, retire into my cell,
> And there repose. A turn or two I'll walk
> To still my beating mind.
>
> (Act IV, scene 1, lines 156–64)

My question was simply: Can this speech support a coaching conversation on power? Coaching and noncoaching students alike envisaged how the words the magician Prospero uses to draw the play's action to a close illuminate a chamber of motifs such as loss, reality, play, fantasy, unreality, and identity – all of which would be useful and fitting to explore in a coaching relationship. Prospero's speech also raised questions of thematic interest for coaches: What does it take to survive? What is the justification of one person's rule over another? Is obedience to authority willing or forced? Some of the students were familiar with the play, others not, yet Shakespeare's words had the effect of capturing everyone's imagination: "The words have an almost erotic power," someone observed. Shakespeare's words commanded the attention of all. This was a brief exercise but one that taught me that even the briefest experiment can yield striking results. A speech of eighteen lines produced the startling recognition that coaching and language are mutually reinforcing, which is, to my mind, unavoidable and immensely exciting for the future of coaching.

Note

1 Permission to use the Leopard: "From *The Leopard* by Giuseppe Tomasi Di Lampedusa, translated by Archibald Colquhoun, published by Harvill Press. Reprinted by permission of The Random House Group Limited. © 1986."

References

Balmer, John. 2011. "Corporate Heritage Identities, Corporate Heritage Brands, and the Multiple Heritage Identities of the British Monarchy." *European Journal of Marketing* 45 (9–10): 1380–98.

Becker, Ernest. 1997. *The Denial of Death*. New York: Free Press. First published in 1973 by Simon and Schuster.

Busco, Cristiano, Paolo Quattrone, and Angelo Riccaboni. 2007. "Management Accounting: Issues in Interpreting Its Nature and Change." *Management Accounting Research* 18 (2): 125–49.

Correia Jesuino, Jorge. 2008. "Lost in Translation: From Influence to Persuasion." *Diogenes* 55 (1): 107–19.

Evans, Kate. 2013. *Pathways Through Writing Blocks in the Academic Environment*. Rotterdam: Sense.

Gilbert, John. 1966. "The Metamorphosis of the Gods in *Il Gattopardo*." *MLN* 81 (1): 22–32.

Khalil Saucier, Paul, and Tryon Woods. 2014. "Ex Aqua: The Mediterranean Basin, Africans on the Move, and the Politics of Policing." *Theoria: A Journal of Social and Political Theory* 61 (141): 55–73.

Koubova, Veronika, and Aaron Buchko. 2013. "Life-Work Balance. Emotional Intelligence as a Crucial Component of Achieving Both Personal Life and Work Performance." *Management Research Review* 36 (7): 700–19.

Lampedusa, Giuseppe Tomasi di. 2007. *The Leopard*. Translated by Archibald Colquhoun. London: Vintage.

Lampedusa, Giuseppe Tomasi di. 2010. *Letters From London and Europe (1925–30)*. Translated by J.G. Nichols and foreword by Francesco da Mosto. London: Alma Books.

Lansing, Richard. 1978. "The Structure of Meaning in Lampedusa's *Il Gattopardo*." *PMLA* 93 (3): 409–22.

Leavy, Patricia. 2013. *Fiction as Research Practice*. Walnut Creek: Left Coast Press.

Matravers, Derek. 2011. "Empathy as a Route to Knowledge." In *Empathy: Philosophical and Psychological Perspectives*, edited by Amy Coplan and Peter Goldie, 19–30. Oxford: Oxford University Press.

Nolan, David. 1966. "Lampedusa's *The Leopard*." *Studies: An Irish Quarterly Review* 55: 403–14.

O'Mara, Richard. 2008. "*The Leopard* Reconsidered." *The Sewanee Review* 116 (4): 637–44.

Perschel, Anne. 2010. "Work-Life Flow: How Individuals, Zappos, and Other Innovative Companies Achieve High Engagement." *Global Business and Organizational Excellence* 29 (5): 17–30.

Quint, David. 2010. "Noble Passions: Aristocracy and the Novel." *Comparative Literature* 62 (2): 103–21.

Saccone, Eduardo. 1991. "Nobility and Literature: Questions on Tomasi di Lampedusa." *MLN* 106 (1): 159–78.

Smith, Murray. 2011. "Empathy, Expansionism, and the Extended Mind." In *Empathy: Philosophical and Psychological Perspectives*, edited by Amy Coplan and Peter Goldie, 99–117. Oxford: Oxford University Press.

Smith, Steven B. 2010. "The Political Teaching of Lampedusa's *The Leopard*." *The Yale Review* 98 (3): 30–48.

Visconti, Luchino. 1963. *DVD. Il Gattopardo*. Performed by Burt Lancaster, Claudia Cardinale, Alain Delon, Serge Reggiani, Mario Girotti, Pierre Clementi, and directed by Luchino Visconti. Produced by Goffredo Lombardo and Pietro Notarianni and distributed by 20th Century Fox.

Conclusion

Coaching with Shakespeare?

In the foregoing chapters, I have put forward an argument for the value that literary works can bring to coaching. I have chronicled a series of pedagogical experiments in using literature with coaching students to build up a qualitative picture of what coaching with literature looks like and how and why it works. We have seen that literary works can act as powerful stimulants of the reflective process and can serve, simultaneously, as a simulative threshold of affective experience, a safe space for emotional openness within the formal context of the workplace. The value literature can bring to coaching derives from these intersecting cognitive and emotional axes: literary works make us think about ourselves and the world we inhabit; at the same time, they trigger and manage our emotional responses to linguistic and imagistic stimuli. In a coaching context, reading literature can galvanize coachees' thought processes, encouraging them to reflect more deeply on the situations they encounter in their lives and in the workplace, and, at the same time, literature can enhance their emotional intelligence. In an optimal coaching scenario, literary works are a natural companion for peer dialogue and can be integrated into coaching practice with minimal effort and maximal potential gain. Of course, literary works bring their own challenges too. We saw some of the challenges brought about by this innovative coaching methodology in Chapter 1 on Herman Melville's "Bartleby." In particular, it is worth noting that no given work of literature is universally applicable to different coaching scenarios. Part of my aim in the foregoing chapters has been to illustrate the role of the coach in selecting and pairing literary works with their coaching audience in order to ensure the compatibility and efficacy of the literary intervention.

I have argued that the rationale for using works of literature as a coaching tool is predicated, to some degree, on the analogies shared by the processes of writing and coaching. Both processes are predicated on the attainment of similar skills; both are creative acts that contain blocks and frustrations; both are skills that can be refined and developed by reflective practice. In Chapter 1, I used my students' reactions to an excerpt from "Bartleby" to illustrate how reflection on a piece of writing can be used to trigger reflection on the process of communication. As a communicative act, coaching is dependent on the quality of the linguistic and gestural expression through which it is conducted. Using Melville's text to show how the description of office dynamics could be enriched through the use of imagery enabled my coaching students to discover their own poetic license. The figures of speech we find in great writing are transferable to great coaching because metaphor plays such an important role in our conversations. Julian Jaynes (1990) argues that metaphor is in fact central to how our mind conceives the world. Jaynes (1990, 52) hypothesizes that our consciousness is expressed as metaphor and that we understand the world only in metaphorical terms: "Understanding a thing is to arrive at a metaphor for that thing by substituting something more familiar to us." If consciousness can be conceived in terms of metaphor, then it follows naturally that coaching has much to gain from opening the doors of literary perception. Just as Melville's metaphors enable readers to perceive his world, the metaphors deployed in a coaching dialogue can help to capture the experiences of the participants in that dialogue. And if coaching is contingent on the capacity of self-expression, which, in turn, can be enhanced through the practice of reading and writing, then the relevance of literature for contemporary coaching practice seems a logical conclusion.

Although I have reiterated in the preceding chapters the distinction between coaching and therapy, it is undeniable that integrating literary writing into coaching has therapeutic benefits. As a space for our emotions, the process of reflecting on literary works provides us with the emotional competence to discuss our personal issues. In Chapter 4, we saw how Arthur Miller's play *Death of a Salesman* can be used to cultivate emotional intelligence. Willy Loman is the kind of character we all feel we know, although most of us would not want to be thought of as possessing similar qualities to Miller's protagonist. My coaching students were enthusiastic about using the drama in their own coaching conversations. They testified to its value in opening up discussions on self-awareness and on the management of expectations. When we empathize with Miller's tragic protagonist, we get to know ourselves a little better. The critical scalpel Miller takes to his characters' deficiencies encourages an introspective gaze in the audience. As the flaws in Miller's characters are revealed, our own deficiencies are thrown into a harsh, unforgiving light. Miller's play is also an excellent text to explore family dynamics. One of my students argued that discussing Willy Loman was the antidote to the perennial coaching problem of "wanting to be liked." Unsurprisingly, because of the play's sales themes of success, failure, and money, the students reported direct and very emotional responses when they used the play as a discussion tool in their coaching practices. A work of art like *Death of a Salesman*, by obliging us to reflect on our emotions, trains us to be more attentive to what makes us and others tick.

Each of the texts discussed in the earlier chapters – "Bartleby," "Neighbor Rosicky," "The Swimmer," "Notes of a Native Son," *Death of a Salesman*, and *The Leopard* – interacted with different readers in variable, sometimes unpredictable ways. The variability of the literary coaching methodology outlined here and the difficulty of predicting how coachees might interact with the reading materials constitute the principal challenges coaches might face when adopting the ideas set out in the preceding chapters. In the final chapter, I reported on my endeavor to mitigate the problem of variability by appealing to the work of a dramatist frequently considered universal. Shakespeare is so popular and pervasive that his plays seem a versatile alternative to more obscure and lesser-known authors. They have been performed, read, studied, analyzed, deconstructed, and argued over for centuries. Shakespeare's plays are so well known that it is as if they existed in our collective consciousness. They are malleable and elude attempts to define and reduce them. Shakespeare's dramas are an abundant mine of ideas about human nature. They deal with sex, marriage, gender, class, commerce, consumption, relationships, and the whole spectrum of human emotions – and that's just the tip of the iceberg. His language displays a potent exuberance, a generosity, an ever-present verbal brilliance. Might there be a way of incorporating Shakespearian plays into coaching or accommodating his soliloquies or sonnets?

Shakespeare, in a sense, represents my final frontier in coaching with literature: the ultimate linguistic challenge coupled with the greatest potential for enhancing how coachees think about themselves and their world. In my final chapter, I discussed how I used one of Prospero's speeches from *The Tempest* as a touchstone to discuss power and control, two concepts that figure prominently in workplace politics. Shakespeare's ability to resonate with the feelings that human beings have experienced in all cultures over the centuries makes him the premier coaching voice. One direction in which I intend to advance in my future coaching practice is to use Shakespeare's writing – a play, an act, a scene, a soliloquy, a passage, a poem, a sonnet – as a theoretical framework within which to view and describe our emotions, our coaching development, and a range of phenomena in our working lives. I want to show that using Shakespeare can inform and develop our coaching in a creative, introspective, and distinctive way. In our psychological need to experience autonomy and competence in our professional lives, we need Shakespeare more than ever to discuss how to achieve the richest and most transformational outcomes in coaching. Shakespeare's exploration of the human soul through his writing is the ideal vehicle to support clients' motivation and self-actualization. In *The Tempest*, Prospero announces, "Now does my project gather to a head/My charms crack not, my sprits obey, and time/Goes upright with his carriage" (Shakespeare 1997, Act V, scene 1, lines 1–3). Like Prospero, coaches have the ability to transform the coaching interaction through space and time. The words that we use should reflect the beautiful and sacred duty entrusted to us. I urge you to bring the alchemy of Shakespeare to bear on your coaching practice. Coaching deserves no less magic.

References

Jaynes, Julian. 1990. *The Origin of Consciousness in the Breakdown of the Bicameral Mind*. Boston: Houghton-Mifflin.

Shakespeare, William. 1997. *The Norton Shakespeare*, edited by Stephen Greenblatt. New York: W. W. Norton.

Index